365 GUITARS
AMPS & EFFECTS YOU MUST PLAY

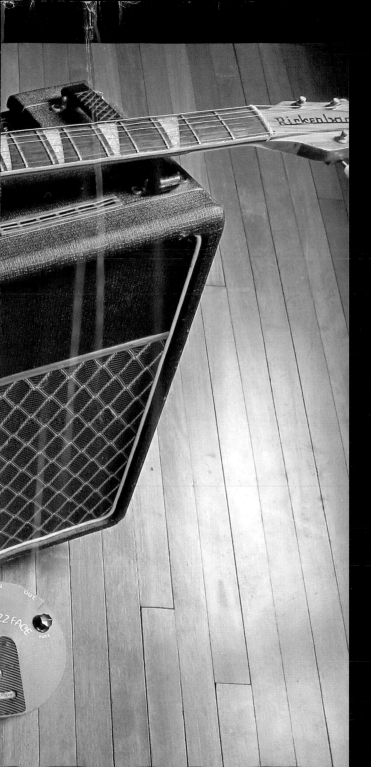

365 GUITARS

AMPS & EFFECTS YOU MUST PLAY

DAVE HUNTER

Voyageur Press

First published in 2013 by Voyageur Press, an imprint of MBI Publishing Company,
400 First Avenue North, Suite 400, Minneapolis, MN 55401 USA

Voyageur Press titles are also available at discounts in bulk quantity for industrial or sales-promotional use. For details write to Special Sales Manager at MBI Publishing Company, 400 First Avenue North, Suite 400, Minneapolis, MN 55401 USA.

To find out more about our books, visit us online at www.voyageurpress.com.

Library of Congress Cataloging-in-Publication Data
Hunter, Dave, 1962-
  365 guitars, amps & effects you must play : the most sublime, bizarre and outrageous
gear ever / Dave Hunter.
     pages cm
  ISBN 978-0-7603-4366-1 (softcover)
  1. Guitar—Miscellanea. 2. Guitar amplifiers—Miscellanea. 3. Effects pedals—Miscellanea.
  I. Title. II. Title: Three hundred sixty-five guitars, amps and effects you must play.
  ML1015.G9H856 2013
  787.87'192—dc23
                          2012040561

Front cover photo: © Fender Musical Instruments Corporation

Page 3 and 5 photos: © Michael Dregni

Editors: Dennis Pernu and Michael Dregni

Design managers: James Kegley and Cindy Laun

Design: Simon Larkin and Chris Fayers

Layout: Chris Fayers

Cover design: Simon Larkin

Printed in China

1866 Torres Classical

The most hallowed name in the history of classical guitar, Antonio de Torres consolidated the best work of luthiers of the mid-nineteenth century to bring the guitar forward to the twentieth century and beyond. As such, Torres is widely recognized as the father of the modern classical instrument and, essentially, the Stradivarius of the guitar. The thinner and more responsive soundboard, livelier and more structurally sound strutting, and simultaneously more ergonomic and tone-enhancing design of the best contemporary classical guitars can all be credited, to some degree, to Torres' work. Unsurprisingly, Torres' guitars are extremely rare and highly prized today, so getting your grubby hands on one is extremely unlikely. Nevertheless, any professional classical guitarist playing a top-shelf classical instrument will have had daily contact with Torres' legacy in the guitars of later makers, such as Ramírez, Romanillos, Hauser, Hernández, Fleta, Simplicio, and others who owe a great debt to the master. *Should* you get your fingers around a genuine Torres, however, note how the understated, even rather plain appearance gives way to a sublime voice mellowed and enhanced by the sonic patina that only 150 years of beautiful music can provide.

1910 Bohmann Harp Guitar

Freak of nature? Medieval torture device? *Au contraire*, it's the Bohmann Harp Guitar, and as finger-twistingly unplayable as it might appear, this beast can produce sublime, almost otherworldly music in the right hands. Relatively few acoustic aficionados today are likely to have heard of Chicago guitar maker Joseph Bohmann, who immigrated to the United States in 1878 from Neumarkt, Bohemia (in present-day Germany). Bohmann was considered one of the most skilled luthiers working in the late nineteenth and early twentieth centuries, winning eight major international instrument-making prizes between 1888 and 1904. Once you realize that the bass strings on this guitar's upper neck aren't intended to be fretted but are harp strings plucked to resonate with the chord or melody being played on the lower neck, this monster becomes somewhat more approachable. Even so, this odd instrument that looks even more archaic than its century-old lineage would suggest is a work of art in wood and wire even before you approach it as a musical instrument.

Courtesy Outline Press Limited

1920s Dyer Symphony Harp Guitar Style 8

Like the Bohmann harp guitar, this elaborate instrument was designed as a somewhat conventional acoustic guitar with its own bass accompaniment. The enthusiasm with which many makers addressed the form in the early part of the twentieth century might have led guitarists to think that these were the real next step forward, and of all the various designs on the table at the time, the harp guitars sold by the Dyer company were possibly the most advanced. Rather than supporting the several heavy-gauge bass strings under tension with just a sturdy upper neck, a Dyer like this elaborately decorated Symphony Harp Guitar Style 8 had an entire body extension through which those drone strings would resonate, producing a haunting, ethereal sound. Dyer, based in St. Paul, Minnesota, didn't actually manufacture these harp guitars. Early examples were designed by Chris J. Knutsen, a Norwegian guitar maker working in the northeastern United States, and most were manufactured by the Larson Brothers of Chicago. Dyer harp guitars are exceedingly rare today; the instrument's most acclaimed proponents include Stephen Bennett and Michael Hedges, who died in a car accident in 1997.

Courtesy Outline Press Limited

1920s Washburn Style A

Every player needs to have one of these little parlor guitars lying around, right? Preferably in that remote mountain cabin where you noodle endlessly in front of a crackling fire to renew your inspiration. (You *do* have a remote mountain cabin, too, right?) From the 1880s, Washburn guitars were manufactured by Chicago's Lyon & Healy of Chicago in styles clearly much inspired by Martin. Many were perfectly good little instruments right from the start, but by the post–World War I period the company more consistently used X-bracing for their guitar tops, broadly improving their tone as a result. Aside from the great North American spruce and Brazilian rosewood that many of these petite beauties employed and the deluxe mother-of-pearl inlays that the top models carried, there's just something magical about coaxing a sweet, mellow tune out of such a tiny, old flat-top guitar. And while few such parlor-size Washburns offer much by way of volume, their tone can often be sublime.

Courtesy Outline Press Limited

Weissenborn Style 1

Born in Hanover, Germany, in 1864, Hermann C. Weissenborn immigrated to California in 1900 and by 1920 was well positioned to capitalize on the Hawaiian music boom sweeping the United States at the time. Although Weissenborn also built traditional "Spanish" guitars, he has become best known for the acoustic lap-style Hawaiian instruments built with hollow sound chambers extending through the entire length of the neck in an effort to increase the instruments' volume, addressing a constant need for early guitarists. Even more volume was soon produced by resonator guitars from the National and Dobro companies, and soon after by electric guitars, but the haunting, atmospheric sound of Weissenborn's hollow lap-style slide guitars earned them a devoted following and a place in music that remains valid to this day. Noted slide artists such as Ben Harper and David Lindley have brought the Weissenborn into the twenty-first century and present some of the best available examples of how sonically effective this unusual guitar can be.

1920s Gibson L-5

Orville Gibson pioneered the archtop guitar in the late 1800s, but the instrument took a major step toward embodying its full potential in the 1920s after the company's sales manager, Lewis Williams, hired mandolin virtuoso and instrument designer Lloyd A. Loar to develop a new high-quality line in 1922. The mandolin was still more popular than the guitar at the time, and when Loar applied his thinking to the 6-string, the result was the new L-5. Upgrades came in the form of revised bracing, a height-adjustable bridge, the first adjustable truss-rod commonly used on a guitar, and various considerations intended to improve resonance and overall tone. Also, more obviously, the L-5 and other Gibson guitars adopted the mandolin-like f-holes in place of the previous round or oval sound holes. Original Loar-era L-5s can feel like real antiques, but when in good condition, they should produce a warm, sweet, rather mellow tone with some sparkle and harmonic shimmer. In its day, this was state-of-the art, and a 1920s L-5 is still an impressive work of art today.

1931 National Tricone

Less than a decade after National introduced its first models in 1927, the resonator guitar's original *raison d'etre* was made redundant when the electric guitar took amplification to new heights, but in seeking simply to make guitars louder, inventors George Beauchamp, Adolph Rickenbacker, and John Dopyera also created a haunting tone that remains as expressive today as it was in the age of Sol Ho'opi'i. The single-cone National is more familiar today, but the tricone was the first to hit the scene. It was actually a rather more complex contraption, too, with three smaller cones that open toward the inside of the guitar body, all connected to the strings via a T-shaped bridge. This trio of smaller spun-aluminum cones gives early tricones a slightly more complex and articulate sound, with plenty of characteristic bell-like zing and a slightly strident honk from that body of German silver (a nickel alloy). The beautifully etched Style 4 (and the Style 3, for that matter) had an exotic exterior to match their intricate construction. Even a "roundneck" model, which is intended to be played in the standard upright position, still sounds its best when attacked with a bottleneck slide and, ideally, a set of steel fingerpicks. Tune to open G or D, lay into it, and it's like your own lap-size reverb chamber and orchestra all in one.

Courtesy Outline Press Limited

1935 Rickenbacker B-7

Three decades before Rickenbacker-branded 6- and 12-string guitars made a major splash in the hands of the Beatles, The Who, the Byrds, and other '60s legends, the original team behind the name was pushing the envelope with groundbreaking electric designs. The Ro-Pat-In company, which branded its guitars Rickenbacker, married George Beauchamp and Paul Barth's groundbreaking magnetic pickup design to Adolph Rickenbacker's stylized guitar body of the early- to mid-'30s—first in aluminum, then in Bakelite—to produce one of the first viable amplified electric guitars, although it was more often played in the Hawaiian or "lap" style with a steel slide. The large magnets and relatively heavy wire gauge of Rickenbacker's "horseshoe" pickup give this instrument a thick, gutsy tone, with a snarly edge that nevertheless remains fairly clear, unless you drive the amp excessively. This is the singing, muscular, electric sound of Sol Ho'opi'i, the Sweethearts of the Air, and later, several early Western swing artists who quickly became the envy of their Spanish-style cohorts. As industrial as this pickup might look today, it still yields a ballsy tone that can't really be replicated by any "evolution" of the form in the past eighty years of guitar development.

1930s Dobro

Whereas National resonator guitars have always been tied to Hawaiian and blues music, the Dobro seems to have made its warm, woody way into the country and bluegrass scenes almost from the start. Dobro did make many metal-bodied guitars in the image of the classic Nationals that Dobro cofounder John Dopyera pioneered before his split with the company in 1928, but the company is far better known for its wooden-bodied instruments, which were perhaps just more befitting of the image and sound of the scene where they found their home. In order to avoid copying National too directly, Dopyera gave his Dobros (Dopyera Brothers) a single resonator cone installed in the reverse of the National style, which is to say it opened toward the top of the body rather than into it. As such, it required the very different eight-legged "spider bridge" that became another characteristic of the Dobro build and tone. Although well-aged Dobro and National guitars might seem to have more in common than they do apart, this vintage example exhibits a somewhat rounder, softer, more organic tone than will be heard from most Nationals, yet it still puts out plenty of zing thanks to that forward-facing spun-aluminum cone.

Courtesy Retrofret Vintage Guitars/www.retrofret.com/photo by George Aslaender

1931 National Style O

After cofounder John Dopyera split from National to launch his rival Dobro brand in 1928, the company responded with its own wood-bodied, single-cone resonator guitar, known as the Triolian. The model fared poorly initially, but an upgrade to a steel, then a bell-brass, body in the early '30s signaled the arrival of a new classic. This 1930s Style O has a nickel-plated bell-brass body that gives it the visual appeal of the upper-echelon tri-cones, although these single-cone Nationals tended to appeal more to blues players, eventually at least, than to the Hawaiian players the breed was aimed at. Naturally, the single-cone resonator guitars sounded quite different than the tri-cones, and the single-cone Dobros, as well. Rather than directly copy the Dobro's outward-firing cone, National mounted its cone firing into the body (picture an inverted speaker cone), with the strings passing over a saddle set into a round, wooden "biscuit bridge" mounted at the apex of the cone. The combination of this spun-aluminum cone's resonance within the metal body and the tone projecting forward from it through the sieve-like cover produces a powerful sound that is simultaneously homey and haunting, instantly recognized as one of the most evocative sounds in music.

DIRE STRAITS   WALK OF LIFE

STEREO

The Legendary
Son House   Father of the Delta Blues
The Complete 1965 Sessions

Paramount
ELECTRICALLY RECORDED
13096-B
Vocal
Guitar
Clarksdale Moan
(House)
Son House
L 407
THE NEW YORK RECORDING LABORATORIES · PORT WASHINGTON, WIS.

Paramount
ELECTRICALLY RECORDED
13096-A
Vocal
Guitar Acc.
Mississippi County Farm
Blues
(House)
Son House
L 401
THE NEW YORK RECORDING LABORATORIES · PORT WASHINGTON, WIS. TRADE MARK REGISTERED

1931 Martin 000-45

The big D-45 might make a more common example, from later years at least, of Martin's ornate showpiece guitars, but if you ask us, the beautifully rounded 000 body shape makes a more elegant aesthetic statement. For many years the Style 42 had been the Pennsylvania maker's fanciest offering, for a time with a genuine ivory bridge, but the stately Style 45 upped the ante with a bound headstock and abalone fountain inlays in addition to its other notable adornments. The snowflake fingerboard inlays are a Martin classic, and note how the abalone inlay within the body-top binding traces the entire fingerboard extension, even cutting into the abalone sound-hole rosette. The attention to detail isn't limited to the guitar's front, either: flip it over, and admire the colored-wood marquetry that joins the beautifully figured two-piece Brazilian rosewood back. Strummed, fingerpicked, or flatpicked, this 000-45 offers a sonic elegance to match its appearance. An X-brace allows that solid Adirondack spruce to sing sweetly, and while more compact than the larger dreadnoughts soon to come, the 000 has more than enough acoustic muscle to produce a deep, rich tone.

1932 Martin D-28

Mention the term "acoustic guitar" today and most people are likely to picture a dreadnought: the big-bodied, square-shouldered style invented by Martin early in the twentieth century. Martin made its first dreadnoughts as a special-order item in 1916 for Ditson Music, which had stores in Boston and New York City, but the refined Martin dreadnoughts that are archetypal of the form didn't hit the company's lineup until 1931. The D-28 is the flagship of Martin's dreadnought line, and a prewar example like this one is likely the "dream guitar" of countless acoustic performers. This D-28 features the subtly elegant herringbone trim that Martin dispensed with after 1947 as well as distinctive snowflake inlays in its ebony fingerboard, a top of Adirondack spruce, and Brazilian rosewood back and sides. You could just about say this guitar was born to play bluegrass: its rich, muscular voice is equally suited to banging out the rhythm behind a steam-train-paced fiddle, banjo, and mandolin arrangement as it is to singing its own flatpicked solo when its turn rolls around. Arguably a perfect marriage of form and function, a D-28 is all that many legendary artists required to make a career's worth of great music.

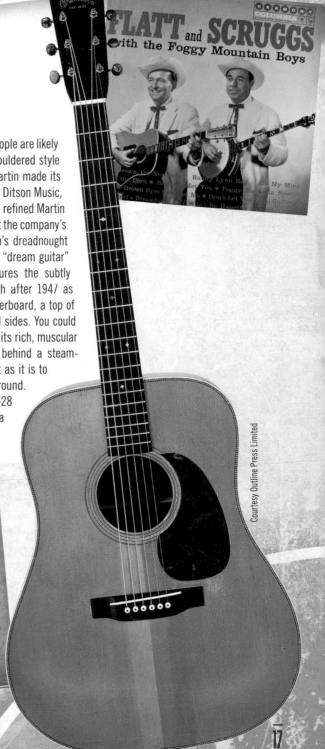

Courtesy Outline Press Limited

1932 Julián Gómez Rámirez Steel-String

This revolutionary—and somewhat bizarre-looking—guitar was crafted by renowned Spanish luthier Julián Gómez Ramírez. Ramírez apprenticed with the famed guitar maker José Ramírez I in Madrid, then set up shop in Paris around 1914. Here he built classical guitars before trying his hand at this novel steel-string model. This guitar was revolutionary in marrying classical guitar with mandolin and banduria features to create a steel-string model that was loud enough to cut through the sound and fury of accordion dance bands and, later, jazz ensembles. The body is made of Brazilian rosewood with a softwood soundboard featuring large open sound holes designed to project the guitar's voice. It's incredibly light weight with a warm, woody, and bright tone. This guitar was specially made for the Gypsy jazz maestro Pierre "Baro" Ferret, who often loaned it to his friend Django Reinhardt. Django used it in his early days before adopting the Selmer-Maccaferri.

Django Reinhardt (second from right) plays the Rámircz steel string seen here.

1936 Gibson ES-150

The humble ES-150 is notable for being both Gibson's first production electric guitar (and therefore the first production electric from a major maker) and the guitar that carried the hallowed "Charlie Christian pickup." Which means, of course, that it's also a fast road to achieving that fat yet biting Charlie Christian tone. We think of these old archtop electrics as being dark and boomy, and they can be, but that impression possibly comes as much from the circumstances of the recordings of the day as from the instruments themselves. Plugged in today, a good ES-150 will definitely be thick and warm, but it should have a surprisingly clear, snarky edge, too. A vintage amp such as the EH-150, with which the ES-150 was originally partnered, will enhance the compressed and midrange-y nature of the guitar itself, but a good contemporary tube amp will extend the pickup's frequency range in both directions and reveal some unexpected harmonic sparkle, too. The guitars' necks can be rather club-like, and playability is often cumbersome—making you appreciate all the more what Christian himself achieves on a song like "Air Mail Special"—but there's definitely a personality to these archaic electrics that can be hard to find elsewhere.

Courtesy Retrofret Vintage Guitars/www.retrofret.com/photo by George Aslaender

1940s Gibson EH-150

Plenty of attention is paid to Charlie Christian's use of an early Gibson ES-150 guitar, with the blade pickup dubbed colloquially in the jazz guitarist's honor, but the EH-150 amplifier of the mid- to late 1930s also deserves credit for helping plenty of formative electric jazzers be heard. The notion of amplified electric guitar was truly in its infancy when these amplifiers were made, and both guitars and amps would evolve a long way before the match was optimized, but the EH-150 is pretty impressive for its day. We often think of vintage amps as being warm, muddy, and even rather dull—and perhaps that's how many tired, out-of-shape old amps sound when you try them out today—but plug into a late-'30s EH-150 that has been put into good electrical condition, and you have a real surprise in store. These amps have a good amount of clarity to them and an appealingly edgy, raw bite—characteristics that helped Christian's tone cut through beautifully on the several early recordings that exist. Back when this was one of the few options available to help you get heard above the horns on the bandstand, it did the job admirably, and the EH-150 still offers a stirring trip back to the jazz age.

Prewar D'Angelico New Yorker

For many archtop aficionados, the zenith of the craft can be found in a single name: D'Angelico. After taking over the instrument shop of his uncle, Signor Ciani, in which he oversaw fifteen employees at its peak, John D'Angelico decided he was more cut out for the path of the lone craftsman and opened a shop in New York City in 1932. D'Angelico had studied classical violin making and learned Italian-style flat-top guitar making under his uncle, but he largely followed in Gibson's footsteps with his own work, although his instruments were widely considered superior to those of the larger manufacturer in terms of style and tone. The New Yorker is clearly the flagship of the line, and this early example has a gloriously rich, complex tone that takes you back to cigarette-hazed nights at Birdland. Upon close examination, many of D'Angelico's guitars might even be considered to be rather rough-hewn, given their status, but they are glorious creations nonetheless and seem to exude some mystic, ineffable presence that virtually hums within their spruce and maple form. After thirty-two years in the business, producing a maximum of around thirty-five guitars a year at his peak, D'Angelico passed away in 1964, and his guitars passed into the pantheon of legendary instruments.

1935 Gibson Super 400

Ah, for the simplicity of an age when manufacturers named their guitars after the prices they charged for them. Following a war with Epiphone that began in the early 1930s, in which each maker sought to outdo the other by introducing larger and larger archtop models, Gibson finally played its trump card in 1934 in the form of the Super 400, a mammoth 18-inch-wide tone machine that quickly became the premier jazzbox on the scene. Unlike its predecessor, the rather sparsely adorned L-5, the Super 400 was given ornate dress befitting its status. Highlights included a five-piece mother-of-pearl "split diamond" headstock inlay; a multiply body; fingerboard, headstock, f-hole, and pickguard binding; an elaborately engraved gold-plated tailpiece; and large split-block mother-of-pearl fingerboard inlays. And while we often think of this supreme archtop as a blonde beauty today, Gibson shipping records from the era show that, of the mere 401 non-cutaway Super 400s made before production was suspended for World War II, only 7 were given a natural finish. Chop out the changes on this one and you're rewarded with an archetypal driving big-band rhythm tone, but its X-braced top (which would be parallel-braced by 1940) also resonates sweetly beneath your speedy bop solo lines.

Prewar Prairie State Acoustic

It's easy to think that Martin and Gibson dominated the flat-top game from the late 1800s right up through World War II, but a lot of other significant and respected players took the field, particularly in the years between the World Wars. Prairie State flat-tops are rarely seen today, but they have many devoted followers. Built by Maurer & Company and later by Euphonon, the Chicago companies of brothers August and Carl Larson (who also made many instruments wearing the Dyer, Stetson, W. M. Stahl, and Leland labels), Prairie States were often elaborately decorative instruments that frequently boasted equally elaborate design notions, too. Within their fancy, abalone-festooned shells lurked devices such as steel support tubes running from tail block to neck heel to help ease string tension across the tops of their mammoth 20- or 21-inch-wide bodies, as well as steel clamps to aid neck attachment. Attack this guitar with a heavy pick, and you're rewarded with a stout, muscular voice that lives up to the maker's efforts to take the acoustic guitar to the next level in the volume wars.

Stella 12-String

For a second-tier brand name, Stella guitars—their 12-strings in particular— would gain significant kudos for their use by two major names at very different ends of the musical spectrum. Although, upon consideration, these artists were perhaps extremely well aligned in terms of energy and attitude. Folk originator Huddie Ledbetter, better known as Lead Belly, was a major proponent of the 12-string acoustic guitar and most frequently played a Stella once the models hit the scene. Some sixty years later, grunge icon Kurt Cobain of Nirvana would use a later Stella 12-string (though often with fewer than twelve strings) to record the song "Polly" on the *Nevermind* album as well as other tracks and demos. As the budget brand of instrument maker Oscar Schmidt, the Stella name landed on guitars made from cheaper woods and using more basic constructional techniques. Many of the flat-tops featured simple trapeze tailpieces with a basic floating bridge, a far less costly method than the glued-down pin bridge used on better flat-tops. Regardless, hit 'em in anger like Lead Belly or Cobain, and that old Stella will churn out a chugging, thumping jangle, producing more than enough noise to make some seriously moving music.

1937 Rickenbacher M11

The name Rickenbacker is most closely associated with the guitars of George Harrison and John Lennon of the Beatles, Pete Townshend of The Who, and Roger McGuinn of the Byrds, but long before those more familiar 6- and 12-string designs took shape, it appeared—sometimes spelled with the "ch" as here—on early lap-steel guitars and the amps they were played through. This 1930s Rick might have the "electronic suitcase" appearance of its day—a look that conjures images of archaic circuitry and soft, flabby tones—but the M11 packs some surprises in both departments. Its cab is made of thinner panels than contemporary amps, 3/8-inch pine in this case, and its chassis is a crude, top-mounted, folded-steel contraption loaded with old-world 6SJ7 and SN7 octal preamp tubes and a pair of 6V6

output tubes, but crank it up to the sweet spot and it packs a few surprises, too. Keep the volume down and it is sweet, clean, and just compressed enough to thicken up your tone. Crank it, and it sings with a complex and musical tone that particularly suits single-coil guitars. It might have been born more than seventy-five years ago, but it's a tone that still proves viable today.

Amp courtesy Steve Olson/
photos Dave Matchette/Elderly Instruments

1937 Gibson Advanced Jumbo

A rare and precious beast, the Advanced Jumbo was produced for only four years, from 1936 to 1940 (company records show that only two shipped in 1940) and was, upon its introduction, Gibson's largest flat-top prior to the impending arrival of the Super Jumbo (a.k.a. SJ-200). Often quoted as having a body that was 16 inches wide—although careful measurement often shows it closer to 15.75 inches—the Advanced Jumbo might appear an archaic flat-top today, but it was state of the art for its day and remains a thing of timeless beauty either way. With a spruce top, solid Brazilian rosewood back and sides, an "advanced" X-brace moved forward toward the sound hole for improved resonance, and a large 25.5-inch scale length that belies later Gibson specs, this vintage piece really puts out some volume with a rich, chocolaty warmth that's hard to equal with a modern acoustic. Thanks to its elegant dress—notably the diamond-and-chevron fingerboard and headstock inlays, "firestripe" tortoise pickguard, and sunburst finish with Cremona-brown outer edge—it's a marvelous showpiece from a bygone era, too.

Courtesy Retrofret Vintage Guitars;
www.retrofret.com/photo by George Aslaender

1937 Gibson SJ-200

From its original status as the "Cadillac of acoustics" for country crooners to its role as the ultimate rhythm cannon for seminal rock 'n' rollers, the SJ-200 has proved itself one of the most powerful flat-tops on the planet, time and time again. The model was originally designed by custom order for "Singing Cowboy" Ray Whitley with the same dimensions and neck as Gibson's big L-5 archtop. Later examples are known for their bright-toned solid maple back and sides, but rare prewar SJ-200s like this one had a solid spruce top married to solid rosewood back and sides for a voice that was still bold and bright but with a nuanced depth and richness besides. Given the aged tonewood and bountiful proportions, a great SJ-200 will sound sweet and sultry for gentler acoustic moments, too, but it is really suited to hammering out the big open chords behind the band and gives that Nudie-suited frontman a means of being heard, rather than just looking good. Whether you're Roy Rogers, Gene Autry, Elvis Presley, or Johnny Cash, the "King of the Flat-tops" gets you there in style and never leaves you in danger of failing to be heard . . . or seen.

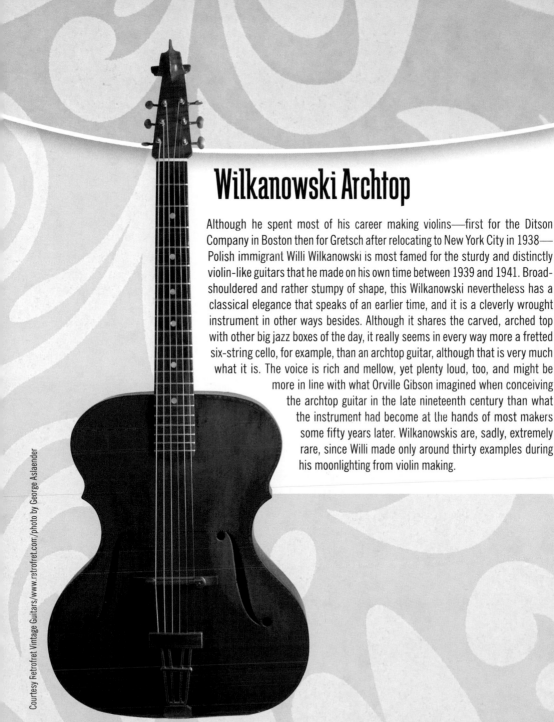

Wilkanowski Archtop

Although he spent most of his career making violins—first for the Ditson Company in Boston then for Gretsch after relocating to New York City in 1938—Polish immigrant Willi Wilkanowski is most famed for the sturdy and distinctly violin-like guitars that he made on his own time between 1939 and 1941. Broad-shouldered and rather stumpy of shape, this Wilkanowski nevertheless has a classical elegance that speaks of an earlier time, and it is a cleverly wrought instrument in other ways besides. Although it shares the carved, arched top with other big jazz boxes of the day, it really seems in every way more a fretted six-string cello, for example, than an archtop guitar, although that is very much what it is. The voice is rich and mellow, yet plenty loud, too, and might be more in line with what Orville Gibson imagined when conceiving the archtop guitar in the late nineteenth century than what the instrument had become at the hands of most makers some fifty years later. Wilkanowskis are, sadly, extremely rare, since Willi made only around thirty examples during his moonlighting from violin making.

1940 Selmer *Petite Bouche* Modèle Jazz

In the quest for volume in the days prior to electrical amplification, Italian luthier Mario Maccaferri was a true revolutionary. He built mandolins, harp guitars, and classical guitars before trying his hand at a steel-string guitar that combined features of a classical with a mandolin. He showed it to French musical instrumental magnate Henri Selmer, who immediately set up a small atelier for Maccaferri to produce the guitars in a corner of his Mantes-la-Ville factory near Paris. The earliest Selmer-Maccaferris from 1932 featured a *grande bouche* D-shaped sound hole and an interior resonator box to better project the guitar's voice and slice through the volume of a full band without amplification. The cutaway and long fretboard offered the player easier access to a broader palette of notes. And the guitar's tone was quite trebly, perfect for the bass-heavy recording process of the day. Gypsy jazz legend Django Reinhardt adopted the Selmer early on, eventually favoring the later *petite bouche* models with the smaller sound hole and neck that joined the body at the 14th, instead of 12th, fret. In fact, this guitar, serial number 503, was one of Django's last personal instruments.

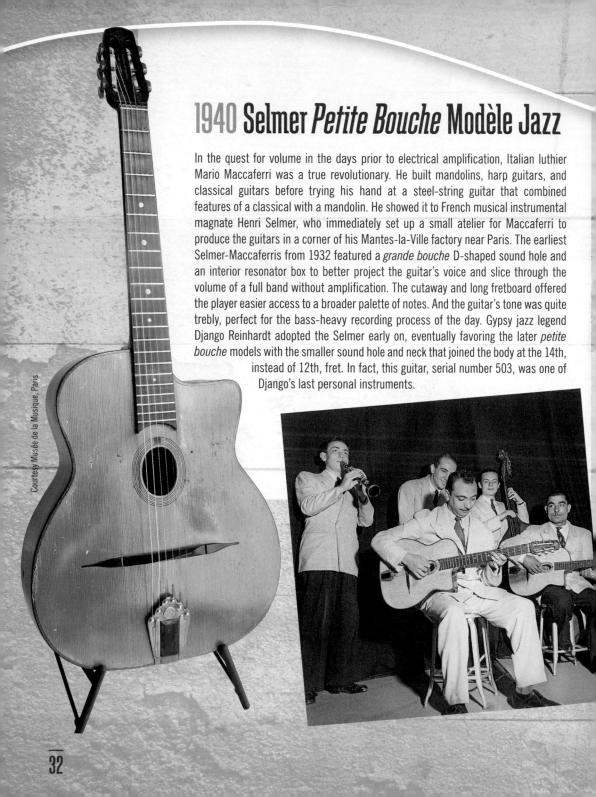

DISQUES
SWING
ANDRÉ 41
DJANGO
REINHARDT
Imp. A. KARCHER_Paris

1942 Martin 00-21

Courtesy Outline Press Limited

Martin's dreadnoughts get lots of attention today, but back when the bigger, squarer flat-top was still just the youngster in the catalog, Martin's 0, 00, and 000 models constituted the meat of the lineup. The predecessors of the 1932 00-21 first appeared in the late 1890s and originally had gut strings, but in 1930 Martin fortified the bracing and bridge construction to enable the guitars to take steel strings, thus giving them a bigger, bolder voice. Not only was the early-'30s 00-21 a sweet looker among its Depression-era siblings—with its subtle snowflake fingerboard inlays and herringbone sound-hole rosette—but it was a sweet-voiced performer, too, as the ghosts of Jimmie Rodgers, Woody Guthrie, and several other notable players would no doubt attest. The 00-21's 12th-fret neck joint gives this relatively small-bodied flat-top a deep, rich voice, and the combination of an Adirondack spruce top and Brazilian rosewood back and sides presents a luscious blend of clarity and complexity. Whether played finger-style (considered by many to be its forté) or with a flat pick, after some eighty years of aging and mellowing, this 00-21 will yield as magical a voice as you could hope to hear in an acoustic instrument.

1942 Epiphone Emperor

Long before Epiphone was a byword for "affordable Gibson," the Emperor made a serious run at living up to its name in jazz circles. Based right there in jazz central, New York City, Epiphone put guitars in the hands of many of the top players on the scene in the 1930s and early 1940s and presented a serious rivalry to Gibson until the World War II manufacturing slowdown (which coincided with the death of company president Epi Stathopoulo) delivered a blow from which Epiphone would never quite recover. The Emperor was introduced in 1935 in answer to Gibson's Super 400 of the year before, and the company clearly intended for this massive 18.5-inch-wide archtop to show who was king of the castle. By 1941 many Emperors were given an innovative rounded cutaway, and the line had also gained adjustable truss rods and two-piece Frequensator tailpieces. With its carved solid spruce top and impressive dimensions, these later Emperors chug out a girthsome rhythm tone and prove nimble, pliant soloists, too. Crafted in an age when the archtop wars were far from over, it also looks pretty darn good with its multi-ply body and headstock binding, inlaid abalone and mother-of-pearl V markers, and floral headstock inlay.

1943 Gibson Southerner Jumbo

One of the great flat-tops of Gibson legend, the Southerner Jumbo—later known as the Southern Jumbo—has origins tinged with an air of mystery. Long documented as having been introduced in 1942, some assessments now claim the model didn't arrive until 1943. In any case, the original production run was extremely short before the wartime slowdown. According to *Gruhn's Guide to Vintage Guitars* by George Gruhn and Walter Carter, the first batch of Southerner Jumbos was constructed with solid Brazilian rosewood backs and sides, although mahogany would be more common from early 1943 onward, with a few wartime examples constructed with more readily available maple. Several early guitars were also made without truss rods, which became standard from 1945 onward. Wood variations aside, the Southerner is a classic example of Gibson's jumbo-sized dreadnoughts, with the 16-inch-wide body styled in the elegant round-shouldered shape. Extremely similar to the more common J-45, the Southerner Jumbo is distinguished by its split-parallelogram fingerboard inlays and offers the same succulent tone and power with a rich organic depth that comes from carefully aged tonewood.

Courtesy Mandolin World Headquarters/www.vintagemandolin.com

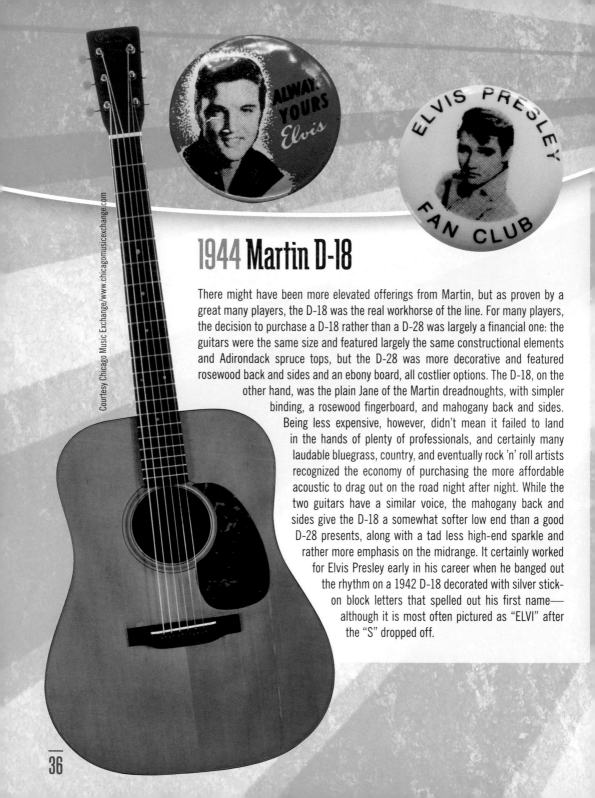

Courtesy Chicago Music Exchange/www.chicagomusicexchange.com

1944 Martin D-18

There might have been more elevated offerings from Martin, but as proven by a great many players, the D-18 was the real workhorse of the line. For many players, the decision to purchase a D-18 rather than a D-28 was largely a financial one: the guitars were the same size and featured largely the same constructional elements and Adirondack spruce tops, but the D-28 was more decorative and featured rosewood back and sides and an ebony board, all costlier options. The D-18, on the other hand, was the plain Jane of the Martin dreadnoughts, with simpler binding, a rosewood fingerboard, and mahogany back and sides. Being less expensive, however, didn't mean it failed to land in the hands of plenty of professionals, and certainly many laudable bluegrass, country, and eventually rock 'n' roll artists recognized the economy of purchasing the more affordable acoustic to drag out on the road night after night. While the two guitars have a similar voice, the mahogany back and sides give the D-18 a somewhat softer low end than a good D-28 presents, along with a tad less high-end sparkle and rather more emphasis on the midrange. It certainly worked for Elvis Presley early in his career when he banged out the rhythm on a 1942 D-18 decorated with silver stick-on block letters that spelled out his first name—although it is most often pictured as "ELVI" after the "S" dropped off.

DeArmond Tremolo Control

One of the most productive pickup makers in the early history of the electric guitar and right up through the 1960s, DeArmond was also responsible for what might be the first genuine standalone effects pedal. The Tremolo Control (also "Trem-Trol") was produced as early as 1946, according to research by Dan Formosa, and housed an electro-mechanical mechanism for inducing tremolo in the guitar signal when plugged in between guitar and amplifier. This unit contained a motor that shook a small container of what DeArmond referred to somewhat redundantly as "hydro-fluid" (errantly called a "mercury switch" in some descriptions, although the unit contains no mercury whatsoever), causing the conductive fluid to rhythmically ground out the signal introduced within the canister by a contact wire. However obtuse the description of its workings, the result was a smooth, buoyant, and, yes, very liquid tremolo, best heard on many of Bo Diddley's early recordings. Most vintage Tremolo Controls require some restoration, and the "hydro-fluid" usually needs to be replaced at the very least, having dried up over the years. But putting one into working condition (Formosa recommends Windex as the perfect conductive replacement) is well worth the effort.

Amp and photos courtesy Jason Lollar

1946 Masco MAP-15

The Masco name is best known in guitar circles for an entirely un-guitaristic use of its products, that being the converted Masco PA head through which legendary harpist Little Walter produced his bluesy wail. It's no surprise, though, that the company's lesser-seen guitar combos, this MAP-15 for one, produce a similarly creamy, bluesy tone unlike quite anything else out there today. This one, in fact, despite its age and apparent fragility, remains a favorite gigging amp of notable pickup maker Jason Lollar, who tells us it wipes the smirks from the faces of other players as soon as they hear the fury that comes out when fired up. Two unusual 7F7 preamp tubes fire up the front end, while a pair of 6L6s provides a far lower output level than expected, at about 15 watts. But who needs volume anyway, right? Stick it up in front of a mic, and the sky's the limit. You're sure going to sound more original than the guy next to you riffing through the similarly rated Pro Junior.

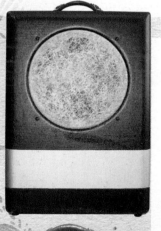

Amp and photo courtesy Terry Scarberry

Late-1940s Silvertone 1304

We often hear of how Danelectro provided guitars and amplifiers for Sears, Roebuck and Co.'s Silvertone brand in the 1950s and '60s, but the start of that story is rarely told. Silvertone existed *before* Danelectro, but as in the case of this Model 1304 amplifier, it was often the product of Nathan I. "Nat" Daniel, who would famously found Danelectro in Red Bank, New Jersey, in the late 1940s. Peruse the back panel of this rarity and you will find no mention of Danelectro, only the Silvertone name and the Sears connection. What you will also find, however, in addition to the Volume and independent Treble and Bass controls (often credited to other later makers), is a Tremolo control not seen on a Fender amp, for example, until the middle of the following decade. Powered by a 12SJ7 pentode preamp tube in the front end and a pair of 6L6s in the back for around 18 cathode-biased watts, the 1304 pumps a thick, juicy tone through its single Jensen PM P12T speaker. And like a lot of early vintage amps, it handles single-coils far better, exuding a dirty near-freakout tone when humbuckers are introduced—although that might just be the kind of freakout you dig.

1946–1947 Fender Dual Professional

As hard as it might be to believe today, the concept of a dual-speaker amp was radical in the mid-1940s—so radical that Fender's early Dual Professional is credited as being the first commercially produced guitar amplifier to be so equipped. Even if not for its two 10-inch Jensen PM10C alnico speakers, however, this combo from Fullerton's young upstart was a groundbreaking design. It was also among the earliest amps to feature a top-mounted control panel. For firsts within Fender, it boasted easier access to the inside of the chassis through a removable back panel; it was covered in the enduringly popular tweed (though a more linen-like variety); it carried a tube chart; and, as John Teagle and John Sprung point out in *Fender Amps: The First Fifty Years*, it was the first built in a finger-jointed pine cabinet. And let's not forget the toothsome tone that this unusual angle-fronted beauty is capable of—it's a major favorite of ZZ Top's Billy F Gibbons (who has snatched up more than his fair share of good 'uns). The Dual Professional is clean yet complex down low, and woody and creamy when cranked, with a voice and body that prefigures better-known Fender tweed amps to come.

Amp and photos courtesy Mark Watson/Amwatts Amps

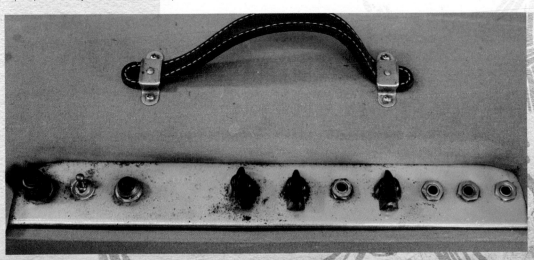

Late-1940s Bigsby Merle Travis

Paul Bigsby's early custom-made solidbody electric guitars were most famously seen in the hands of country star Merle Travis in the late 1940s and the 1950s, but Bigsby made several roughly similar instruments for a number of different artists (although all of these are extremely rare). Bigsby, foreman of the machine shop at the Crocker Motorcycle Company of Los Angeles in the 1940s, became known for his side business repairing the newfangled instruments used by country-and-western musicians. Bigsby made his foray into guitar making after Travis sketched out a rudimentary solidbody electric guitar in 1946. The result featured a thin maple body and hand-carved wooden arm rest, tailpiece, and pickguard; the hardware was machined almost entirely by Bigsby himself. The original Merle Travis guitar had a single pickup in the bridge position, but others often had two pickups. In fact, no two Bigsby guitars are quite alike. One of Travis' original intentions for the solidbody guitar was that it had the singing, sustaining tone of the lap-steel guitars popular in country music at the time, and the Bigsby delivers in spades. The solid maple body and neck give it plenty of sparkle and cut, although that wide, hand-wound pickup packs some snarl, too. All in all, it's a glimpse into the definition of twang before Fender's 6-string even hit the scene.

Courtesy Outline Press Limited

1950 Gibson ES-5

It might seem no great shakes today, but upon its debut in 1949, Gibson's ES-5 grabbed the honors of being the first three-pickup electric guitar from a major manufacturer and was clearly intended to be a market leader in its day. The maple-bodied guitar also emphasized, like the ES-175 introduced the same year and the ES-350 of two years before, Gibson's commitment to archtops built primarily as electric guitars. Had the original ES-5 offered some form of pickup switching rather than just individual Volume controls for each pickup, it likely would have made even more of a splash. As it is, the pickup selection is balanced by rolling back the volumes of those you don't want in the blend, while the overall output level is controlled with the Master Volume mounted on the Venetian cutaway. Awkward though this might be, the ES-5 still sounds grand, with a plummy, rich jazz tone from the neck pickup and plenty of rockabilly twang when you isolate that bridge P-90. In the hands of the great T-Bone Walker, the versatile ES-5 could pretty much do it all simultaneously.

1949 Gibson ES-175

Big carved-spruce archtops like Gibson's Super 400 or D'Angelico's New Yorker might win the day for pure acoustic tone, but Gibson's ES-175 set a benchmark for amplified jazz tone that remains the standard today. While Fender was developing a solidbody electric to combat feedback and improve sustain, Gibson's more traditional approach was to retain the fully hollowbody, but reasoning that an amplified guitar didn't require the same niceties of acoustic tone, constructed it with rigid laminated maple. This wood could be pressed into an arch for the top and back rather than having to be carved, so savings were realized on several fronts, alongside a genuine improvement in performance for many styles of playing. Of course, we tend to think of the ES-175 as loaded with one or two humbucking pickups, which it received from 1957 onward, but at its birth in 1949 this guitar carried a single P-90 in the neck position, with two P-90s available from around 1951 onward. As such, our ES-175 is still characteristically warm and rich, with a round, blooming tone, but has an appealingly gritty edge to it, too, which offers a little more bite than the traditional ultra-smooth jazz tone. Throw it a few seventh and ninth shapes and dig in.

Courtesy Chicago Music Exchange/
www.chicagomusicexchange.com

c. 1950 Oahu 230K Tone Master

Oahu of Cleveland started out as a publisher of how-to-play books aimed mainly at the Hawaiian boom of the 1930s through early '50s, but soon found itself selling lap-steel guitars and amplifiers to go with them. It sourced this gear from Chicago manufacturers such as Kay and Valco, with the latter producing this groovy little Tone Master, a design that it supplied to other re-branders in similar form. Although many Valco-made amps of a few years later would migrate toward more modern (or at least early modern) designs, this 230K really is a throwback to a previous era of tube electronics. There's no circuit board, just a somewhat chaotically cobbled rat's nest of point-to-point connections with relatively few components populating the chassis, two octal preamp tubes, and a pair of 6V6s generating around 10 watts. What it does offer, though, is a chewy tone that just begs you to put a mic in front of it and make it the centerpiece of your next hit recording.

1952 Gibson GA-50T

Here's another amp that starts off looking like something a traveling salesman might throw into the back of his Ford Coupe for a swing through the Midwest, but the 1952 Gibson GA-50T was a sophisticated amp for its day, and its features hold up well even 60 years later. The amp was conceived with jazz in mind (Jim Hall says a GA-50 was responsible for the best tone he ever had) and capable of acquitting itself well on the country bandstand, too, although it can get the juke jumpin' if you turn it up. A 12-inch Jensen P12P and an 8-inch Jensen P8P speaker chuck out a broad tonal range with plenty of complexity, and even with the thick octal preamps and cathode-biased 6L6s, there's still surprising clarity and articulation in this old brown box. But the real joy comes from its rich, syrupy midrange and touchy-feely dynamics. All that, and there's tremolo, too. Back in 1952, before rock 'n' roll was even close to being a household word, this was quite an amp to reckon with, and if you were a serious pro guitarist you very likely conspired to do so.

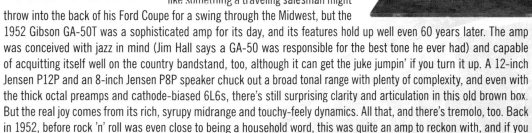

1950 Fender Broadcaster

It wasn't the first solidbody electric guitar ever made, but Fender's Broadcaster certainly was the first *production* solidbody made in any numbers, and in your hands, this electric still has the feel of something seminal, groundbreaking, trendsetting—*revolutionary*. You can't claim that the Broadcaster—the forerunner to the Telecaster—invented rock 'n' roll (a music that has plenty of hollowbody electrics in its early history), but it certainly was built to make rockin' a lot easier while also forging the archetypal sound of electric country guitar. Simple ingredients such as resonant swamp ash, a responsive maple neck, and a hot, snarly bridge pickup combine to forge musical history. Hit the low-E string down near the bridge, bend it up at the 3rd fret, and pick the octave E (D string, 3rd fret), and the Broadcaster makes you feel like you're giving birth to rock 'n' roll and country music in one gut-thumping twang. By February 1951 Fender had decided to change the Broadcaster's model name to Telecaster in deference to a request from Gretsch, who claimed the name infringed on their Broadkaster (with a *k*) banjos and drums.

Fender fine electric instruments

- Amplifiers
- Guitars
- Covers
- Cases

207 OAK STREET
SANTA ANA, CALIF.
CATALOGUE No. 2   1950

This Broadcaster was signed by the legendary guitar-and-steel-guitar team of Jimmy Bryant and Speedy West. Bryant was instrumental in the Broadcaster's development.

1950s Maccaferri

Italian Mario Maccaferri was one of the musical world's true visionaries. Working in France in the 1930s, he created the radical Selmer-Maccaferri steel-string. Immigrating to New York City, he patented a plastic woodwind reed in 1941, part of an eventual empire of pioneering plastic products, from clothespins to 8-track cassettes. Maccaferri believed in plastic, not just as a cheap substitute for wood, but as a miracle product. Turning back to his luthier days, he launched the plastic Islander ukulele in 1949, selling for just $5.95. This was followed by the Maccaferri plastic guitar, which looked similar to the Selmer jazz guitars but with f-holes and either steel or plastic strings depending on the model. The guitars sounded good, too—they were not just a cheap plastic imitation of a "real" guitar. But by 1969, sales had slowed and the small plastic guitars were no more. Still, Maccaferri never gave up: he crafted a plastic violin that was debuted at Carnegie Hall in 1990.

Both Courtesy Outline Press Limited

1952 Kay Thin Twin K161

While plenty of Kay electrics of the 1950s and 1960s linger on the sub-$1,000 bargain rack, the Thin Twin K161 (a.k.a. the "Jimmy Reed model" for its use by the Chicago bluesman) is one of a handful of Kays that has attained an elevated status for playability and tone. Plug in this beauty, and you're greeted with a voice that's simultaneously thick and biting, a product of an enclosed hollowbody construction, unusual pickup configuration, and further constructional oddities hidden under the hood. The "Thin" refers not to the semi-full-depth body, but to the pickups, only the thin blades of which project through the fire-stripe pickguard, with the coils hidden beneath. A steel reinforcement bar stretching from neck heel to tail block purportedly adds sustain to the entire brew. An iconic-looking guitar from a bygone era, the Thin Twin was one of few catalog-grade instruments to knock on the door of the big makers and earn respect not only from Reed, but from the likes of Howlin' Wolf, Hubert Sumlin, Bob Dylan, and T-Bone Burnett.

Early-1950s Flot-A-Tone

No, not Flaunt-A-Tone—*Flot*-A-Tone. Though you might be flaunting it when you get this odd duck cranked and rippin'. You'd be forgiven for guessing, at first glance, that this groovy construction was a Valco product, with its compact cabinet, rigid handle, and slant-mounted rear control panel, but Flot-A-Tone amps were manufactured in Milwaukee, Wisconsin, from the late 1940s through the late 1950s or early 1960s and sold by accordion importers Lo Duca Brothers (with a Wisconsin locale, there just *had* to be an accordion in there somewhere, right?). As simple as most tube amps were back in the early '50s, though, the same circuits that worked for an accordion proved pretty effective for guitar, too, and these can be smokin' little sleepers when hit with some 6-string attitude, as notable artists such as Ry Cooder and G. E. Smith—both Flot-A-Tone fans—have proven. A 6SC7 preamp tube and a 6SN7 phase inverter, both octal tubes, hit a pair of 6L6s for approximately 25 watts, all governed by dual Volume and Master tone knobs that go all the way to . . . nine. But, hey, sometimes less is more in Flot-A-World.

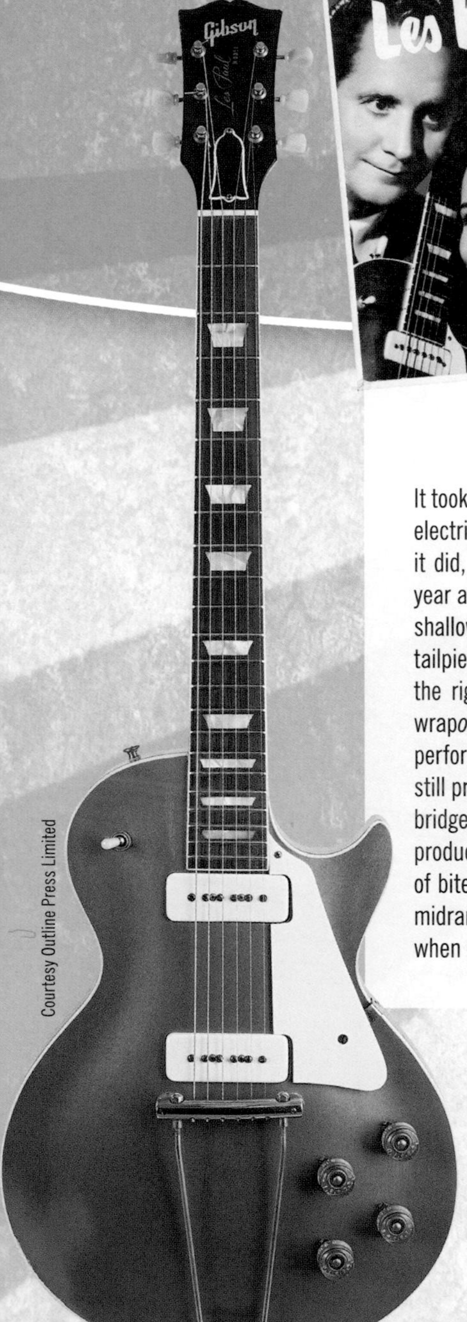

THE HIT MAKERS!

EAP 1-416 PART 1

Capitol

Les Paul and Mary Ford

Mockin' Bird Hill
Josephine
Whispering
How High The Moon

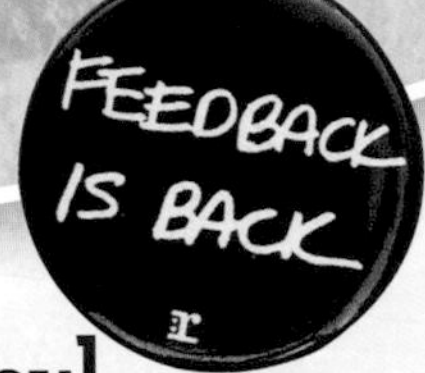

FEEDBACK IS BACK

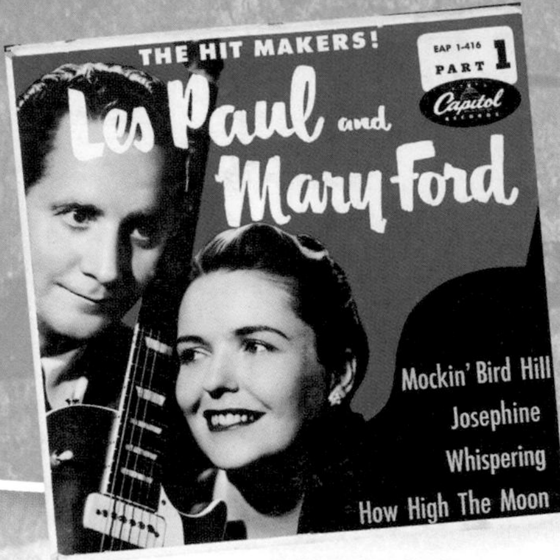

1953 Gibson Les Paul

It took Les Paul several years to convince Gibson of the viability of a solidbody electric guitar before the original "Goldtop" hit the streets in 1952, and when it did, it had an odd flaw that made it far less playable than it would be a year after its debut. Gibson made the first Les Paul models with an extremely shallow neck angle that required running the strings under the trapeze bridge/tailpiece configuration rather than over it, yielding an unconventional feel at the right hand. Once this was remedied with a simple wraparound (a.k.a. wrap*over*) bridge in late 1953, the Goldtop proved itself the thick, meaty performer that it remains known as today. Plenty of rock and blues players still prefer this configuration to anything that followed: the simple wraparound bridge enhances resonance and sustain, while the P-90 single-coil pickups produce a thick, rich tone that also presents plenty of bite and grit in the upper frequencies and a midrange girth that just screams rock 'n' roll when played through a cranked tube amp.

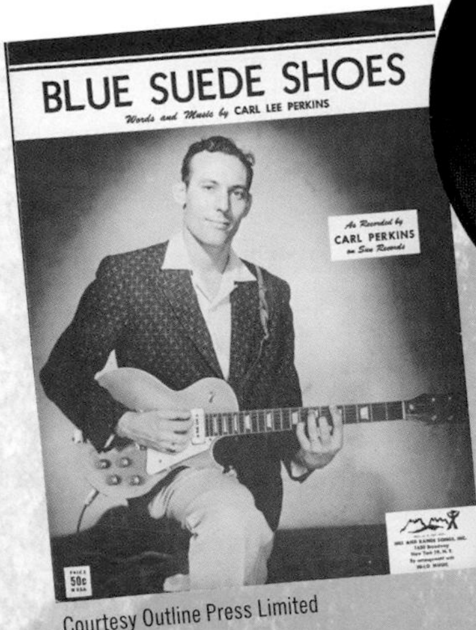

BLUE SUEDE SHOES
Words and Music by CARL LEE PERKINS

As Recorded by
CARL PERKINS
on Sun Records

PRICE 50¢

SUN

HONEY, DON'T!
CARL PERKINS
MEMPHIS, TENNESSEE

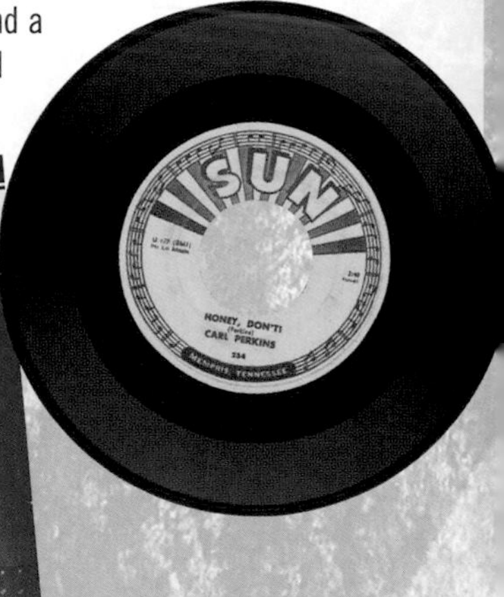

The Guitar That Changed The World!
Scotty Moore

Heartbreak Hotel
Hound Dog
Don't Be Cruel
Mean Woman Blues
Love Me Tender
Money Honey
Don't
That's All Right
My Baby Left Me
Mystery Train
Loving You
Milk Cow Blues

Scotty Moore was there when it happened. He heard the screams. There was Elvis in the spotlight. And at his right hand from the beginning—from ragged rehearsals in a boardinghouse room and first record sessions to barnstorming the flatbed truck circuit, from flat-broke to that historic first appearance with Tommy Dorsey, from roadhouse to the glittering spotlight in Las Vegas, from hillbilly honky-tonk to Hollywood—Scotty was there.

EPIC

1953 Gibson ES-295

Before the solidbody electric guitar had risen to prominence in popular music, players were breaking the molds and blasting out new sounds on archtop electrics, and the stunning Gibson ES-295 was right there at the head of the pack. It's amazing to think that a guitar like this, that just screams rock 'n' roll, was issued in 1952 before the looming new music revolution even had a name. Just a year later, though, an ES-295 was picked up by Scotty Moore—who had previously played a Fender Esquire—and it proceeded to make musical history behind Elvis Presley. Despite the look, and the fact that we now know it to be behind the most formative rockabilly playing of all time, the ES-295 is essentially an ES-175 jazz box with gold paint and a fancy pickguard. But when it comes to rock 'n' roll, looks are half the battle—attitude is the rest. Plug the ES-295 into an old tube amp turned up just a little too hot for jazz, put some attitude into a scattershot of fired-up bop runs and driving double stops, and you can bet they never danced like this to *jazz* music.

1953 Fender Telecaster

Here we are only three years beyond the arrival of Fender's plank, but the seminal solidbody has already evolved in several notable ways. The early steel bridge saddles are now warm, round brass; the pickup just beyond them is wound with somewhat fewer turns of a heavier-gauge wire; the neck is a little less clubby but still a full, round "D" in your left palm; and, of course, the name on the headstock is finally, firmly, forever *Telecaster*. Plenty of major Tele slingers will tell you that the '53s are the zenith of vintage blackguards. Telecasters made in 1953 have been played by Roy Buchanan, Danny Gatton, Waylon Jennings, Vince Gill, and Duke Levine, so there might just be something to the theory. Plugged into, ideally, a tweed Fender combo, the '53 Telecaster gives you a pliant, slightly snarly breed of twang with a big, round, piano-like attack at the center of its low notes and a multidimensional shimmer in the highs that is never harsh or piercing. In short, this is exactly what a player seeks in a great Tele.

ARMADILLO WORLD HEADQUARTERS
PRESENTS

ROY BUCHANAN
The Bugs Henderson Group

AUSTIN, TEXAS

FRIDAY
9:00 P.M.

01468
SEC   ROW   SEAT
GEN. ADM.
SEPT 1, 1978
ADMIT ONE ON ABOVE DATE ONLY

S
E
P
T   1   1
              9
              7
              8

NO REFUND PRICE NO EXCHANGE
$6.00
ADVANCE

SEC   ROW   SEAT
GEN. ADM.
01468

Robert Gordon with
Danny Gatton - Live

"The Humbler"

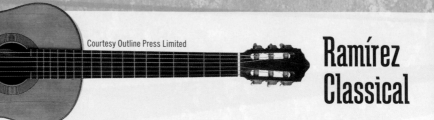

Ramírez Classical

As appended to Spanish brothers José and Manuel, initially together, then separately after a rift forged by a longtime feud, the Ramírez name is one of the most significant in all of classical-guitar making. After the split to two rival shops in 1891, José continued making the large, loud, heavy-topped guitars traditionally used by entertainers in nightclubs while Manuel refined the art in the image of Torres's great instruments, producing the concert-hall-worthy instruments that won favor with Andrés Segovia and others. Following Manuel's death in 1916, the Ramírez style flowed, through two successive generations of Josés, more toward the elegant, sweet-voiced instruments of "Uncle Manuel." José Ramírez II brought new heights of craftsmanship to the guitars, while José Ramírez III further advanced the template upon taking control of the company in the late 1950s, introducing the western cedar tops that have since become popular in the field. This Ramírez guitar purrs with a rich, confident tone that quickly reminds us why so many major artists have been drawn to the name, and which would certainly have put a smile on disenfranchised cofounder Manuel Ramírez's face.

Hauser Classical

Before encountering renowned classical guitarist Andrés Segovia in 1925, German maker Hermann Hauser was building the thin, heavy, rather strident guitars in the European nightclub tradition (see the José branch of the original Ramírez brothers' approaches to the instrument). At Segovia's urging, however, and following a heavy dose of inspiration from the virtuoso's Manuel Ramírez guitar, Hauser completely revised his approach to the art to become one of the most significant European makers of the twentieth century. Hauser's turnaround took the form of a new, scientific approach to guitar making, one in which he maximized the effectiveness of his guitars' bracing patterns, which in turn allowed thinner, livelier soundboards and a better and more responsive overall tone. The results are heard clear as day in this Hauser, a descendent of the guitar that Segovia declared one of the finest ever made.

Hauser's son, Hermann II, carried on in much the same tradition after his father's death in 1952 and passed the baton to his own son, Hermann III, in 1988.

1954 Gibson J-45

Introduced alongside the Southerner Jumbo in 1942, Gibson's round-shouldered J-45 dreadnought is one of the most beloved flat-tops of its type. The J-45 was available only in its sunburst finish initially, although the J-50 model designated a natural finish from 1947 onward. The guitar's solid spruce top and solid mahogany back and sides teamed up for an appealing blend of depth and clarity, and the J-45 and J-50 became known as especially effective rhythm instruments, finding their way into the hands of players banging out everything from country to blues to rock 'n' roll. The Gibson flat-top's distinctive look kept it separate from its dreadnought rivals over at Martin, whose "square-shouldered" D-18 and D-28 were also big players, while the Kalamazoo brand had always boasted its own following regardless. That said, even aside from their more rounded upper bout, the J-45 and J-50 have always been very much their own beasts, with a clear character and vibe that set them in their own little corner of flat-top history. Now, as then, they remain great alternatives in storied American-made acoustic guitars.

Courtesy Rumble Seat Music/www.rumbleseatmusic.com

1954 Fender Stratocaster

So universal is the Fender Stratocaster today that it's almost impossible to truly appreciate how this guitar must have appeared to a scene populated by only a few solidbodies, like the Telecaster, Les Paul, and Gretsch's semi-solid Duo Jet, as well as a plethora of big jazz boxes. In a word, it was revolutionary. In another word: sexy. Pick up an original 1954 Strat today, though, with its early Bakelite pickguard and pickup covers and its chunky maple neck, and it really does feel like the origin of the species; that, and it's *still* far sexier and more revolutionary than so many other guitars out there. The ash body and maple neck of Fender's debutante Stratocaster gives the guitar degrees of snap and twang that more closely ally it with its predecessor, the Telecaster, while those relatively low-output vintage pickups prove beautifully detailed and trenchant, artfully translating the well-aged depth and harmonic richness of the woods into the overall tone. Leo Fender built this guitar for the country-and-western crowd, but it begs to rock 'n' roll—which it does with unparalleled style.

Ike Turner (center) and his Kings of Rhythm, 1956. Gilles Petard/Redferns/Getty Images

1954 Gretsch Rancher

Gretsches have earned a large chapter in the electric guitar annals, and the company's acoustic archtops had a place in their day, but a Gretsch flat-top? Perhaps this one won't win any prizes for tone or playability when put up against market leaders of the day from Martin and Gibson, but the Rancher has proven rather collectible at least, thanks primarily to its western appointments. Intended as a match for the original-issue Roundup electric, the Rancher (also introduced in 1954) displays the same kitschy "G" brand, steer's-head headstock inlay and block fingerboard inlays engraved with various western motifs. The pick-shaped sound hole is also an eye-catcher, and the adjustable bridge saddle with metal string retainer makes for an excellent conversation piece, if only a mediocre coupler of vibrational energy from strings into body. By late 1956, the western appointments would disappear from the Rancher entirely, which makes it, in our opinion, rather closer to pointless. Strum this roughrider with vigor while your lead guitarist applies some Travis picking to his matching Gretsch Roundup electric, and you're at least guaranteed some attention down at the rodeo.

1955 Gibson Les Paul Custom "Black Beauty"

While the Les Paul Standard is a classic, the mid-'50s Les Paul Custom is totally *classy*. There's something about a black guitar with aged binding, ebony fingerboard, and mother-of-pearl block inlays that stirs the heart of any hot-blooded player, and this one gets the juices flowing more than most. Les Paul and then–Gibson president Ted McCarty conceived of the Custom as the "black tie" Les Paul for musicians performing in formal settings, and the look certainly fits the part. Beneath the gloss-black finish, the Custom hides an all-mahogany body rather than the Standard's carved maple top. There's a story, perhaps apocryphal, that this is another of Les Paul's ideas that got twisted around: the Standard should have been the simple mahogany guitar, the Custom the more complex multi-wood construction. Either way, the result gives this top-of-the-line solidbody a sound that's a little warmer and smoother than its Goldtop sibling, although the added crispness and clarity of the Alnico (a.k.a. "staple") pickup in the neck position helps to narrow the gap a little. A Black Beauty, indeed, this model was also known as the "fretless wonder" for its low frets. Intended to be superbly playable, they actually lack the necessary "grab" to many modern fingers, but the 1955 Les Paul Custom's trenchant, earthy tone makes the effort worthwhile.

1955 Gibson Byrdland

Although its name might imply otherwise, Gibson's Byrdland had nothing to do with the famous New York City jazz club, Birdland, nor was it inspired by Charlie Parker, whose nickname put the "i" in that bebop mecca. Unveiled in 1955, the Byrdland was the result of consultation with first-call Nashville session musicians Billy Byrd and Hank Garland, and its design incorporated a number of "advancements" that the two saw as beneficial to the player of the day. Like its predecessor, the L-5CES, which evolved from acoustic archtops, the Byrdland has a carved solid-spruce top and a big 17-inch-wide body, but—designed from the ground up as an *electric* guitar—is considerably thinner, at only 2.25 inches deep. It's also shorter, with the scale length of 23.5 inches along its extremely thin neck, which Garland and Byrd reasoned would ease playing speed and reach of those complex jazz chords. Amped up, the shorter scale lends plenty of warmth and roundness to the Alnico (a.k.a. "staple") pickups that the early examples were born with, yielding a surprisingly full, rich tone. Indeed, it's an easy ride, too, and makes you feel rather nimble once you adjust to its dimensions.

1955 Gretsch 6120 Chet Atkins

We often think of solidbody electrics as having launched rock 'n' roll, but hollowbodies like the seminal Gretsch 6120 Chet Atkins arguably played a bigger role than any single-plank guitar in transitioning hot-riffsters from country and swing over to rock. The 6120 debuted as the signature guitar of Gretsch's hot new endorsee, Chet Atkins, a star on the country and pop scenes, but its charms quickly won over many names in the younger, rowdier scene—Eddie Cochran and Duane Eddy among them. As a result, it has become an eternal rockabilly archetype. Although the 6120 has a relatively deep, fully hollowbody made from laminated maple, its Dynasonic (a.k.a. DeArmond Model 200) single-coil pickups are cuttingly bright and quite powerful. The result is a guitar with an inherent acoustic airiness and "thickness" to it, yet one that presents plenty of spank and sparkle at the amp. These pickups drive enough to break up an old tube combo but not so much as to flatten out the detail and harmonic content of the guitar itself; add a judicial wobble of the Bigsby vibrato to that unparalleled meaty twang and you've got a great theme tune for the birth of rock 'n' roll.

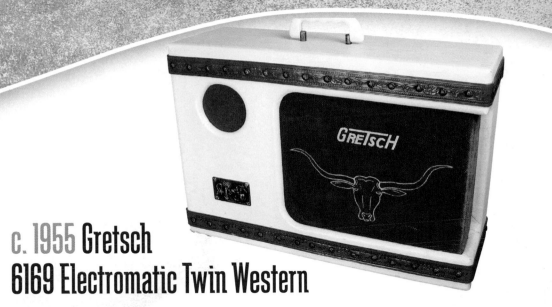

c. 1955 Gretsch
6169 Electromatic Twin Western

We can't tell you how many workaday cowhands were carting electric guitars and amps out on the range for the cattle drive, but Gretsch must have figured the look worked. The same steer's-head and tooled-leather motif that briefly adorned the Roundup renditions of the Chet Atkins and Duo Jet guitars gave these amps a look all their own. Thanks to the gnarly—and snarly—Valco-made circuitry behind it all, though, the country kitsch turns to rock 'n' roll bluster proportionate to your turn of the Volume knob, proving the 6169 Electromatic Western Twin more than just a conversation piece when you plug in and give it some gumption. The eight-pin 6SC7s preamp tubes sound a little thicker than their ubiquitous nine-pin cousin, the 12AX7, and the duet of 6V6s kicks out a delectable crunch through two elliptical 6x9-inch speakers and a 4-inch tweeter. The Tremolo knob governs the rate of that haunting effect (depth is preset) and only adds to the atmosphere that this cowboy can kick out.

c. 1955 Danelectro Twin Twelve

You want funky? You got it: two diagonally mounted 12-inch speakers in a chipboard box front a diagonally mounted chassis with four 6L6 output tubes (producing a mere 40 watts of power) along with oddball 6AU6 and 6FQ7 preamp tubes through two independent output transformers. Several of these ingredients equate with the bones of Fender's "high-powered" tweed Twin of several years later, and yet the Dano circuit doesn't squeeze anywhere near the Fender's 80 watts from the brew. But watts aren't everything. For bluesy or garagey grunge and grind, this vertically challenged combo certainly holds its own. The aforementioned dual output transformers, one feeding each speaker, are each about the size of the OT found on a much smaller tweed Fender Deluxe or similar, so this won't give you much low-end girth (we already mentioned the shallow chipboard cabinet, right?), but for all that, it was an impressively sophisticated amplifier, too, with independent Volume controls for each of two channels, individual Bass and Treble controls, and Vibrato with both Speed and Strength. In a word, *funky*.

c. 1955 Montgomery Ward 55 JDR 8473

Although amps such as Fender's Pro, Super, Twin, and Deluxe, and Gibson's GA series already existed in the mid-1950s, not every maker was ready to accept that these would set the pace for the look and layout of 90 percent of combo amps to come. Danelectro, maker of this unusual Montgomery Ward model, clearly figured the future might just come in the shape of a hinged suitcase that split into two cabinets with four 8-inch speakers each and 25 feet of wire between them so you could really spread the sound around the stage. Speaker configuration aside, it's an interesting amp in many other ways, using four 6V6GT output tubes (where many would have turned to a pair of 6L6s) and a top-mounted preamp section with two 12AX7s—one as a first gain stage for each of two channels and the other for gain makeup after the independent Treble and Bass controls (another deluxe early Dano feature). Even in quintuples these smaller speakers don't give a lot of low-end oomph, but the amp sounds pretty darn good regardless, moving more air than you might expect, with plenty of snarl amid the detailed response.

1955–1956 Fender Pro 5E5

The 5E3 tweed Fender Deluxe has become a benchmark for small-amp tone done American style, and one of the classics that every guitarist needs to experience at least once in his or her lifetime. And once that happens, many will enjoy the experience but walk away wishing they had just a little more power and a heap more headroom and imagining that adding such to the brew might well conjure up the best-sounding guitar amplifier of all time. Welcome the 5E5 Pro, a short-lived model at the front of the "narrow-panel" tweed wave that possibly embodies everything a player wants from a 5E3 Deluxe and more. While the other medium-size tweed amps advanced to tighter-sounding, fixed-bias output stages and more complex preamps with independent bass and treble tone stacks in the cathode-follower configuration, the 5E5, for all its 6L6 output tubes, 15-inch speaker, and chunky output transformer, retained a circuit that was essentially the same as the 5E3 Deluxe. This means a simple yet toothsome volume and tone complement rammed straight into an oh-so-sweet cathode-biased output stage with no negative feedback. In other words, a blues amp to die for, and possibly the archetypal tone for classic country or rock 'n' roll—with a Telecaster or a Les Paul Special injected, respectively.

1956 Gibson Les Paul Junior

Introduced in 1954, the Les Paul Junior wasn't fully appreciated until the late 1960s and early 1970s when garage rockers and, later, punk rockers discovered the minimalistic appeal and unassuming power of this erstwhile "student model." The slab mahogany body and single P-90 pickup made it far more affordable to produce than the flagship carved-top Les Paul, but these elements also contributed to a voice and performance that led some players to actually prefer a Junior over its big brother. The solidbody gives a Junior a round, woody voice, and the lack of a neck pickup means there's more wood present at the crucial neck/body joint, resulting in enhanced resonance. Plugged in, the single P-90 in the bridge position really screams, and there's a pliant snap and grind to this guitar that just begs you to churn out some power chords. Its thick, round neck still feels entirely like a vintage '50s Gibson and, kept in good condition, should render this no-frills beauty just as playable as any Goldtop worth ten times the price.

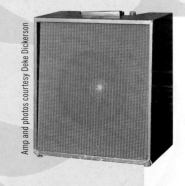

Amp and photos courtesy Deke Dickerson

1956 Ray Butts EchoSonic

Plug in and crank up for a one-stop source of the seminal sound of rockabilly. Although Ray Butts built relatively few of his EchoSonic amps with built-in tape-look echo, the list of players who owned them in the mid-1950s reads like a veritable who's who of early rock 'n' roll. Chet Atkins, Scotty Moore, Luther Perkins, Carl Perkins, Roy Orbison—all had to have an EchoSonic, and once they did, that meaty slap-back echo was enshrined for all time as *the* sound of classic rock 'n' roll. The basic amp itself doesn't have a whole lot of punch, putting out about 25 watts max even after Butts stepped up the design to a pair of 6L6s from the original 6V6s (Butts built Scotty Moore a pair of 50-watt "satellite" amps that fed off the original combo so he could be heard onstage behind Elvis Presley), but it does its thing like no other amp. Plug in, roll it up to a point just shy of breakup, and get that echo happening (which has a longer delay time than traditionally associated with slap-back echo today), and it's "Mystery Train" in a box, baby.

1950s Gretsch 6128 Duo Jet

Despite a subtle bit of deception at the heart of Gretsch's marketing strategy for this guitar, the Duo Jet is one of the truly formative instruments in the birth of rock 'n' roll. Gretsch's bid to enter the solidbody arena, the Duo Jet, isn't truly a solid at all. Duo Jets have mahogany body backs topped with pressed arched tops made from laminated maple, and between the two is a significant acoustic chamber. Regardless, a great Duo Jet performs much like a solidbody and is quite a bit lighter than many. The Duo Jet first found its way into rock 'n' roll history in the hands of Gene Vincent and the Blue Caps guitarist Cliff Gallup, who played a 1955 model. But arguably, the guitar made an even bigger splash after Beatle George Harrison purchased his own secondhand 1957 Duo Jet

in Liverpool for £75 in 1961. As can be heard both on Gallup's late-'50s recordings and Harrison's early Beatles recordings, the Duo Jet has a little more bite and sting than its fully hollowbodied sibling, the 6120, with a bright, gritty snarl that can really push a semi-cranked tube combo. In other words, another classic voice of rock 'n' roll.

1957 Fender Stratocaster

In the minds—and ears and hands—of many Stratocaster players, the '57 is the archetypal '50s Strat. This is the Stratocaster of seminal rock 'n' roll (Buddy Holly) and hard-bitten Chicago blues (Buddy Guy), of sultry two-tone sunburst and play-worn, nicotine-stained maple neck. Plug it in and you're rewarded with a little more snarl and edge than you might expect if you're more familiar with '60s Strats. The winding of the '50s pickups was somewhat less consistent than in later years, and as a result, you occasionally stumble on a relatively hot set. The swamp ash bodies that Fender was still using beneath this finish were also rich and resonant, and the one-piece maple necks contributed a crystalline shimmer that nevertheless refrained from any icepick-in-the-ear brightness. Plenty of players feel these are some of the best necks Fender ever made: a gently V'd (some call it a "soft boat") profile that really measures fairly thin if you put the calipers on it but feels magical in the hands of most players, whether they like 'em beefy or slim.

1957 Fender Champ 5F1

You want to hear what an electric guitar sounds like when amplified through a vacuum tube? Fender's 5F1 Champ takes you there with fewer components between input and output than almost any other conventional amplifier out there. One 12AX7 preamp tube, one 6V6 output tube, and a handful of capacitors and resistors (only a few of which the signal actually passes through), and there you are. Of course purity doesn't always equal quality, but fortunately the tweed Champ has seduced many players over the years despite its potential failings as an amplifier (its easy breakup, the heavy compression, and the overt midrange content in its less-than-balanced frequency response). Eric Clapton, for one, recorded several tracks on Derek and the Dominoes' *Layla and Other Assorted Love Songs* through a tweed Champ, and it has been a favorite studio amp of countless others. This little 4-watter with a single 8-inch speaker might have trouble keeping up with a drummer on stage, of course, but pop it up in front of a good studio mic, and the end listener won't have a clue how small a box is creating that superlative tone.

Courtesy Retrofret Vintage Guitars/www.retrofret.com/photo by George Aslaender

1957 Guild M-75

Too often forgotten among the Fenders, Gibsons, Gretsches, and Rickenbackers of the day, Guild only got up and running in 1952 but was producing first-class instruments virtually from day one. Much like Gretsch's Duo Jet, the M-75 Aristocrat had a semi-hollowbody made from a chambered mahogany back capped with a carved solid spruce top. It was clearly launched as competition for both the Duo Jet and Gibson's Les Paul, but original examples are usually a few pounds lighter than either at well under 5 pounds. Also like the other "Big G" makers of the day, Guild targeted both the jazz and rock 'n' roll crowds with this model, which ultimately became best associated with electric blues and took the name Bluesbird in later reissue incarnations. The pickups look outwardly like Gibson P-90s and are similarly designed, but they tend to have a little less of the gritty midrange hump and somewhat more snap and upper-midrange crackle. Combined with the unusual construction, these pickups help give the M-75 Aristocrat a voice all its own, which is to say some of the airy richness of a good archtop but with more bite and definition. The unusual 23.25-inch scale further influences the tone, adding a soft roundness in addition to the easy-playing feel.

1958 Gibson LG-2

For several years, the diminutive LG-2 was the only smaller-bodied Gibson flat-top worth its salt, and it remains a popular vintage acoustic today. Introduced in late 1942 or early '43, around the hubbub of America's entry into World War II, the LG-2 was intended as a more affordable Gibson, a little brother to the big Jumbos, Super Jumbos,

and L-5 archtop and its brethren. Even so, it was the only Gibson its size to be made with a proper X-braced top, and had a nice solid-spruce top and solid mahogany back and sides, in addition to other classic, traditional Gibson touches. As such, it offered a rich tone and volume with gumption that defied its 14.25-inch body width, while retaining that appealing playability of Gibson's shorter 24.75-inch scale length, and the comfortable, rounded neck carve that often went with it. Because it was a "real Gibson" that could be had at a more affordable price, the LG-2 appealed to many folk and blues players, and was even a favorite of Woody Guthrie for a time.

1958 Rickenbacker 325

If not for John Lennon's use of a couple of these guitars early in his career with the Beatles, the diminutive Rickenbacker 325 might have slipped to the B- or C-list of vintage collectibles, along with so many other "student-size" guitars. Lennon associations aside, and despite its short-assed 20.75-inch scale, this thing sounds utterly groovy if you whack it with gusto in the course of bopping out some hormone-fueled, teen-beat dance rhythms. Lennon acquired his first 325 in a Hamburg guitar shop in 1960, then his second, a gift from Rickenbacker, in 1964. One way or the other, the loose, rubbery, short-scale vibe and gritty-bright "toaster-top" pickups defined the Fab Four's electric rhythm-guitar sound for the first five years of the band's recording career. These so-called three-quarter-scale guitars (which actually aren't quite as short as that implies) take some getting used to, playability-wise, and the decreased string tension can send the attack of the note or chord slightly off pitch when you hit them hard, but that too is part of their mojo. For all its drawbacks, the 325 is a performer to be reckoned with.

Late-1950s Gretsch 6120

While the debutante 1955 Gretsch 6120 had undergone a number of minor alterations by 1958, mostly cosmetic, a change of pickups was the biggest differentiator between the introductory Chet Atkins models and those produced later in the decade. As with Gibson's move from P-90 to humbucker, the replacement of the DeArmond Model 200 (a.k.a. Dynasonic) pickups with the new Gretsch Filter'Tron humbuckers of 1957 splits 6120 fans into two distinct camps. Although they are humbuckers, Filter'Trons aren't any hotter than their single-coil predecessors; in fact, their specs read a lot cooler, and they often exhibit less poke and snarl through a semi-cranked tube amp, too. What they do offer, however, are excellent clarity, plenty of twangy brightness, just enough edge to put some hair on your tone when you dig in, and, of course, the hum-canceling performance that Chet Atkins requested of them in the first place. Good vintage Filter'Trons have a sound and feel all their own, and while they can do classic rockabilly (Brian Setzer prefers his Gretsches thus equipped), they can also rock out when you show them some gain (see AC/DC's Malcolm Young or the Cult's Billy Duffy). Strap on, dig in, and experience what many consider the last valid stage in "that great Gretsch sound."

Late-1950s Gibson GA-40T Les Paul

If you ever want to document the bias toward guitars versus amps in vintage collectability, look no further than a late-1950s Gibson Les Paul pair. While a good Goldtop 1957 Les Paul Model guitar with humbuckers might be worth $125,000 and a sunburst '58 with figured top more than twice that, a mint GA-40T from the same years will fetch, oh, around 1 percent of the Goldtop price. But make no mistake, these are hallowed tone machines and collectibles in their own right. The key to the fat, meaty GA-40T tone lies in the 5879 pentode preamp tubes that goose the single gain stage in each channel, ramming a little more breadth and depth into the dual-6V6 output stage. The tremolo on these amps is a thing of beauty, too, a lush, bubbly effect produced by a fairly complex circuit driven by an eight-pin 6SQ7 tube. Crank it up, and the Les Paul amp gives you an overdrive tone often described as creamy and chocolaty, with just enough bark and honk to cut through the mix.

1958 Gibson ES-335

The sunburst Les Paul Standard, Explorer, and Flying V of 1958 to 1960 all proved way ahead of their time and were rewarded with early demises. But the new ES-335 knocked it out of the park. Designed as an electric that benefited from many of the advances found on new solidbody models, but with a look and feel that would appeal to archtop-loving traditionalists, the ES-335 quickly proved more than the sum of its parts. A great dot-neck ES-335 with the rounded "Mickey Mouse" ears that were also characteristic of the early models, this version offers much of the grunt and muscle of a Les Paul but with a certain airiness in the midrange and an appealingly hollow thunk to the attack. The neck profile of the rare 1958–1959 examples is a little chunkier and more rounded than that of the early-'60s ES-335s most players are likely to be familiar with and, as a result, offers a meaty, girthsome playability. Caress it all through the bite and complexity of a pair of PAF humbuckers, and you've got a tone for the ages—and a guitar that can do anything you ask it to.

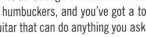

1958 Fender Telecaster

You could start counting on your fingers the ways in which the Telecaster evolved from 1950 to the early 1960s and not finish the task until you run out of toes, too. One of the more significant changes lasted only a short while before players' objections inspired Fender to revert to an earlier template. Midway through 1958 Fender simplified the bridge and string-anchor configuration on the Telecaster and Esquire by dispensing with the through-body stringing (and, as a result, the steel ferrules in the back of the guitar for the strings' ball ends) and instead drilling six holes for the strings into the back lip of the bridge plate. This seemingly minor adjustment simplified the manufacturing process and saved the cost of the six steel ferrules; it's surprising Fender didn't build the guitars this way in the first place. However, through-body stringing is one of the crucial ingredients in the Tele magic, imparting a depth and thickness to the resonance that some players clearly missed. That said, plug in a great "top loader" like this one, and you'll find 99 percent of the archetypal Tele spank and twang still there, with perhaps just a little less meat and a little more sparkle. Either way, it's another great variation on the theme, even if it only lasted less than a year or so in production.

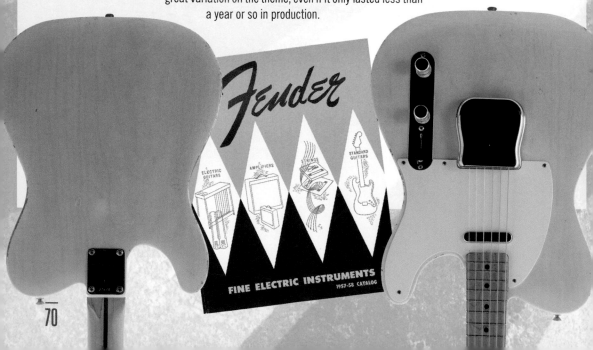

1958 Fender Twin 5F8-A

As far as many aficionados are concerned, this is where the guitar amplifier got serious. Other amps that existed before Fender's high-powered tweed Twin arrived in 1958 had some of the same ingredients in place—four output tubes, two speakers—but none put them together in a manner that produced the bold and cutting, yet sweet and juicy tone of the 5F8-A. And most failed to generate anything close to this amp's stout 80 watts. While the 40-watt 5E8-A Twin is a great amp, this big boy, which put out about as much power as Fender could conceive of producing at the time, set a standard that has remained in place even through several evolutions of the breed: ask for "a Twin" in any studio or venue around the globe, and people know exactly what you're talking about. B. B. King played through a 5F8-A Twin for much of the early '50s. The amp was also a mainstay of virtuoso Danny Gatton and remains a favorite of Keith Richards. Put simply, if you want tweed, but you need it big, it's got to be a high-powered Twin.

1958 Gibson Flying V

One of the rarest production guitars on the planet, the original Flying V, produced from 1958 to 1960, set a new standard for Rock(et) Age cool. Yet it was so underappreciated in its time that a lack of uptake led to its deletion from the catalog in 1960 after, according to many estimates, fewer than 100 units were sold. Playing an original example is a breathtaking experience, and while you might think a vintage V sounds much like a Les Paul or SG of the late '50s or early '60s, it is really very much its own beast. The two PAF humbucking pickups and Tune-o-matic bridge work toward a distinctive Gibson mojo, for sure, but add to these tested ingredients a light Korina body and neck and unusual through-body stringing, and this Flying V has more pop and zing than you tend to hear in either of Gibson's other major contenders. You'll have trouble playing this one sitting down, but why sit when you can strut across the stage? Light on the strap and made to be seen, this is a guitar for declaring your rock-god intentions loud and proud . . . then selling to finance your kids' college education.

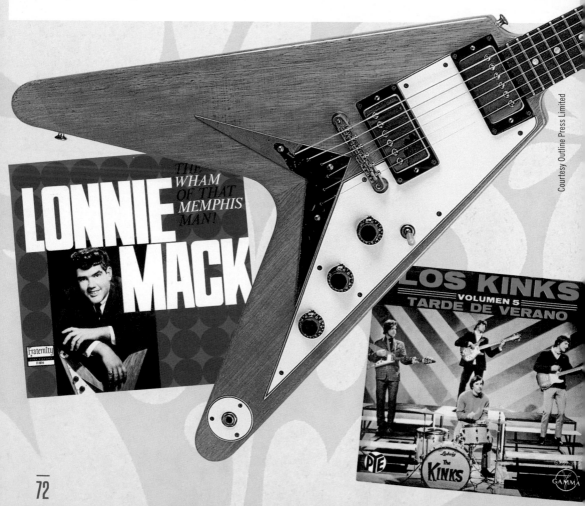

Courtesy Outline Press Limited

albert king years gone by

Keith Richards, 1969. Peter Sanders/Redferns/Getty Images

Maestro Echoplex

With the arrival of the Echoplex in 1959, tape echo finally became easily accessible, and if you wanted to rock like Elvis Presley in Memphis' Sun Studios, you were just the spin of a dial and a tape loop away. And that doesn't begin to describe the sonic adventures Led Zeppelin or Pink Floyd would take the Echoplex on. It was basically a tape recorder with a second, adjustable playback head that slid on a track, allowing adjustment to the echo spacing. The first Echoplexes were retroactively known as the EP-1, followed by the EP-2, which added a combined instrument and echo volume blend oscillator to its control panel alongside the Echo Repeats knob. It also featured Sound-on-Sound recording, allowing infinite looping—at least for the tape's two-minute length. The early tube models create a slapback echo with a warm, rich sound. Adding more repeats and spacing out the echoes creates an otherworldly vibe, and the sky's truly the limit. These days, analog and digital delay pedals are less expensive, more hardy, and easily replaceable. But the Echoplex has become the standard by which everything is measured.

1957 Fender Duo-Sonic

Many "student-size" models fall flat with serious players, but the original short-scale Fender Duo-Sonic, introduced midway through 1956, has found a place in plenty of guitarists' hearts. Of course, part of that appeal might be that you can acquire this nifty little pre-CBS electric for less coin than any other vintage Fender, but many significant artists' use of the Duo-Sonic proves that there's more to it than the novelty factor. Steely Dan's Walter Becker played one for a time, and the petite Duo-Sonic was also beloved of Rory Gallagher, David Byrne, Liz Phair, Patti Smith, and John McLaughlin; it was even the choice of a young Jimi Hendrix during his days backing the Isley Brothers and Curtis Knight & The Squires. Plugged in, this little electric has a loose, slightly furry vibe to its tone thanks to the short 22.5-inch scale length, but there's plenty of quack and chime in those Strat-like single-coil pickups, too. There's also something sweetly dated about its looks: the gold anodized pickguard, enclosed pickup covers, Desert Sand finish, and one-piece maple necks on the pre-'59 models all make it look somehow "other," yet still distinctly Fender.

Courtesy Southside Guitars/www.southsideguitars.com

Amp courtesy Grumn Guitars/photos Eric C. Newell

1958 Magnatone Custom 280

The liquid, warbling "true vibrato" of the larger Magnatone amps is a thing of legend, even if relatively few players have had a chance to experience its lusciousness firsthand. For recorded examples, look to Lonnie Mack, some of Bo Diddley's work (although he used other amps before and after), and late-period Buddy Holly, who discovered that addictive Magnatone pulse following an early love affair with tweed Fender amps. Not only did the Custom 280 conceal an extremely complex vibrato circuit, it reproduced it in stereo when desired, splitting its output to individual transformers through individual 12-inch speakers, each paired with its own 5-inch tweeter to broaden the effect. Set this thing rolling and it's the aural equivalent of a day out on the open sea. In fact, are those seagulls flying through the sky of the grille cloth's lower-right corner? No, merely the double V symbol reminding us of the Custom 280's "Vibrato Vastness," as Magnatone dubbed it. They weren't lying.

1957 Kay Barney Kessel

It's a clear injustice that one of the first things many players note about this guitar is that it has a headstock that reminds them of a 1950s refrigerator. By any standards, the 17-inch-wide Kay Barney Kessel model is an impressive archtop packed with fascinating features. That said, the enormous gold-and-pearl plastic "Kelvinator" headstock sure is a head turner, ain't she? But check out the exquisite Grover Imperial tuners, as used on some of Gibson's high-end guitars, or the complex Melita bridge, more commonly seen on Gretsch 6120s and Duo Jets of the era, as well as the ornate, German-made nickel tailpiece. Unlike so many Kay guitars, this model has a set neck and was otherwise crafted with utmost attention to detail—truly an effort by a B-list guitar maker to punch it out with the A-list boys. Plug it in, though, and what you'll notice most is the warm, juicy tone exuded by those P-90-like "Kleenex box" pickups. Whether you're playing jazz, blues, rockabilly, or vintage rock 'n' roll, the Kay Barney Kessel offers a fast track to doing it in your own style.

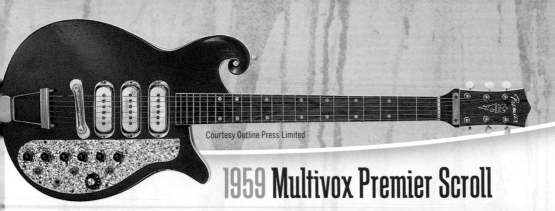

1959 Multivox Premier Scroll

Fun and funky and even rather artfully DIY-looking, the Premier Scroll of the late 1950s and early 1960s is not the trade-embargo-era European creation that it might appear, but a genuine made-in-the-USA solidbody electric manufactured by Multivox of New York, which also made Premier amplifiers. As groovy as these things are, the design looks—and we say this with love—somewhat *behind* its time, a little like it was rendered by a guitar maker who had ignored everything Fender and Gibson had achieved with solidbodies over the previous decade, like some pioneer who had taken a crate of wood, wire, and assorted components into his workshop in 1948, closed the door, ordered in lots of take-out, and emerged in 1957 to declare, "Ah-ha, I've *got* it! Oh . . . I see. . . ." For all that, though, dagnabbit if these things aren't cool. Scrolls came with one, two, or three pickups, and some of the upmarket models even had solid rosewood necks, though specs tended to change without notice as Multivox appeared to source parts from a wide range of suppliers. Fire this one up, and the marriage of chunky tonewood and honkin' fat single-coil pickups delivers some distinctive beef and bluster, with a dollop of quacky snarl for spice.

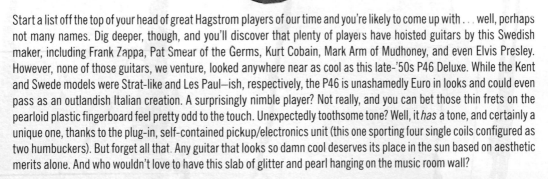

Late-1950s Hagstrom P46 Deluxe

Start a list off the top of your head of great Hagstrom players of our time and you're likely to come up with . . . well, perhaps not many names. Dig deeper, though, and you'll discover that plenty of players have hoisted guitars by this Swedish maker, including Frank Zappa, Pat Smear of the Germs, Kurt Cobain, Mark Arm of Mudhoney, and even Elvis Presley. However, none of those guitars, we venture, looked anywhere near as cool as this late-'50s P46 Deluxe. While the Kent and Swede models were Strat-like and Les Paul—ish, respectively, the P46 is unashamedly Euro in looks and could even pass as an outlandish Italian creation. A surprisingly nimble player? Not really, and you can bet those thin frets on the pearloid plastic fingerboard feel pretty odd to the touch. Unexpectedly toothsome tone? Well, it *has* a tone, and certainly a unique one, thanks to the plug-in, self-contained pickup/electronics unit (this one sporting four single coils configured as two humbuckers). But forget all that. Any guitar that looks so damn cool deserves its place in the sun based on aesthetic merits alone. And who wouldn't love to have this slab of glitter and pearl hanging on the music room wall?

1958–1960s Fender Bassman 5F6-A

Thanks not only to its own achievements, but also those it inspired as the template for Marshall amplifiers in 1960s Britain, the tweed Bassman of the late '50s has been justly hailed as one of the ultimate tone machines of all time. Given this status, it was also one of the prime instigators—and most emulated designs—of the early "boutique" amp boom of the 1990s, rivaled only, perhaps, by the Vox AC30 and AC15. Since it pumps a beefy 45 watts into four articulate 10-inch speakers, it is capable of moving some serious air and needs to be turned up pretty loud to hit the sweet spot. Get it there, though, and you are rewarded with a dynamic and multidimensional tone that has just the right blend of low-end thump, midrange growl, and high-end sparkle. From blues, to country, to jazz, to rock 'n' roll, and even indie rock and grunge, the Bassman has been there and done that—and will undoubtedly keep doing so for another half century or more.

1959 Fender Telecaster Custom

With its rosewood fingerboard, bound body, and sunburst finish, the Telecaster Custom looks a little like a bid for some Gibson-esque tradition—or maybe a subtle counterattack after Gibson's bid to out-snazz Fender with its ultramodern Flying V and Explorer designs. Clock the slab body, though, or that distinctive bridge plate and pickup, and the 1959 Telecaster Custom remains far less removed from Fender's wheelhouse than its maker might have intended. The addition of a rosewood fingerboard to the formerly all-maple neck slightly rounds out the bright pop of the Tele's tone, compared to our 1950 Broadcaster and 1953 Telecaster, and smooths the attack just a hair, but the classy look is what really gets the attention. Word is, Fender had some trouble getting the binding to work properly early on in the life of the Custom, and was given help in the process by none other than C. F. Martin, maker of some of the world's finest acoustic guitars (and, we might add, a longtime rival to Gibson's flat-top acoustics). While it might be a twang monster with some class it's still a roughrider at heart.

Late-1950s Hofner Club 40

Perhaps best known for the small-bodied 500/1 that Paul McCartney played during his tenure with the Beatles, German maker Hofner logged a different piece of Fab Four ephemera before its "violin bass" made a splash. In the pre-Beatles combo, the Quarrymen, both John Lennon and George Harrison played Hofner Club 40 guitars for a time, one of which is occasionally seen—upside down—in the hands of Paul McCartney in very early photos of the Beatles in Hamburg before Macca took over bass duties from Stu Sutcliffe. The Club 40 and Club 50 were identical other than their one and two pickups, respectively, and differences in related controls. Both were quality guitars for their time, with light, compact, semi-hollowbodies with solid spruce tops. With an import ban of U.S. goods in full force in the late 1950s and early 1960s, Hofner was one of the better makes a British guitarist could acquire, and despite certain "European peculiarities"—a zero fret, odd controls and switches, and a floating bridge that uses snippets of fret wire as bridge saddles—this is a surprisingly playable guitar with a rich, lively voice of its own.

1959 Gibson Les Paul Special

Man, Gibson was busy in the late 1950s. In addition to unveiling mammoth changes to the Les Paul Standard and introducing the ES-335, ES-330, Explorer, Flying V, and a few others, Gibson enacted significant alterations to the lesser slab-bodied Les Paul siblings, namely the double-cutaway design of 1959 that makes this one a very different guitar from the Special of just a year before. The ever-so-slightly asymmetrical double-horned design hints at more modern touches to come at Gibson. And while constructionally it represents only a bite out of the upper shoulder of the same flat-top, solid-mahogany body as the Special, the alteration changes the look, feel, and perhaps sound of the guitar more than the simple loss of a mere chunk of timber might lead one to expect. Obviously exposing the fingerboard right up to the 22nd fret improves playing access, but the decreased wood mass at the critical neck joint can also give these Specials a somewhat lighter, zingier tone, if only slightly. It can also lead to easy neck-joint fractures when a double-cut Special slides off the amp that you propped it against. As a result, unrepaired, original-condition examples are getting harder and harder to come by. Regardless, with two P-90s and plenty of resonant, well-aged solid tonewood, this guitar remains a thick, gnarly rock 'n' roller for the ages.

Courtesy Outline Press Limited

1950s Supro Dual Tone

The use of broadly similar models by Jack White of the White Stripes and Dan Auerbach of the Black Keys has helped elevate the Dual Tone above its longtime B-list status, and more's the shame for the rest of us. This Supro remains a supercool, ultra-funky alternative that is not only a good player when set up right, but also exudes a snarky, gutsy tone all its own. Not that the Dual Tone is a recent rediscovery, by any means, as this wooden-bodied wonder, and the similarly styled Res-O-Glas model, the Belmont, made significant music in the hands of David Bowie, Jimmy Page, Link Wray, and other notables several decades ago. The irresistible style blends rock 'n' roll bluster with an earlier art deco chic, and the sound—well, the sound really compares to nothing else. While those pickups look outwardly like humbuckers, they are really just wide single coils with six pole pieces positioned toward the outer edge of the assembly. Show them a vintage tube amp set to the edge of breakup, and they give you a thick, surprisingly complex tone, with a slightly grating attack that really cuts through the mix, and no end of crispy crackle when you roll on into genuine overdrive. Definitely an instrument primed to make a statement.

Courtesy Outline Press Limited

81

1959 Gibson Les Paul Standard Sunburst

Amid so many fun and funky, queer and quirky instruments, the good old Les Paul Standard might seem, well, almost rather *tame*. But spend a few minutes with a good vintage example, and you are quickly reminded why this is one of the most desirable, and most expensive, electric guitars ever made. We have seen carved maple tops, mahogany bodies, and dual humbucking pickups on so many iterations of the Les Paul by now, yet the original effort—achieved with selected and well-aged tonewoods, and PAF pickups that are among the finest electromagnetic creations known to man—yielded a powerful yet elusive magic that continues to weave its spell on all who come near one even 50-odd years down the road. If you've never plugged in a good set of PAFs, particularly as installed in a late-'50s Les Paul, there's a zing and liveliness here not heard in other humbuckers, along with a certain indescribable biting, slightly metallic edge that puts the attack of each note exactly where you want it to be. If you ever get the chance to try a good vintage Les Paul Standard . . . don't. It can be an otherworldly experience, and it might just spoil you for all time.

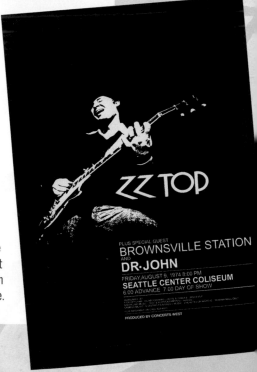

Gretsch White Falcon

The White Falcon emerged in 1955 as Gretsch's top-of-the-line guitar and eventually exploded into all kinds of stereo-wired and knob-bonanza'd excess, and the early-1960s models are good examples of why these guitars might just be the most elegant electrics ever produced. Compared to true white, these vintage beauties are a sedate ivory-cream that goes easy on the eye, and even the gold-sparkle binding comes off more as "exotic" rather than "gaudy." Poised at a transition period for Gretsch, this 1959 model has the Filter'Tron humbuckers that had become available just a few years before and retains the single-cutaway body styling with a simple floating-bar bridge and Bigsby vibrato. Less obvious to the naked eye is the longer 25.5-inch scale length that Gretsch gave this impressive flagship model, making its voice somewhat more akin to the full-size archtops that dominated the jazz world in the 1930s and early '40s before guitars like Gibson's ES-175 and Gretsch's own 6120 established a norm at slightly under 24.75 inches. As a result, this White Falcon has a taut, piano-like low end when amped up, with a little more high-end harmonic sparkle and an outstanding chime through those clear, low-powered Filter'Trons. Gretsch continued production through 1980 and the type was notably played by Stephen Stills, Neil Young, Johnny Thunders, and the Edge.

GRETSCH GUITARS

NEIL YOUNG

Neil Young, circa 1974. Michael Ochs Archives/Getty Images

GRETSCH Guitars

1959 Gibson ES-330

Often misperceived as "an ES-335 with P-90s," the ES-330 is actually a very different guitar with different intentions. Released a year after its solid-centered sibling, the ES-330 is, we might say, the inverse of the ES-335: a genuine jazz guitar disguised as a thinline rock 'n' roller, rather than vice versa. As such, the ES-330 has a fully hollow—if thinline—body as well as a neck joint at the 16th fret, a position a little more akin to an old-school archtop, which also placed the guitar's bridge farther into the meat of the body, right amid the two f-holes. This early ES-330 has a warm, round, airy tone, despite its shallow dimensions, and makes an outstanding jazzer for the player seeking an easier girth than the full-depth archtop affords, as Grant Green proved on several recordings in the early 1960s. Those snarly, gritty P-90s can rock with the best of 'em, too, as a close cousin of the ES-330 would prove with the Fab Four, although the guitar's hollow construction can induce some serious feedback howl in front of loud amplifiers.

1958 Gibson Explorer

Unveiled in 1958 as the Modernist sibling of the Flying V, Gibson's Explorer shared the V's Korina construction and had its own pair of glorious PAF humbuckers, but somehow it seems to sound subtly different—or is that just your eyes telling your ears this is a beast of a different color (even though, uh, that golden-hued natural finish looks pretty much identical, too). Gibson's records tell us that the original production run of 1958–1960 Explorers didn't even reach the 100 mark, so opportunities to try the pair side by side are going to be few and far between, even if the V is relatively more "plentiful" at a hair over 100 units. Befitting its radical rock image, though, the Explorer is meaty and thick plugged into a suitable amp like a vintage Marshall or a later high-gain tubester, but the Korina's slightly enhanced upper-midrange bark through the PAFs' glorious clarity gives the guitar enough cutting power to avoid muddying out where a Les Paul or SG might start to go swampy. Imagine for a moment you were fortunate enough to own such a beauty, didn't need to sell it and had the cojones to take it out of the house: could there be a better weapon with which to strut the rock stage?

1960 Silvertone U-2

The electric guitars made by Danelectro under the Silvertone name and sold in Sears, Roebuck and Co. catalogs, were among the earliest of the B-list makes to attain collectible vintage status. Hip and extremely stylish, these guitars also have their own sound that works surprisingly well in many contexts. In this example, the "dolphin" headstock is an immediate giveaway this is a Silvertone U-2; Danelectro U-2s featured the now-classic "Coke bottle" headstock. (The cowgirl is an "aftermarket" addition.) Danelectros and Silvertones like the U-2 (denoting two pickups) are made from Masonite with a solid wood core (usually some indifferent timber such as poplar), leaving air pockets throughout the body. With strings anchored at one end by a simple bridge comprising a steel base and a one-piece rosewood saddle and at the other end by an aluminum nut, the U-2 yields an unexpectedly zingy tone to which the bright, low-output "lipstick tube" pickups add a further helping of chime. These guitars prove that a total lack of tonewood can still result in an interesting tone. Also, while they aren't characteristically thought of as hard-rockin' electrics, Jimmy Page's adoption of a later double-cutaway Danelectro as his main squeeze for slide or Jimi Hendrix's use of one early in his career should put to rest even that bias.

1961 Airline P-3

The Airline brand pops up on a range of guitars made by other manufacturers, with this hip P-3 hailing from Kay in Chicago. While some elements of this instrument are still rather catalog grade—the bolt-on neck, the austere headstock, the chintzy tailpiece and floating bridge—its sharp double-cutaway design is fairly forward-looking, and the laminated maple construction exhibits some tasty flame front and back. The 25.5-inch scale helps give it a slightly bolder, firmer tone than some of its shorter brethren, and while you get the feeling Kay (via Airline) wasn't sure whether this was intended as a jazz, blues, or rock 'n' roll machine, this instrument does any of the three pretty nicely, from the perspectives of both style and tone. The laminated construction and body depth (under 2 inches) help cut down feedback somewhat, but crank your amp and those hot "Kleenex box" pickups will give you some squeal. These, by the way, are the same pickups we saw on the Kay Barney Kessel model, and at times this P-3 has been known as the Airline Barney Kessel Swingmaster.

Courtesy Outline Press Limited

1960 Harmony Jupiter Stratotone

The name might have been a bid to horn in on the status of Fender's successful Stratocaster with the budget-guitar crowd, but Harmony's Stratotone has achieved cult status in its own right. A close study of this instrument finds its bolt-on neck rather crudely attached and less sultry of profile than Fender's creations of the era, while its single-cutaway, seemingly solid but in reality hollow, spruce-topped body is more roughly hewn than anything from the likes of Gibson or Gretsch. Yet there's an undeniable vibe resonating in the sum of these parts—one that really breathes fire when you throw in the pair of Rowe/DeArmond "goldfoil" single-coil pickups. Highly sought-after by garage-rock, blues, and slide players today (who often pull them from their original guitars to reinstall in more refined instruments), these surprisingly hot pickups have a brash, raw, edgy sound that is nevertheless extremely expressive and free from any harshness. These aren't guitars for your fleet-fingered shred or nuanced voicings, but dig in through a tube combo cranked just to the edge of breakup, and the Jupiter Stratotone provides a throaty, slightly clanky voice that makes you want to play all day.

1959 Ampeg Jet 12

Ampeg founder Everett Hull's aversion to rock 'n' roll is well documented, but you can't prevent a player from plugging into a small combo intended for accordion or jazz guitar and cranking it up, can you? This groovy Jet 12 from 1959 carries a pair of cathode-biased 6V6 tubes just like a tweed Fender Deluxe, although Ampeg added a little negative feedback around the output stage to tighten it up slightly. Still, get it smokin' and it's only so tight, and those octal 6SL7s in the front end are pretty fat-sounding preamp tubes, too. The late, great tube-amp guru Ken Fischer, himself a former Ampeg engineer, once explained that the company viewed these more easily distorting 6V6 amps as somewhat of a glitch in the product line, but if they had marketed them as rock 'n' roll amps, they might have been extremely successful. As it is, few true rock 'n' rollers played through Ampegs until the Rolling Stones employed the company's larger amps to cut it on mammoth arena stages in the late '60s, and more's the shame.

1959 Fender Deluxe 5E3

Ah, the 5E3 tweed Deluxe——can we say enough about this amp? Once players got over the notion that they needed 100 watts and a pair of 4x12 speaker cabs, or——heaven forbid——a rack-mounted preamp and multi-FX unit through massive Crown power amps or the like, this was the beauty that reminded many how simple pure tone could be. The magic of the late-'50s Deluxe's circuit comes from the fact that it has just enough guts to fill a medium room with sound——around 15 to 18 watts through a 12-inch speaker, courtesy of two cathode-biased 6V6s——and just enough give to sound nasty and delicious while doing so, thanks to its lack of negative feedback, filthy little cathodyne phase inverter, and rather small output transformer. Set the volume to around 10 o'clock and inject a Telecaster for honkin' roadhouse twang, or choose somewhere past noon with a Les Paul for reedy, creamy ZZ Top—style boogie. As countless players have discovered, you really can't go wrong . . . unless, of course, you need a little more headroom and a tighter bottom, in which case see "tweed Pro" (a.k.a. the Fender Pro 5E5).

Paul Burlison (seated) with the Rock 'N Roll Trio, 1956.

1961 Fender Jazzmaster

Little did Fender know when they took this broad shot at the jazz crowd in 1958 that they were unleashing what would become one of the most popular guitars of the later punk and indie-rock scenes, not to mention the surf scene of the day. Other than featuring Fender's move to a more traditional (and therefore presumably jazz-certified) rosewood fingerboard and wider single-coil pickups with an *ever so slightly* warmer tone than previous Fender offerings, any observant guitarist can tell you that there's not much here to appeal to a genuine jazzer. Look beyond this misfire of sorts—as most Jazzmaster fans have—and you see a stylish new offset body design, a clever and smooth-feeling new vibrato unit, outstanding playability, and a unique and versatile tone that cuts through the mix for all kinds of musical styles. Fortunately for those who dig 'em, Jazzmasters never really hit the mark with many rock or blues players, which for a long time helped keep them within reach, price-wise, of less well-heeled players. However you slice it, a good Jazzmaster is many players' embodiment of cool, as Nels Cline, Elvis Costello, Tom Verlaine, Lee Ranaldo, Thurston Moore, J Mascis, and so many others will tell you.

1960 Fender Super Amp

The brown 6G4 Fender Super Amp is often considered a way station on the road from tweed to blackface, but actually it has more of the characteristics of the latter than the former, even if their earlier transformers and other components—including the tasty yellow Astron coupling capacitors—can make them look pretty tweedy inside the chassis. When compared to the tweed 5F4 Super, however, with its

cathode-follower tone stack and cathodyne (a.k.a. split-phase) phase inverter, the extent to which the 6G4 had evolved becomes more apparent. Indeed, judging by the fine points, it is virtually an entirely different amplifier. With the tone stack sandwiched between the two 12AX7 gain stages on each channel, a long-tailed-pair PI, and higher voltages on the plates of the 6L6s, you can expect the brown Super to be tighter, punchier, and louder overall than its tweed predecessor. And have we mentioned that luscious "harmonic vibrato" that now comes loaded in as a bonus? We should, since many players consider it to be the epitome of wobble. Plug in and enjoy another stop on Leo Fender's road toward loud, clean, and clear—then crank up and put all that nonsense behind you.

1960 Fender Tremolux 5G9

Search the ultimate real tremolo, rather than the more complex Fender or Magnatone approximation of "harmonic vibrato," and many roads will lead you to the tweed Tremolux of 1959–1960. It is often touted as "a tweed Deluxe with tremolo," and for earlier iterations such as the 5E9 or 5E9-A, that was close to true, but the 5G9 had the fixed-bias output stage and long-tailed-pair phase inverter of the larger Fender amps, which gave it a somewhat tighter, bolder tone as a result. What we are here for, though, is that sublimely undulating bias-modulated tremolo effect, which arguably reached its zenith in this amp. Created by a relatively simple circuit powered by one full 12AX7 that interrupted the bias voltage applied to the 6V6s, this tremolo is warm and plummy, with a great touch sensitivity that lets the note punch through when you pick a string hard—even when the Depth control is turned up pretty high—and brings the effect pulsing back in the note's decay. It is thoroughly groovy stuff, and thanks (or not) to the fact that more and more players over the past decade have discovered what a cool tweed Fender this amp is, it is becoming harder and harder to come by.

1960 Fender Showman 6G14

Leo Fender had cut his teeth on the country-and-western scene of Southern California, but he needed a more bombastic test bed for his next great leap in amplification. The burgeoning West Coast surf scene would prove just the laboratory, and Dick Dale's bludgeoning of prototypes night after night would eventually result in Fender's development of the company's first "piggyback" amp: the Showman. The new model didn't really reach its zenith until its accompanying cab was loaded with the high-powered JBL speakers that would become key to its signature sound and impressive volume, but this extremely early example carries a single 15-inch alnico Jensen P15N that would not even have been capable of handling the Showman's full 85 to 100 watts of power (perhaps part of the reason for Dale's claims of having blown up 49 amps before the JBLs joined the formula). Even so, this meaty head-and-cab rig pumps out a big, bouncy tone with fat lows and crispy highs, with the added bonus of Fender's complex "harmonic vibrato." Ready to hang ten and hit that curl?

Amp courtesy Lee and Donna Scaife/Vintage Tone Music/www.vintagetonemusic.com

Early-1960s Harmony Rocket

If you were, shall we say, a non-rich kid playing the guitar in the 1960s or '70s, it's unlikely you escaped without playing, and very likely owning, a Harmony—and there's a good chance it was a Harmony Rocket. Sadly (although hopefully you valued the privilege of owning *any* playable electric guitar), you very likely yearned for a Gibson, Gretsch, Fender, or Rickenbacker at the time and perhaps therefore—other than subconsciously grooving on it in the tube-saturated heat of a sweaty garage-jam moment—never fully appreciated the stellar tone that this thing put out. Sure, the "tone" woods weren't much to speak of, the neck was bolted on, and the bridge likely sproinked out of place and sent the whole thing out of tune just when you were laying into your big solo, but add together the whole funky package, message it through those almost-too-good-for-it pickups, and there's a character here that can stand with the best of 'em. Note that this is another excellent undersung pickup from Row/DeArmond, the Model 6812, which is related to the goldfoil pickups in our Stratotone, but with adjustable pole pieces and slightly fewer turns of coil wire for a little less sting, but a meaty, biting tone nevertheless. Now you want it back, right?

1960 Guild Starfire III

So, you're a raw rockabilly slinger in the early '60s who just doesn't dig Gretsch's move to humbuckers and double cutaways on the 6120, but what are you to do? Jump on over to a Guild Starfire III, that's what. Crafted with utmost skill and top components in Hoboken, New Jersey, early Guild guitars were easy rivals to Gibson and Gretsch for tone and playability, and this one is spec'd out in very classic mid-'50s Gretsch style, too. A pair of genuine DeArmond Model 200 alnico-pole pickups gives a broad, meaty twang, while a fully hollow, thinline mahogany body tames the harsh highs that a maple-bodied electric with the same single coils might threaten and offers a sultry visual twist beneath the faded, weather-checked, cherry red finish. Grab that Bigsby-licensed vibrato for some emotive wobble, dip, and warble, and you're really ready to shake, rattle, and roll. As it happens, Gretsch artist Duane Eddy moved over to Guild in 1960, endorsing a similarly equipped, though more poshly executed, model. You can't get much more twang-certified than that.

Amp and photos courtesy Michael Tamposi

1960 Vox AC30

All JMI-built Vox AC30s of the early to mid-1960s are rare, prized, and collectible amps today—so imagine just how collectible this veritable hen's tooth of a combo must be. It's one of somewhere between 49 and 146 TV-cab AC30/4s ever built, and fewer than a dozen examples are known to have survived, according to Jim Elyea, author of the excellent *Vox*

Amps: The JMI Years. With the soon-to-be-abandoned EF86 in the front end, lifted from the AC15's preamp, and no Top Boost tone stack on the horizon, the AC30/4 hit its four EL84s and two Celestion alnico speakers with a thick, meaty breed of Class A chime that is rarely heard in any amplifier today. The more common breed of AC30 later loaded with the cathode-follower Top Boost circuit (which gave the 12AX7—a.k.a. ECC83 —now in the preamp a little more oomph on its way through the works in addition to providing a highly interactive bass and treble pairing) is known for a little more sparkle and shimmer, although it still gnashes and grinds like a cornered badger when you wind it up.

The Duchess, circa 1959. Michael Ochs Archives/Getty Images

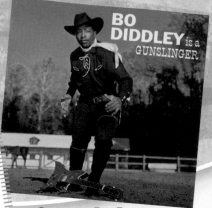

BO DIDDLEY is a GUNSLINGER

Gretsch Jupiter Thunderbird

Plenty of guitars have been designed in recent years with the input of major artists, but only a handful of guitarists put their stamp on a guitar in the formative years of rock 'n' roll. The 1952 Les Paul was one, of course, and this rare Gretsch Jupiter Thunderbird was another. The Jupiter Thunderbird might not have fared as well as the Les Paul, but in embodying Bo Diddley's stylish 1959 spin on the perfect tool for boppin', beat-infused rock 'n' rhythm 'n' blues, it darn well should have. Essentially a Duo Jet with rocket-ship body styling, the Jupiter Thunderbird got right down to business through a pair of bright yet meaty Filter'Tron humbuckers. TV footage exists of Bo Diddley performing at the Santa Monica Civic Auditorium in 1965 with a Jupiter Thunderbird, a second in the hands of "The Duchess" (a.k.a. Norma-Jean Wofford, see photo) in his backing band. The combination of radical guitar meets Bo Diddley beat is simply groove incarnate. The closest we're likely to get to one today is in the form of Gretsch's reincarnated Billy-Bo model, based on an original Jupiter Thunderbird Bo gave to ZZ Top guitarist Billy F Gibbons.

BO DIDDLEY/CHUCK BERRY
TWO GREAT GUITARS
BO DIDDLEY/CHUCK BERRY

Early-1960s
Rickenbacker 360

A little quirky and arguably slightly behind the times in the mid- to late 1950s, Rickenbacker pushed the envelope in the late '50s and early '60s in several ways. As a result, the maker soon found itself rivaling Fender, Gibson, and Gretsch in the design stakes—if not quite in sales (something the endorsement of a certain pop group from Britain would soon seek to change)—although the sound was particularly designed to take a bite out of Fender's market. Initially known as the Capri 330 and the fancier Capri 360 upon their introductions in 1958 and '59, respectively, Rick's semi-hollows were known by their numbers alone by the early '60s and were on the way to some major exposure, too. The chambered maple bodies, rigid through-neck construction, and bright yet hot "toaster-top" single-coil pickups work together toward the archetypal California jangle, although the 360—or the import variant brought into the U.K.—is probably best known for its dynamic *kerrang* and impressive splintering in the hands of The Who's Pete Townshend.

Courtesy Outline Press Limited

Post-1960 Vox AC15

Designed by Dick Denney in 1957, the AC15 was the flagship of Tom Jennings' Vox guitar amplifier line at the time, and it served as the building block for bigger things to come. When popular British bands of the late 1950s such as the Shadows needed more powerful amps to be heard in the bigger and bigger venues they were playing, Denney simply doubled the power of the AC15 and coupled its preamp to the new AC30, although the latter element soon changed. As such, the AC15 post-1960 was the largest Vox offering to carry the fat EF86 pentode preamp stage, and with that pumping through two hot-running EL84s and a tactile EZ81 rectifier, well, the AC15 was just waiting to rev up and wail. As popular as the AC30 would become, many players have since discovered that the AC15 really is the premier Vox tone machine of all time, a combo that's hard to beat for sparkling chime, three-dimensional tonal swirl, and all-out overtone-rich grind. And where these were pretty easy to come by just 15 or 20 years ago, AC15s now often bring in more than their larger siblings on the vintage market. Harrumph.

Amp courtesy Jim Elyea/photo Jennifer Cheung/Steve Nilsson

Mid-1959 to Mid-1962
Fender Stratocaster

It's eternally fascinating to us guitar nuts how the several subtle changes enacted upon any particular design through the years evoked gentle alterations in its tone and performance. Born in 1954 with a one-piece maple neck with integral fingerboard, the Stratocaster gained a rosewood fingerboard partway through 1959—a change seen, apparently, as a step up for Fender—and both its playing feel and sonic character changed ever so slightly as a result. Until midway through 1962, these guitars carried what has become known as a "slab board": a rosewood fingerboard made from a thicker piece of timber milled flat on the bottom. Naturally, the change that year from slab to "round lam" (a thinner rosewood board with a curved underside glued to a radiused maple neck) serves as another demarcation point in vintage Fenders, but the slab-board Strat has earned a certain mystique among players. The notion that the thicker piece of rosewood imparts a thicker, warmer tone might be based largely in myth, but the combination of rosewood and the slightly deeper, rounder neck profiles of guitars close to the end of this era make them beloved by many players. Whatever the science behind it, flip the switch to the neck position, lay into it good through a black-face Super Reverb, a tweed Pro, or indeed a '60s or early-'70s Marshall anything, and you have one of the finest electric guitar tones known to man.

1961 Gibson
Les Paul Standard

It's still one of the great perplexities of guitar history that the all-time, most desirable, general-production vintage electric—the Les Paul—was dropped from Gibson's catalog after a run of just three years in its most revered form. In 1961 it was replaced with the new Les Paul, a guitar that, despite carrying the same type of pickups and bridge, was really something entirely different. Yet the Les Paul Standard of 1961, soon and forever after known as the SG for "Solid Guitar," itself established a new classic that would particularly come into its own in the hands of heavy rock and metal players of the late '60s and early '70s and prove itself a versatile performer in several other genres besides. Wrap your hands around this ultra-slim neck (fans and marketing departments call it "fast"), keep clear of the awkward "sideways" vibrato if you want to stay in tune, and you're rewarded with a tone and feel that's really very different from the Les Paul of just a year before. There's more slap and spring in the attack, as well as a pleasantly woolly mahogany-inspired midrange chunk.

Cranked up, you can go pretty much anywhere a Les Paul will go, but it's an undeniably different voice. And to think, while a 1958–1960 Standard would cost you the price of a nice four-bedroom home in the Midwest, you can make this '61 your own for the mere price of a new Honda Civic.

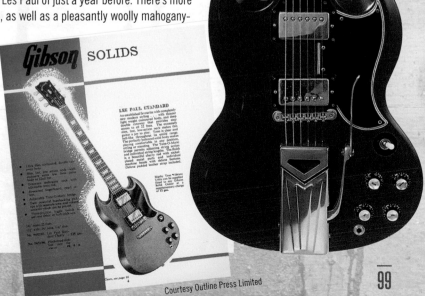

Courtesy Retrofret Vintage Guitars, www.retrofret.com / photo by George Aslaender

c. 1961 Gibson GA-79RVT

Many Gibson amps of the 1950s and early '60s are billed as "poor man's Fenders," propped by their proponents for how well they equal or surpass the sound of similar, but more expensive, tweed Fender models. The GA-79RVT, however, is a Gibson entirely unto itself. You might even argue that Gibson amps fared best, commercially, when they did follow Fender's look, format, and sound, but given Gibson's brief but enthusiastic support of the stereo guitar fad, there needed to be an amp to go with it, and this boggle-eyed freak was it. In truth, the GA-79RVT is really two amps in one unit designed to reproduce a stereo input signal, rather than an amp intended to *create* a stereo sound, like the Magnatone 280 or the later Roland Jazz Chorus. As such, it is actually pretty simple: two independent preamps in each of two channels with Volume, Bass, and Treble controls (the latter two on stacked knobs), plus Tremolo and Reverb on Channel 1. Each channel can produce 15 watts through its own dual-EL84 output stage, or they can be linked for a total of 30 watts in mono. Either way, the widely spaced Jensen 10-inch speakers inside the angle-front cab throw out a broad soundstage. Whether mono or stereo, it's a unique-sounding—and looking—amp, for sure.

Fender Reverb Unit

Although Fender was slow bringing reverb to the table (both Gibson and Ampeg, among others, featured it before Leo installed it in his amplifiers), the company would set the standard with its first wet offering in 1961. The Fender Reverb Unit offered more control than most, with knobs for dwell, mixer, and tone, and a deep, lush, watery sound thanks to an uncompromising tube-driven circuit. As a result, this became *the* sound of surf guitar and a must-have effect for guitarists—and indeed vocalists—in several other styles of the day. A few minutes with a great vintage unit like this one quickly reveals what a wonder this effect must have been in its day: when set just right, the reverb unit adds an ethereal dimension to your guitar tone and takes you on a sonic trip rarely bettered by more dramatic delay or modulation effects. Still a major classic—and little wonder.

1961 Selmer Truvoice Selectortone Automatic

Automatic? Well, it didn't play your guitar for you, but this Selmer Truvoice Selectortone amp did offer the option of five "automatic" tone presets, plus traditional Rotary control, and for 1961 that was apparently automatic enough. Whether you selected High Treble, Treble, Medium, Bass, or Contra Bass (or, indeed, Rotary) wasn't really the point, though; more important to this amp's vibe was the meaty 30 watts it belted out from two cathode-biased EL34s pushing a big 15-inch Goodmans speaker. This was an age, remember, when Selmer was still running to stay neck-and-neck with upstart Vox, and with a mighty performer like this on the track, you could see how Henri's company might just take the gold now and then. Channel 1 is a more traditional affair, with just a Volume and Tone control, but to tap the hypnotic tremolo effect, with both Speed and Depth controls, you have to jump into Channel 2 or jumper the two together. Each opens the bidding with a chunky, broad-voiced EF86 pentode preamp tube, so the Truvoice Selectortone Automatic really is a smoldering dark horse of juicy, dripping tone.

1961 Ampeg M-15

Ampeg always made sturdy, good-sounding amps, and the company's founders strictly avoided jumping on any bandwagons design-wise or copping the look or sound of other makers, even when those makers were leading the field the way Fender was in the late 1950s and early '60s. This nifty 1961 M-15, covered in navy "random-flare" vinyl, is a case in point. It might have been at home sitting behind Wes Montgomery or Kenny Burrell on a small club stage, or maybe gracing accordionist Dick Contino's back line, but bent toward friskier applications, it can rock 'n' roll when it wants to. A look inside the back shows, rather surprisingly, a grab-bag of topologies that Fender, for one, had moved away from several years before. Many makers had ditched the octal 6SL7 preamp tubes used here for the less microphonic nine-pin 12AX7 and the like, but chances are Ampeg knew many jazz players that preferred the 6SL7 tone. The two cathode-biased 6L6GCs would have pumped more volume through the single 15-inch Jensen C15Q if configured in fixed-bias, but the quirks are what make this amp fun, and this tubester has very much its own tone as a result.

1960 Epiphone Wilshire

When is a Les Paul Special *not* a Les Paul Special? When it's an early-'60s Epiphone Wilshire, of course! And yet, for all intents and purposes, a Wilshire is virtually just that. Gibson bought up Epiphone in 1957 and made it into more of an entry-level line as the years progressed, but for the first several years after the consolidation, Epiphones were manufactured in Kalamazoo right alongside Gibson models and shared many of their specs and features while being on par with their parent brand quality-wise to boot. While the Wilshire's body lines, pickguard, and headstock are all its own, the most important ingredients of this early example—the chunky mahogany body, glued-in mahogany neck, dual P-90 pickups, and Gibson hardware—represent a re-blending of the main ingredients in the Les Paul Special formula. Hell, the Wilshire even gives you an upgraded Tune-o-matic bridge and stop-bar tailpiece versus the Special's basic wraparound bridge. As a result, the Wilshire presents the same gritty, mid-humped rock 'n' roll grind and bite as a Special, with perhaps a touch more articulation and certainly more precise intonation thanks to those adjustable, sharp-peaked bridge saddles. At one time we would have added "for less money" to that last sentence, which was long the case. However, for many years now, the Wilshire's relative scarcity, combined with players' realization of what it has to offer, have brought prices right up into LP Special territory.

1962 Gretsch Corvette

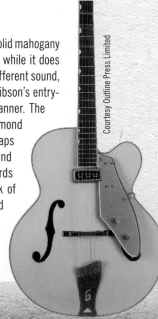

The ingredients might tell you that this should make a great LP Special alternative—solid mahogany body with beefy glued-in neck, vintage single-coil pickups, simple hardware—but while it does pull up at many of the same pit stops on paper, the Corvette ends up having quite a different sound, and therefore feel, when fired up. Clearly Gretsch was aiming to take a bite out of Gibson's entry-level solidbody market but went about it in its own slightly quirky Gretschified manner. The Gretsch HiLo'Tron pickups (Gretsch's go-to single-coil unit after dropping the DeArmond Model 200) constitute one of the main differences in the formula. HiLo'Trons perhaps should have stood for "high tones, low powered"—make no mistake, they can sound pretty darn glorious in many applications where clarity and twang are the watchwords (as can Gretsch's surprisingly low-powered Filter'Tron humbuckers), but their lack of oomph throws some players off their stride. Still, blend the warm, resonant, well-aged mahogany body and meaty neck with the 24.65-inch scale length and a bright, clear pickup, and this Corvette yields another individual voice with a character best defined, yet again, simply as "that great Gretsch sound."

1964 Airline Res-O-Glas

Prior to the late 1990s, this guitar might have been known—to the relatively few players who took a real interest—as the "J. B. Hutto model" after the Chicago bluesman who made one his main squeeze for many years. One glance at that synthetic red beauty today, though, and you're likely to declare, "Hey, that's Jack White's guitar!" Although White has played other electrics, the Airline Res-O-Glas is the one with which White Stripes fans most closely associate him. And it makes sense: this oddly shaped, molded fiberglass creation (also dubbed the "Jetsons model," understandably) is the perfect representation of the White Stripes' music and garage rock in general. Loud of look, garish of tone, it's one rasping, grinding, honking music machine, especially when cranked via fuzzbox through one or several smoking B-list tube amps. The neck and general playability might require a little wrestling, the pickups are cruel single-coil impersonations of humbuckers, and the controls are, well, odd—but oh what a glorious noise she makes.

We're not sure quite what the actual sales figures were, but wouldn't you love to know just how many kids in the early 1960s flipped through that Montgomery Ward catalog (where these guitars were originally retailed), pointed to the space-aged red beauty on the page, and said, "I'm having *that* for Christmas!"

Courtesy Outline Press Limited

103

1965 Gibson Country Western

Gibson's popular, long-running Country Western was introduced in 1956 as a round-shouldered dreadnought and was essentially a Southern Jumbo with a natural finish. It evolved into its better-known incarnation as a square-shouldered dreadnought in 1962, but in both forms this guitar was designed to deliver the goods as its name declared. With its solid spruce top and mahogany back and sides, this big-bodied flat-top was primarily designed for booming out the rhythm, and it does so with aplomb. Hit your chords hard, and that chunky, slightly compressed characteristic Gibson midrange tone blasts forth with enough body to drive the band forward so that no one's going to drop the tempo. Like many of the other grand Gibson flat-tops, these are lookers, too. The split-parallelogram fingerboard inlays brought over from several upmarket archtop models look particularly classy here, as does the "crown" (a.k.a. wheat) headstock inlay, while the three-point pickguard "westerns" up the whole shebang somewhat (though some might argue that the understated single-point pre-'62 'guard was more elegant).

Courtesy Rumble Seat Music/www.rumbleseatmusic.com

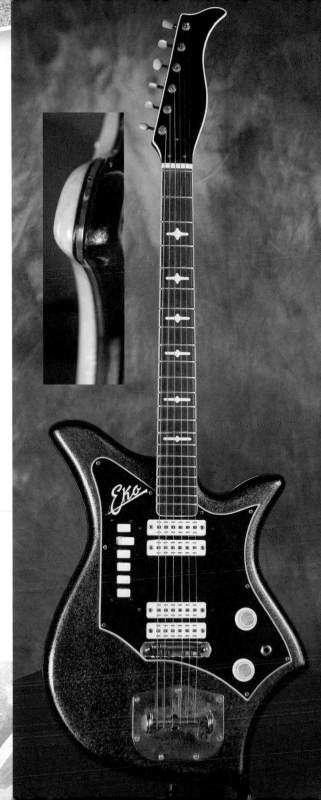

Early-1960s Eko 700 3V

The Eko guitar company was founded in Italy in 1959 by accordion manufacturer Oliviero Pigini and fairly rapidly grew to be one of Europe's largest guitar manufacturers. While many fledgling guitar makers developed their lines through years of rather crude, beginner-grade models, Eko, thanks to its experience in the squeezebox industry, was knocking out impressively stylish electric guitars almost immediately, and—with their many pushbuttons and glitter and pearl finishes—these remain among the archetypal Italian "accordion guitars" to this day. For all of its undeniably groovy retro-chic, installation-art looks, this Eko 700 3V has a surprisingly decent playing feel, and with its bank of switches, three funky pickups, and simple vibrato tailpiece, it knocks out some hip and original tones, too. Long scoffed at in a guitar scene dominated by upmarket U.S. makes, and therefore a dime-a-dozen on the used market for many years, these old Ekos are becoming far more appreciated lately, and their prices are appreciating as a result. Their stylish Italian looks have also inspired several homages from the likes of Italia and Eastwood, as well as a reissue series from Eko itself. Remember when you told yourself you should spend the two hundred bucks if only to hang the thing on the wall? Would have been a wise move.

1965 Supro Tremo-Lectric

Another guitar out of Valco's fiberglass Res-O-Glas stable, the Tremo-Lectric is much like a marriage of a Supro Dual-Tone and an Airline Res-O-Glas guitar, but this instrument is worth experiencing on its own for the sneaky surprise lurking within. Yep—built-in tremolo, baby! As vintage Valco literature puts it, this "new principle enables the artist to selectively embellish his artistry with personalized tremolo expression." A fancy way of saying that if you tug on the little red-tipped toggle switch, perfectly positioned for fingertip access while playing, the guitar's onboard circuit produces a rhythmic fluctuation of the output signal. Of course, such an effect requires battery power, which is delivered via a single whopping old C cell. Ignore the tremolo, as you might be wont to do on occasions, and you've still got a rippin' Valco-made performance tool with two of those hot, mean-sounding 'bucker-looking single-coil pickups, a longer scale length than many of the company's guitars at 24.75 inches, a comfortably chunky maple neck, and a superbly sweet Wedgewood Blue finish. Woah, daddy.

1960s Goya Rangemaster

Ever doubted that those Italian guitar makers loved their buttons? Check out the switchtastic Goya Rangemaster. As a brand name, Goya was passed around like a Christmas fruitcake over the decades, with guitars carrying the label coming from Levin of Sweden, Eko and Galanti of Italy, and Asian makers into the 1970s and early '80s. The '60s was, however, the era of the groovy Italian Goyas, of which this semi-hollow Rangemaster (which came as a solidbody later in the decade) is a fine example. Dig the dual split pickups, which are actually four independently wired units. Selected via the row of pushbuttons on the bass-side bout, they offer the player several odd and unusual tonal combinations, including mix 'n' match neck-position E-A-D strings with bridge-position G-B-E strings (and vice versa), plus all the traditional selections. A revolution in tone? Not really, but what the heck—it offered a novel means of promoting a guitar, and Rangemasters seemed relatively popular for a while. Otherwise, the Goya offered standard Italian playability, which is to say grab the neck tight, hit it hard, and make some noise.

1962 National Glenwood 95

It's a guitar . . . in the shape of a map of the United States of America. What more could you want? Well, plenty, perhaps, and the groovy National Glenwood (a.k.a. the "map guitar") delivers. Made by Valco— which also manufactured guitars with some similar features for Supro, Airline, and others—the Glenwood is characteristic of National's electric style for the '60s, with that jet-aged shape and the fiberglass construction that the company no doubt assumed would forever change the state of guitar manufacturing. Given the Res-O-Glas body and those fat Valco single-coil pickups (sure, they look like PAF-style humbuckers, but don't be fooled), it's no surprise that this thing nails Jack White's Airline tones, but it's also a quick dip into the sound of Bob Dylan circa 1976 with the Rolling Thunder Review and ideal for any mean garage rock you might want to cook up, too. And the secret weapon? Blend in that under-saddle "acoustic" pickup for a sound that, while nothing like your favorite flat-top, works its own odd mojo, either on its own or in combination with the magnetic pickups. In short, one of the hippest "alternative" axes on the planet—it's just a shame the collectors have figured that out, too.

1962 Fender Princeton 6G2

From 1960 to 1961 the Princeton went from being the largest of Fender's bedroom amps to being the smallest of the performance amps, a boost in status that came from bumping the basic format up a notch. With two 6V6GT output tubes in fixed bias for a robust 12 watts versus one tube putting out less than half that a year before, the Princeton was suddenly too loud for the average kid's bedroom but graduated successfully to the basement or garage—where it could hit the sweet spot perfectly with a couple of pals from down the road on drums and bass—or indeed the professional studio, where it offered as much volume as most sessions required, along with all of the tone. Low plate voltages and an easygoing 5Y3 rectifier tube keep the amp sweet and touch-sensitive, so it plays like a great mix of tweed and black-face Fenders, and patched through a larger speaker cab, it offers a surprisingly robust voice. All that, plus cute looks and a succulent tremolo besides.

1962 Ampeg R-12-R Reverberocket

Late amp guru Ken Fischer of Trainwreck Circuits worked as an engineer at Ampeg in New Jersey for many years before setting up shop for himself (with a few years off to ride and repair motorcycles in between), and he was fond of telling stories of Ampeg founder Everett Hull's disdain for rock 'n' roll. Ampeg avoided building anything in the 1950s and '60s that could be considered "a rock 'n'

roll amp" . . . except for one that slipped through the cracks: the early-'60s R-12-R Reverberocket. The Reverberocket was a long-standing model at Ampeg that went through several iterations, most of which aimed at the warm, clean tone and high headroom demanded by jazz players, but a few circuit changes and the use of fat-sounding octal 6SL7 and 6SN7 preamp tubes into easily overdriven 6V6 output tubes put this mainstay combo straight into cranksville for a short period of time. With a great reverb and haunting tremolo on top of its thick, chewy overdrive when turned up, the Reverberocket makes a perfect grab 'n' go combo for anyone who likes it au naturel. Jazzers' complaints eventually got the tight, clean 7591 output tubes reinstated and the fun was over, but it was sweet while it lasted.

1962 Marshall JTM45

The origin of one of the great Marshall sounds, the JTM45 is still quite different from what most players today think of as *the* Marshall sound. In a blind test it might come off to many as something closer to the big-tweed Fender sound. In 1962 Jim Marshall, repairman Ken Bran, and shop assistant Dudley Craven built an amp in Marshall's workshop using Fender's 5F6-A Bassman circuit as a template but employing readily available British components (other than the 5881 output tubes that appeared in the first few runs of amps), and the Marshall line was born. You can virtually superimpose Fender's 5F6-A schematic onto the inside of the chassis of early Marshalls with nary a wire or component out of place, and their control panels are likewise the same, knob for knob. Yet different makes of components and transistors and, more than anything, the use of a big closed-back cabinet with four 12-inch Celestion speakers rather than four 10-inch Jensens in an open-back cab, give the JTM45 quite a different voice when you get down to the fine points. Further variables would soon take Marshall's flagship amps even further from Fender, but it's fun to hear the shadow of Leo in this great, and rare, early example.

Amp courtesy Rick Batey

1962 Fender Jaguar

If Fender's first offset-bodied electric was a jazz guitar that made a hit with the surf crowd, the Jaguar of 1962 was designed as a bid to jump straight in with the West Coast beach-blanket scene. It was also intended as the company's top-of-the-line model, a standing loudly declared by its plethora of bells and whistles, if not by its actual popularity relative to the stalwart Tele and Strat, and even the Jazzmaster. With its many switches and doodads, the Jaguar comes off as the quirkiest of Fender's offerings for the decade, but as such, it seems entirely in keeping with the '60s fondness for fancy switching and sonic variety—even if much of that variety proves of little or no worth in practical playing scenarios. Witness the "strangle" tone accessed by the slider switch positioned alongside the pickup selector sliders on the lower-forward control plate or the built-in, flip-up string mute—perfect for that *ticky ticky* rhythm sound—mounted to the bridge. What this Jaguar does give you, though, are a bright-yet-meaty Fender twang that is indeed fully surf-certified and a smooth-action floating vibrato system that's perfect for gently retro dips and bends.

1962 Crucianelli Tonemaster

Ah, yet another fine Italian "accordion guitar" in yet another design that is entirely lustworthy despite appearing, well, rather unfeasible at first glance. Crucianelli was an esteemed accordion maker dating back to the late 1800s when Santa Crucianelli of the famed Castelfidardo region of Italy began crafting squeezeboxes that stood out from the crowd for their quality and tone. Fast-forward to the early 1960s and suddenly the kids wanna rock, so Crucianelli followed Eko's footsteps into the electric guitar industry, and it did so in grand style, if we may say so. This 1962 Tonemaster has its solidbody and bolt-on neck encased in black pearloid, affectionately known to many as "mother of toilet seat," and might otherwise seem to be rather spartanly kitted out, if not for the bank of pushbutton switches that govern the signal routing of the four pickups (further Italian standards on show). Plugged in, it offers a lively, chiming tone with some bite and, if not a lot of woody resonance, at least some character to cut through the mix. If you can't find the real thing, check current offerings from the likes of Italia and Eastwood—"retro Italian" seems to be all the rage lately.

Meazzi Hollywood

Four pickups? Check! Plentiful knobs and switches? Check! It must be another great Italian electric—and indeed it is not just any old chunk of accordion-inspired ephemera, but a gorgeous 1962 Meazzi Hollywood. Luciano and Fratelli Meazzi of Milan worked with the great Wandré Pioli from the late 1950s into the start of the following decade and, from around 1962, produced their long-running Hollywood series, which included guitars that offered much of the stylistic and sonic veracity of Wandré's own guitars. Although the visual aspects of this one will grab your attention first—the fine marble finish in particular—it's a solidly made guitar with a nice, playable neck, a functional vibrato, and a range of interesting tones. Other Meazzi Hollywoods produced through the course of the decade took multifarious and occasionally radical designs but remained resolutely interesting. Semi-acoustics started out looking much like Hofner's basic offerings but evolved toward some fun and fantastic shapes themselves. Strap it on your back, kick the Vespa to life, and burn out into the piazza, and you'll be cruising in grand *Italiano* style.

Courtesy Outline Press Limited

1960s Gibson Everly Brothers

While the fun and funky shapes of electric guitars might have been grabbing most of the headlines in the early '60s, plenty of interesting acoustic efforts were hitting the market, too, although these often had less veracity than the groundbreaking prewar designs that arguably brought the form to its pinnacle. Gibson's Everly Brothers was an endorsement model that took the attributes of the J-200s the rock 'n' roll duo had been using and transformed them into an interesting alternative. The Everly Brothers guitar has a downsized body similar to that of the J-185 but shallower with star inlays on the fingerboard and enlarged double pickguards virtually engulfing its gloss-black top. In many ways, it's a pretty cool acoustic alternative and puts out an appealing rhythm tone in particular, despite the lesser depth (physically and tonally). The multi-piece adjustable bridge, relatively complex for a flat-top (with pinless retainer designed by the Everlys' father, Ike), is perhaps one of the design's downfalls, although this cumbersome unit impedes the guitar's resonance somewhat less than the clunkier adjustable metal bridges that Gibson added as "improvements" to plenty of otherwise excellent models. Still, the Everly Brothers model is a document of its time and a collectible Gibson at that.

1962 Fender Tremolux

Embodying one of Fender's ever-evolving amp models for a few short years in the early '60s, the blonde Tremolux was the baby of the company's Professional Series piggyback amps of the time, and, as such, it provides many players' favorite avenue to that roaring "transitional" tone. After a brief flirtation with EL84 output tubes, Fender settled on fixed-bias 6L6s for the Tremolux (which had a pair of lesser-powered 6V6s in its mid- to late-'50s tweed incarnation), but its relatively low voltages and small output transformer gave it less muscle than the similarly tubed Bassman or Concert, for example, with a power rating from 30 to 35 watts. As such, this 6G9-B Tremolux goes gorgeously crunchy and creamy at lower volume levels and can even sound kind of "adolescent Marshall" through its closed-back cab with dual 10-inch speakers. Add in a warm, throbbing bias-modulating tremolo circuit and it's a surprisingly versatile performer for a 50-year-old amp with no master volume control. Bags of fun in a groovy and relatively compact package—what more can you ask for?

Courtesy Cowtown Guitars/www.cowtownguitars.com

1963 Gibson Firebird III

While it looks as if it might hang with the Goyas and Supros, the radical "reverse-bodied" Firebird of the early '60s reveals, upon close examination, a Gibson-certified class and solidity that just, let's be honest, escapes so many of the C-list imports and catalog guitars of the era. In fact, in seeking to rob a little of the flash of Fender's Jazzmaster (and perhaps the Stratocaster before it), Gibson really outdid its main competitor in several ways. The result was a radical through-neck guitar with styling by Detroit designer Ray Dietrich and plenty of original new touches, including the six-in-line "banjo" tuners that prevented spoiling the phoenix-head profile and pickups that looked much like mini-humbuckers with enclosed covers but were made especially for the Firebird with coils wound directly around two alnico blade magnets. Bright, snappy, and snarly, the Firebird succeeded in pulling off some Fender-ish tricks, to some extent, but a few minutes with a great original example like this III (identified by its stud-bridge and dot inlays; the V offered a Tune-o-matic and trapezoids) shows that it's very much its own beast. So much so, perhaps, that it was a little too much for many players and was "smoothed out" into the more conventional "non-reverse" rendition just a couple years later.

1963 Epiphone EA-50T Pacemaker

Perhaps it isn't a "great" amp by anyone's standards, or even a "classic," but the Epiphone EA-50T Pacemaker of the early '60s is a fun little also-ran of the era and an interesting study in what an alternative take on the formula can do. And who's to say a little amp like this couldn't help you create your own tone? This combo produces a bold 10 watts courtesy of a pair of 6AQ5 output tubes, which despite being one alphanumeric back from the American nomenclature for the classic British EL84 (a.k.a. 6BQ5) are really quite different sounding, with a smaller seven-pin mounting and less power on tap to boot. The upsides are that the EA-50T segues into the dirt zone far sooner than an EL84-equipped amp, and you can find good new old stock (NOS) 6AQ5s at a reasonable cost, since they were never much in demand in the first place. Two 6EU7 tubes power the preamp and tremolo effect, the totality of which is governed by controls for loudness and frequency (tremolo speed). A 10-inch Gibson Ultrasonic speaker sends it all to the masses.

1963 Fender Vibroverb 6G16

Want to talk about desirability? The Fender Vibroverb of 1963 is perhaps the rarest and most collectible standard Fender production model. Fender was slow in bringing reverb to its amplifiers, and when it finally did in early 1963, it arrived first in the Vibroverb. This short-lived combo was much like the 2x10 Pro of the era, except that it produced a little less power and dispensed with the complex "harmonic vibrato" circuit to make room for its great-sounding reverb. This might sound like a loss to some, but many true tremolo fans prefer the bias-wiggle tube tremolo circuit inside this Vibroverb for its smooth, volume-modulating pulse, which sounds great through the chewy 35-watt output stage with two 6L6GCs. Ramp this one up with Speed and Intensity controls at around 1 o'clock, Reverb at 10 o'clock, and Gain set at the edge of breakup, and it is clear yet forgiving, addictively tactile, and swimming in added aural depths from the onboard effects. Similarly equipped black-face amps that followed would also be great performers, but this one deserved to be with us a little longer.

Courtesy Outline Press Limited

1964 Mosrite Ventures Mark 1

There are endorsement models aplenty out there in Guitarland, but Mosrite's Ventures model took the principle to the next level. Californian Semi Moseley began building guitars in earnest in the late 1950s, and by the early 1960s, his creations were catching the attention of several prominent artists on the instrumental scene in particular. The guitars captured the fancy of Nokie Edwards of hit-makers the Ventures, and in 1963, the band funded production of the Ventures guitar at Mosrite's new facility in Bakersfield, California, after agreeing to a deal that granted them the exclusive rights to distribute the model (which was expected to be Mosrite's biggest seller, given the Ventures' popularity). Although the quirky "reversed Fender" body style has been aped by many cheaper imported copies in the intervening years, the original Mosrites aimed to be the best available, and the Ventures model is no exception. It has a slim, fast neck profile, unique hardware tooled almost entirely by Moseley himself (Kluson tuners aside), and beefy single-coil pickups that contribute to a bold, biting tone. Despite the appeal—and decent sales—of the Ventures model, Mosrite had a bumpy run through the '60s, thanks in large part to Moseley's rather quirky business sense, and folded in 1969. Several efforts at rebirth have resulted in some worthwhile reissues.

RAMONES
ROAD TO RUIN

...visual sound STEREO

THE VENTURES KNOCK ME OUT!

SLAUGHTER ON TENTH AVENUE
OH, PRETTY WOMAN • SHE'S NOT THERE
I FEEL FINE • • • GONE GONE GONE
WHEN YOU WALK IN THE ROOM
SHA LA LA • LOVE POTION NO. 9 • and other hits

DOLTON RECORDS

WALK — DON'T RUN '64
and THE CRUEL SEA
THE VENTURES

DOLTON RECORDS #96

March 1, 1966   S. A. MOSELEY   3,237,502

STRINGED MUSICAL INSTRUMENT

Filed May 11, 1964   3 Sheets—Sheet 1

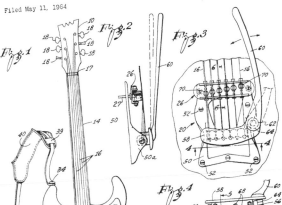

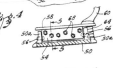

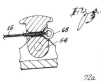

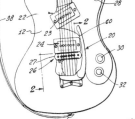

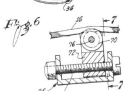

INVENTOR
Semie A. Moseley
By Keith A. Beecher
Attorney

1963 Gibson Hummingbird

The acoustic-guitar market benefited from a significant folk boom throughout the 1960s, yet perhaps ironically, the major makers rarely improved on anything they had nailed down several decades before. Unveiled in 1960, Gibson's big Hummingbird might have been an exception to the rule if not hampered by a few odd Gibsonisms of the CMI era. Rather heavy bracing—intended as an inoculation against guitar returns with "bellied" tops—and the cumbersome adjustable bridge saddle combined to deaden the Hummingbird's resonance somewhat, but it was still a good performer, with a reasonably strong voice for solo work or acoustic rhythm alike. The 'Bird, a whopping dreadnought at 16.25 inches wide, came with elegant split-parallelogram fingerboard inlays and dressed in a vibrant cherry sunburst finish or, less commonly, as a more sedate natural. A fancy three-point engraved hummingbird pickguard just screams for some good old '60s-style communing with nature. One of the more stylish ways to get yer folk on.

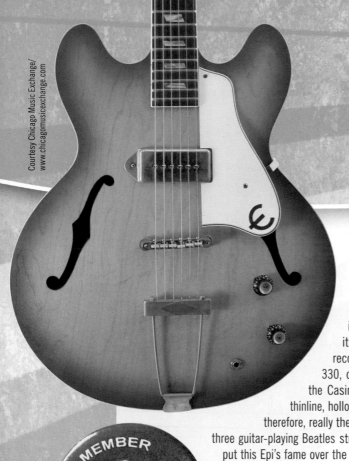

1964 Epiphone Casino

Known largely as Gibson's budget brand, Epiphone offered plenty of worthy Kalamazoo-made guitars after its acquisition by Gibson in 1957. One in particular even outpaced its Gibson equivalent for overall product recognition. Virtually identical to the Gibson ES-330, other than some styling and hardware details, the Casino offered the same dual P-90 pickups on a thinline, hollowbody archtop with a 17th-fret neck joint and, therefore, really the same tone and performance. The fact that all three guitar-playing Beatles strapped on a Casino in the mid-'60s, however, put this Epi's fame over the top compared to the ES-330, which remained something of an also-ran alongside Gibson's more successful ES-335. Bassist Paul McCartney acquired an early Casino in 1964 for "composing," according to Andy Babiuk's *Beatles Gear*, while both John Lennon and George Harrison used their Casinos prominently on the band's final U.S. tour in 1966. This guitar's roundly woody, acoustic-like resonance and meaty, slightly gritty P-90 bite are truly indistinguishable from that of the ES-330, of course, but if you're a Beatles fan, it just *has* to be a Casino.

Early-1960s Epiphone Texan

Gibson's round-shouldered dreadnoughts were shadowed by Epiphone flat-tops, as were several of their electrics, but thanks yet again to a famous Beatles association, the Texan might be the most illustrious of the bunch, due to Paul McCartney's purchase of a natural-topped version in 1964, which he of course converted to play left-handed. Funky Gibson adjustable bridge saddle and all, the large-bodied dread with a solid spruce top and solid mahogany back and sides makes a pretty sweet noise, as famously heard on McCartney's studio Beatles' recording of "Yesterday," which he frequently reproduced live using the same guitar. In the hands, this one feels and sounds much like many similar Gibson models from the same era but offers those Epiphone stylistic touches that tell the world you belong to a more exclusive club—or at least did until the brand appeared prominently on more affordable Asian imports from 1970 onward.

1963 Vox AC10 Twin

The humble and, until recently, underappreciated AC10 is one gargantuan tone machine and arguably a more viable option than the "little" AC15 in this age of downsizing and down-watting. It makes a great recording tool, delivering that Vox chime 'n' grind at levels less likely to freak out your friendly studio engineer and will do just about whatever you ask of it when miked up and put through the mains. Vox released the AC10 in 1959 as a student model under the AC15 (originally the company's largest guitar amp), although the AC10's debutante 1x10 format really wasn't big enough to show what this circuit can do.

The AC10 Twin, with two 10-inch Elac drivers, makes a lot more of the formula, and there's even more poke with an upgrade to more efficient speakers. An EF86 preamp tube in the vibrato channel links the AC10 to the AC15 sound, and the normal channel's ECF82 is more of an oddball, but doesn't sound bad at all. If you aren't afraid to apply a few careful mods, the AC10 can sound even more like a junior AC15 or AC30, but even as it stands, it's one hip little amp.

1965 Gibson ES-125TDC

Before the simple yet effective chooglin' bottleneck barroom blues of George Thorogood brought the snarling tone of a beat ES-125TDC to public awareness in the late 1970s, Gibson's entry-level thinline archtop was a near-forgotten bargain on the used guitar scene. And you know what? Very often it still is. Like the ES-330 (and its cousin, Epiphone's Casino), the ES-125TDC is a fully hollowbody thinline archtop, but it has its roots in the bigger, full-depth Gibson archtops of the 1950s and before, and for that it's a very different beast. Before gaining the "T" in its suffix (for "Thinline," natch), the ES-125 was the more austere member of the laminated archtop family that included the ES-150 and ES-175. Even after it slimmed down, the ES-125TDC retained the floating bridge of the big archtops, with a separate wooden bass "attached" to the guitar's top only by the pressure of the strings. So, thin or no, this guitar has a full, round, woody tone reminiscent of its roots. Give it a little snarl from the right tube amp, though—and stand far enough away to discourage feedback—and those P-90s will growl and bite, making this a formidable rock 'n' roller in jazzer's clothing.

1962 Martin F-55

Work your way down from the tip-top of this Pennsylvania-bred oddity and you're immediately thinking, "D-18, maybe 00-21?" In fact, it's the strangely wonderful Martin F-55 thinline hollowbody archtop electric. Despite having all the right ingredients, it would seem, to make an utter success of it— DeArmond Model 200 pickups, a popular size and shape, and Martin's unquestionably fine workmanship among them—the F-55 and its brethren never quite found a home in the market. It might be that the spartan, flat-top-like headstock that fooled us at the outset just didn't say "rockin' electric" to many players, although the change to a less Martin-esque shape for the GT Series in 1965 didn't meet with any more success. Or perhaps it was that by the time Martin introduced the F series in 1961 or early '62 the wave of thinline hollowbody electrics with single-coil pickups had already passed (in 1954 they might have given Gretsch a run for their money). Whatever the reason for its downfall, this F-55 sounds much as you'd expect: in short, very much like a similarly equipped Gretsch or Guild, with plenty of sting and twang from those DeArmonds and an airy body characteristic of a quality thinline.

1965 Silvertone 1457

Maybe you used to laugh at the kid who dragged his Silvertone amp-in-case rig along to garage jams back in the day when you had your Japanese Strat copy in hand and your solid-state behemoth set up in the corner next to the lawnmower. Today it's painfully obvious there's something so extremely *right on* about these quirky sets from the '60s. The amp itself, which most often had an anemic

Courtesy Retrofret Vintage Guitars/www.retrofret.com/photo by George Aslaender

50C5 output tube, isn't up to much other than some close-miked recording (for which it can sound pretty funky and nasty when cranked), but the guitar itself is an exceedingly hip creation. The necks of these Silvertones, which were made in Neptune, New Jersey, by Danelectro, are comfy players, and though made of poplar, they have a distinctly Fender-ish vibe and feature luscious Brazilian rosewood fingerboards. Pop all that poplar, hardboard, and lipstick-tube goodness into a bigger rig and you get anything from a glassy ringing tone to the kind of pliant, articulate overdrive achieved only when low-output pickups push a cranked tube amp. Now you're smiling . . . if not laughing.

1963 Gretsch 6156 Playboy

The amps on which Gretsch stamped its name have always been among the coolest of the Valco-made stable. This student-size 6156 Playboy model might appear rather diminutive with its single 10-inch Jensen C10R speaker, but its powerhouse carries a whopping surprise and really comes into its own when you give it something a little stouter to breathe through. The two 6973 tubes in the Playboy's output stage were a Valco favorite for many years, and while they might look a lot like nine-pin EL84s, they actually sound quite a bit different. For one thing, they are capable of handling much higher voltages and putting out more power (the Playboy boasts 17 watts, but that is achieved at relatively low plate voltages). For another, they are noticeably thicker, meatier, and perhaps a tad grittier than the classic thin Brit bottles. The result is a tone that is punchy and broad in the clean range, and barky and thick when cranked up. Inject it through a good 1x12 or even a 4x12 and that deeply throbbing Valco tremolo is the icing on the cake.

1963 Fender Twin Reverb

Going on five decades, Fender's Twin Reverb has virtually defined "big cleans with headroom," and yet the amp is far more versatile than this subheading implies. Dig Michael Bloomfield's explosive blues tone on a cranked Twin Reverb, B. B. King's frequent use of the amp, or the fact that Robben Ford swears by one whenever his beloved Dumble is unavailable, and you get an inkling of what this cornerstone of tone can do. With a robust 85 to 100 watts RMS delivered from four 6L6GCs; preamp, tone, and effects stages that were highly advanced when introduced late in 1963; and two 12-inch speakers in a finger-jointed pine cabinet, a good Twin Reverb will take you from honking country twang to smooth jazz to snarling indie rock and beyond without blinking an eye. Roll the volume up past noon, though, and perhaps show it a little booster or overdrive pedal, and just feel the mammoth, room-filling roar that this "clean" amp puts out. One of few amps out there that has justly earned its one-word name.

Amp courtesy Elderly Instruments/ photos Dave Matchette

Mid-1960s Gretsch Silver Jet

There aren't many guitars cooler than a snazzy double-cutaway Gretsch Silver Jet from the early to mid-1960s, and few will grab the same kind of attention on stage, either. Technically any Gretsch solidbody of the Duo Jet family made with a sparkle finish after 1962 was simply a "Duo Jet with Silver Sparkle top," but the individual Silver Jet distinction carried in the catalog in the 1950s tended to stick, so this is how most players think of this guitar today. Only skin deep though it might be, the stunning silver sparkle finish seems to make this guitar *sound* cooler too, unless that's just our imaginations. The "finish" is not a paint application at all, but a sheet of the same Monsanto-made material that Gretsch used to cover its snazzy drum kits. As such, there might be an argument for its inhibition of the guitar top's natural resonance. But who cares? This is an electric guitar, baby, and it looks it—twang and grind with some attitude, and a few boppers in the front row are going to frown at your lack of "natural, woody resonance."

GRETSCH GUITARS

ELECTRIC | Hollow•Solid | • FLAT TOP • FOLK • CLASSIC

THE FRED. GRETSCH MFG. CO.
60 Broadway, Brooklyn 11, N
218 South Wabash Avenue, Chicago 4, Illin

1960s Wandre Soloist

Like some alien electric guitars arrived from another planet to show us how a far-flung race of starmen conceived their own instruments entirely differently from ours, and yet not so differently at all, Wandres are simultaneously works of art and utterly great-sounding guitars. This 1960s Soloist is a classic of the breed, with a semi-hollow "tone chamber" body, eccentric molded plastic parts, wild trapezoidal Davoli pickups, and a fulcrum-adjusting aluminum neck. All of the components, in fact, often led writers to portray Wandré Pioli as some near-crazed madman cum visionary . . . which perhaps he was, although he was also the son of a respected instrument maker in Cavriago, Italy, who learned traditional luthiery at his father's side before taking it to the next dimension several decades later. Best known as the first choice of avant country player Buddy Miller, this Wandre Soloist has a fat yet biting tone and a surprisingly inviting playing feel for a guitar with a neck made from an aluminum rod with a wooden fingerboard attached. From the tail to the whacko vibrato and control fascia to the ingenious slotted aluminum-sided headstock (a thing of beauty in itself), this guitar is truly an out-of-leftfield creation—and a genuine work of art.

Courtesy Rumble Seat Music/www.rumbleseatmusic.com

Early-1960s WEM Copicat

Watkins Electric Music was probably best known for its range of amplifiers—which carried the WEM abbreviation sometime after 1963 because founder Charlie Watkins apparently liked the way the three-letter badge linked them to the more successful Vox company—but the Copicat tape echo certainly ran a close second, and might be considered the company's most successful product in sonic terms, in the opinions of many guitarists. Watkins developed the Copicat in 1958 with the help of engineer Bill Purkiss, and it was the first tape echo to hit the market, ahead of other major European units from Binson, Meazzi, and Vox. Thanks to some advantageous word-of-mouth publicity, Watkins sold out every unit in the first production run of 100 on the day of its introduction in London. A simple, rugged tube-driven tape echo, the Copicat provided the crucial sound of rock 'n' roll for countless British and European guitarists, and singers besides. Several variations on the form came and went, later under the WEM brand, including good-sounding solid-state renditions with sound-on-sound and varispeed, but the early tube unit remains the classic.

1966 Burns Bison

Amid an import embargo on U.S.-made goods in the late 1950s and early '60s, several British and European makers scrambled to fill the demand fueled by the skiffle, beat, and rock 'n' roll booms. In terms of design integrity and overall constructional quality, Jim Burns was one of the more successful. The guitar maker released his first electrics under the Supersound name in 1958, then teamed with Henry Weill to produce a handful of basic, beginner-grade solidbodies under the Burns-Weill brand name. Given the crude nature of these early offerings, it's impressive that just a few years later (and only one year after the unveiling of the basic but vibey Burns-brand debutante, the Artiste) Burns was producing an acknowledged classic in the Bison. Ignore the extreme body horns and ungainly multi-section pickguards that are central to the look of this guitar (Bison . . . horns . . . geddit?), and you discover a well-crafted instrument with a solid-body, a neck with more ergonomic virtue than most European guitars of the time, and several extremely clever proprietary designs in terms of its low-impedance Ultra-Sonic pickups and highly engineered vibrato system. It's a different beast, for sure, but for many, the Bison represents the zenith of amplified early '60s British rock 'n' roll—even if the biggest Brit acts of the time were reaching for Gibsons, Fenders, Rickenbackers, and Gretsches.

Maestro Fuzz-Tone

A sibling of Gibson under the wing of parent company Chicago Musical Instruments, and later Norlin, the Maestro brand was very much an entity unto itself despite its frequent associations with the legendary guitar maker and was more strongly associated with electronic musical effects than was Gibson. The Fuzz-Tone is widely credited as being the first commercially available transistorized fuzz box on the market, although at the time of its introduction it wasn't even promoted as a rock 'n' roll tool. Early promotional efforts plugged the pedal's ability to "make guitar sound like a saxophone," and it was also frequently touted for its "endless, singing sustain" rather than its heavy, distortion-inducing fuzz. It didn't take the rockers long to cotton on, though, and once Keith Richards plugged in a Fuzz-Tone on "(I Can't Get No) Satisfaction" it was all over. The bandwagon filled up fast with imitators, but for thick, hairy, edgy, and slightly grating, there's no mistaking the original.

1964 Custom-Color Fender Stratocaster

Crazy what a lick of paint will do for the value of a vintage guitar. The absence of an original finish from a pre-CBS Stratocaster can knock off nearly 50 percent of its value, even if every other element is original. The change of factory finish from standard sunburst, on the other hand, to one of the rarer "custom colors" can *add* upwards of 50 percent to the market value of what is otherwise the very same guitar. Crazy? Most certainly, but therein lies much of the fun. Of course, to assess the mojo—and therefore, the cosmic worth—of a great custom-color '60s Strat, you really must try one for yourself. While plenty of players rave about the "slab board" guitars of the decade's first years, Stratocasters from early 1964 are excellent guitars by any measure and favorites of many Strat aficionados who have assessed the breed. These guitars usually have chunkier necks than the skinny profiles on early-'60s examples while maintaining all of the highly desirable pre-CBS features, such as the small headstock with spaghetti logo, clay fingerboard dots, and three-ply nitrocellulose pickguard. Naturally, they can sound phenomenal, too, and even better in glorious Daphne Blue, Dakota Red, or Shoreline Gold.

1964 Vox AC4

Like the tweed 1950s Fender Champ across the pond, the AC4 was Vox's gateway amp to young, student, or hobby players, providing a taste of that seminal British rock 'n' roll tone at a fraction of the cost—and volume. And that's exactly what a tasty little vintage AC4 still represents for more advanced, more professional players today. With 4 watts into a single 8-inch Elac speaker, it won't give you the bodacious crunch of the larger Vox amps, but the EF86-powered preamp has a stoutness that belies the AC4's size, and the Class A chime definitely has a familiar character. Unsurprisingly, it's a great recording amp, too, and in this application its size in the track has nothing to do with its footprint on the studio floor. The tremolo is functional, if not particularly lush, and there isn't a lot of tonal versatility here—turn it up for the lead tone, turn it down for the clean tone—but the AC4 offers a nifty means of stepping onto the vintage-Vox ladder.

1964 Sonola Reverb 98-RT

The ever-curious ears behind successful professional recording studios have long understood that the successful sound for the track doesn't always come from the most successful brand name in the gear closet. This humble Sonola Reverb 98-T ripped out a slamming tone time and time again for clients of Camp Street Studios (formerly Fort Apache) and, in doing so, earned its place as a fixture in one of Boston's leading facilities. The origins of the lesser-seen Sonola amp line aren't very well documented, but they appear to have been built by the same Hoboken, New Jersey, manufacturer that provided Guild's amps of the same era and sold by the Sonola Organ Company of Chicago to accompany its amplified squeezeboxes (note the "Acc" input on this amp). Whether

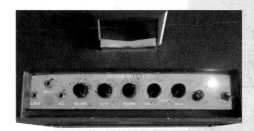

or not the maker was actually Guild or another New Jersey facility isn't entirely clear. What *is* clear is that the amp is nigh on identical to the New Jersey–made Ampeg Reverb Rocket of the era. Enigmatic origins aside, it offers toothsome crunch—courtesy of a 6SL7-loaded front end and a dual-6V6 output stage generating around 15 watts—and the lush atmospheric that the built-in reverb and tremolo allow you to heap onto it.

1964 Fender Super Reverb

After deciding that the late-'50s tweed Bassman was perhaps the all-around best-sounding amp ever made, many players frequently referred to the black-face Super Reverb that followed a few years after the Bassman combo's demise as "a tweed Bassman with reverb and tremolo." Other than its 4x10 speaker complement and dual-6L6 output stage for around 40 watts, however, that description isn't anywhere close to the truth. Leo Fender's quest for a tighter, bolder, cleaner tone led to several changes in the medium and larger black-face (and intervening brown-face) amps from the tweed years, and these make the Super Reverb a very different beast. Higher voltages on the preamp tubes, a tone stack sandwiched between two gain stages (rather than the tweed's cathode-follower EQ), and changes in the output stage all add crispness and cut to this black-face combo, yet you can still crank it for some easy breakup and delectable playing dynamics. And it is the tweed Bassman's equal as a powerful blues and rock 'n' roll machine, if different. The addition of the same reverb and tremolo circuits as in the Twin Reverb is, of course, a great bonus.

Mid-1960s Guild F-30

While churning out some respectable electric rivals, Guild also produced several notable, high-quality acoustic flat-tops, of which this F-30 is a prime example. Guild's dreadnought-shaped "D" range looks much as might be expected, more in the image of the Martin staple, but to our eyes the rounded body of the "F" folk series always seemed more characteristic of Guild's classic steel-string work. This mid-level, mid-size acoustic from the factory in Hoboken, New Jersey, has a solid spruce top with a sweetly aged cherry sunburst finish and solid mahogany back and sides, with Guild's gently arched contour to the latter. It's a great player, with a warm yet lively tone that's perfect for its intended folk but capable of fitting in just about any place a good medium-bodied flat-top is required. A deluxe F-30 with solid rosewood back and sides released in 1967 would become a favorite of Paul Simon, and plenty of other major artists took up the Guild as a viable alternative to Gibson and Martin: Richie Havens, Dave Van Ronk, Johnny Cash, Tim Buckley, and even Howlin' Wolf among them. The company's fortunes were looking good until a general sales slowdown in the 1970s.

Courtesy Golden Age Fretted Instruments/www.goldenageguitars.com

1965 Vox AC30 Top Boost

Any guitarist who doesn't feel a distinct shiver of excitement at the mere thought of a mid-'60s Vox AC30 with Top Boost is clearly dead in the shorts. Vox's cornerstone combo might have evolved through several iterations before reaching this stage in 1964, but the AC30/6 with factory-installed Top Boost EQ undeniably embodies the most desirable form of "that tone," and the most emulated incarnation of the Vox sound, too. This is the amp that Matchless, Bad Cat, Cornell, TopHat, Bruno, Trainwreck, Komet, 65amps, and untold others have used as a springboard for their own contemporary boutique creations, and it remains the veritable definition of Class A tone. The key ingredients here are the elegant ECC83 (a.k.a. 12AX7) gain stage into an ECC83-driven cathode-follower tone stack on the Brilliant channel, then a long-tailed-pair phase inverter into four cathode-biased EL84s with no negative feedback, into a pair of Celestion G12 alnico speakers. You really can't ask for more for chime, bloom, and shimmer at clean volumes. And as plenty who have dared to turn it up past 11 o'clock have discovered, the lead tones offer a sweet, multidimensional, harmonics-laden feast to die for. Dick Denney, it's a job well done.

Mid-1960s Rickenbacker 360/12

Unquestionably the king of all electric 12-strings, Rickenbacker's 360/12 model provided the jangle and chime for two of the biggest hit-makers of the 1960s—as played by George Harrison with the Beatles and Roger McGuinn with the Byrds—establishing a standard that no other maker has been able to knock from its perch. Rickenbacker's legendary 12-string design was born out of a brainstorm by company owner Francis Hall, who saw the growing popularity of the acoustic 12-string in the early '60s at the crest of a major folk boom and figured he could achieve a crossover success in the electric market. His stroke of genius came in guiding Rickie's R&D team to devise a 12-string that played and even looked much like a standard electric 6-string, thereby easing the uptake for players not accustomed to all those extra wires under the fingers. As such, this 360/12 bucks the extreme widths of many acoustic twelves with an easy, comfortable neck and avoids that ungainly elongated headstock otherwise common to the breed by doubling over the six-per-side tuners at right angles to each other. As for the tone, it's pure meaty, crystalline chime—angelically bright, yet never harsh, thanks to the vintage single-coil "toaster top" pickups. No wonder George Harrison, even while languishing in his sickbed in a New York hotel after an *Ed Sullivan Show* appearance in February 1964, was eager to hang on to the 360/12 that Hall had brought him for a trial run.

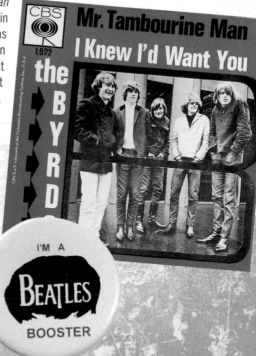

1964 Gibson SG Special

The SG Special inherited the mantle from the Les Paul Special and arguably remained truer to form than its big brother the Standard, given it had always been a pure mahogany solidbody. In retrospect, the once-radical, dual-pointed body design seems entirely more suited to late-'60s rock excess than its more sedate-looking predecessor, primed to move masses of air through towering amp stacks in the hands of a Pete Townshend or a Tony Iommi. The former's thumping, driving rhythm work with The Who in the late '60s and early '70s, as perhaps best heard on *Live At Leeds*, might offer the formative example of what this otherwise humble model can do in the right setting. It sounds fantastic through just about any decent tube amp, especially when you push it toward the point of breakup, but you need to experience an SG Special just once through a big, bold amp much like—or perhaps exactly like—the Hiwatt that was Townshend's go-to live rig in the day. That P-90 grunt and grind retains a deliciously bitey metallic edge at high volume, and when you spank out a few big, open, suspended rhythm chords, you can feel the atmosphere shift throughout the entire room. It's a transformational experience, and all the more glorious when triggered by such a workman-like guitar.

1965 Fender Mustang

Remember that day in junior high when you brought your knockoff Japanese electric in to audition for jazz band, the best guitar you could afford at the time (hell, the *only* guitar), and that rich kid from across town showed up with a shiny silver case, which he opened to reveal an equally shiny red Mustang? No? Well, we sure do. It was a real Fender, and he only let you play it briefly, but never before in your 13 years of existence had you touched such a gorgeous object, and the experience burned a major impression into your brain. Hoist this luscious hunk of vintage Fender, 24-inch-scale student model though it might be, and the thrill remains equally palpable. The Mustang's appeal isn't purely sentimental, either: as a shorter-scale Fender, it maintains plenty of the lively, single-coil Fullerton twang and jangle—but with an extremely easy playing feel, thanks to the reduced tension—and a buoyant roundness in the tone to boot. From surf to garage to good old rock 'n' roll, this Mustang is a surprisingly able performer and an undeniable slice of cool.

1965 Fender Deluxe Reverb

I am small enough to crank up into tone territory for recording, rehearsal, and bar gigs, yet loud enough to fill a room and be heard above the drummer in a medium-size club. What am I? Why, the Fender Deluxe Reverb, of course. Although it evolved from the 5E3 tweed Deluxe via the brown Deluxe of 1961–1963, the black-face Deluxe Reverb that came out later in '63 always felt like "a grown-up amp," and not just because it carried Fender's delectable reverb and tremolo effects, the inclusion of which has made it a one-stop, grab 'n' go sound solution for countless guitarists over the years. Running the 6V6 output tubes at much higher voltages than in the previous incarnations of the Deluxe, as well as continuing the efficient fixed-bias topology with a little negative feedback that had been used since '61, gave the Deluxe Reverb a tighter, bolder presence and considerably more output—up to 22 watts from around 15 to 18. Plug into this one, and even if you never owned or played a black-face Deluxe Reverb before, it somehow feels like coming home.

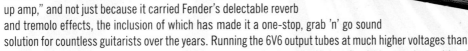

1965 Marshall Model 1958

Ironically, throughout the 1960s, '70s, and beyond, while young players dreamed of graduating to the big stacks their guitar heroes played onstage, the heroes themselves, already hip to the tip, were often recording with the succulent, responsive smaller amps that also doubled as student models. While any close comparisons between this 2x10 Marshall 1958 combo and a JMP50 Plexi stack would clearly render the 18-watt combo quite different from the "low-powered Plexi" it is often described as, it squeezes enough meaty grind and crispy crunch from its dual EL84s to have a distinctly Marshall character nonetheless, and it certainly stands in well for its big brother when lower volumes are required. Plenty of players have discovered this fact lately, too, and a good Model 1958 or similar (and remember these are model numbers, *not* years) can often be more difficult to track down—and more expensive to purchase—than a more powerful Marshall from the late '60s. Whether you get it from this beauty, the 1x12 Model 1974, or the 2x12 1973, the "18-watter," as it has become known, is a gentler road to vintage Marshall heaven.

Mid-1960s
Gibson EDS-1275

The monstrous double-neck guitar is certainly the ultimate icon of late-'60s and 1970s rock excess. It was virtually required that every serious arena rocker of the era carried one in his touring arsenal, certainly every aspiring guitar kid longed to strut the stage with one of these beasts in hand at some point in his or her development—and the mighty Gibson EDS-1275 was the unrivaled king of the castle. Not only did the EDS-1275 enable Jimmy Page to perform the tricky 12- to-6-string shift of "Stairway to Heaven" live on stage, but it accompanied epic excursions from the likes of Family, Rush, and the Eagles, whose Don Felder landed at No. 8 on *Guitar World*'s "100 Greatest Guitar Solos" list with his dramatic Leslie'd 12-string intro *and* climactic dual-solo with Joe Walsh on "Hotel California." Originally offered from 1962 to 1968, with only around 110 made, the EDS-1275 was reissued in 1977 by popular demand. Felder's guitar was from the later batch, while Page's came from the original run. What do the things sound like? Well, unsurprisingly, much like an SG with either 6 or 12 strings, with perhaps more sonic girth thanks to the added body mass. But sound is virtually irrelevant when you look this cool under the spotlights.

rush a farewell to kings

Elvis Presley, 1966. Hulton Archive/Getty Images

1966 Gibson Firebird V

After the radical reverse-bodied Firebird failed to soar, Gibson introduced the somewhat more standard, though still rather nifty, revised "nonreverse" Firebird line in 1965. Not much was made of the change other than the catalog heralding a "new style solid mahogany body and special construction," although by any standards the new Firebird's standard set-neck construction was now genuinely less "special" than that of the previous through-neck design. You could say that the name was the same, but the design had been changed to protect the innocent; even the stylishly reversed six-in-line headstock was flip-flopped to more of a Fender-aping orientation. But never mind all that. This bird still squawks, now with two or three P-90 pickups on the I and III models, respectively (the V and VII retained mini-humbuckers), and a basic but functional Maestro Vibrola whammy unit . . . well, functional if you're not too fussy about staying in tune throughout your performance. Still, this is a hip slice of '60s style by any measure and a great-sounding Gibson solidbody from an era before the company's electrics began to go badly south.

Joseph Branston/*Guitarist*
magazine via Getty Images

1966 Dallas Rangemaster Treble Booster

There seems to be little sense in the fact that one of the simplest commercial effects pedals ever created is also one of the most prized and expensive on the vintage market, but such is the original Dallas Rangemaster Treble Booster. Its circuit contains a mere four capacitors, three resistors, one germanium transistor, plus a boost pot, two jacks, a switch, and a battery. But, as with so many collectibles, complexity

isn't necessarily an indicator of value. Factors that *have* contributed to the Rangemaster's value are the scarcity of good original examples and its use by the likes of Eric Clapton, Brian May, Tony Iommi, and several others in the formative years of rock tone. While the Rangemaster does emphasize treble frequencies somewhat, its simple germanium-fired boost is beloved more for the way it kicks a good vintage tube amp into overdrive. For many players, that alone is enough to justify its rating as the most expensive entry in *Vintage Guitar* magazine's "Top 25 Vintage Effects" list of 2011, although for the rest of us, one of several extremely good copies might work as well at a fraction of the price.

Mid-1960s Teisco Del Ray

From the Space Age body styling to the four/two headstock to the quartet of pickups and related switches, this top-of-the-line Teisco is one of the hippest Del Rays you're likely to find. The model name also graced several lesser one- and two-pickup guitars, however, many of which became the hallowed "first electric" of a surprisingly high number of aspiring young players in the 1960s and '70s. Whether it's the ongoing retro style craze, the fact that these are the closest many players can get to anything smacking of "vintage," or the preposterous notion that—gasp—they really might just be pretty cool-playing and -sounding guitars in the first place, the more elaborate Teisco Del Rays have become mildly collectible in recent years—and, hey, why the heck not? Still easily had for well under a grand, this funky marvel will help you look and sound far more distinctive than your band mate with the expensive reissue Les Paul, Stratocaster, or Gretsch model, and there's a lot to be said even for that.

Courtesy Outline Press Limited

1964 Selmer Zodiac Twin 50

Although Selmer often struggled to hold a footing in the British amp market of the mid-1960s against encroachers Vox and Marshall, the most beloved of its offerings from the era have, after decades in the wilderness, lately become just as collectible as anything from that formidable pair. The Zodiac Twin 30 and Twin 50 were most likely released in direct response to the Vox AC30 and Marshall Model 1962 (a.k.a. Bluesbreaker), respectively, and they sure do remind us how confidently Selmer can play against those more familiar titans of classic-rock tone. This Zodiac Twin 50 produces a pounding 50 watts from two fixed-bias EL34s into a pair of 12-inch Goodmans ceramic speakers, with a front end that's an adaptation of the Truvoice Selectortone visited earlier. An initial ECC83 (a.k.a. 12AX7) gain stage runs into each channel's volume and tone (plus the tone-switch network on Channel 2) before hitting a second gain stage comprising a fat EF86 pentode preamp, then belting on to the power amp, which is laid out in a separate chassis mounted in the bottom of the cab. This unusual configuration gives the amp a warm, thick voice with phenomenal punch when pushed. All this plus silver and black mock croc-skin covering and a front-mounted status light that pulses in time with the tremolo.

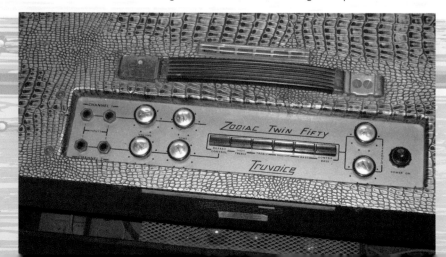

1965 Supro Model 24

Even if a name artist never played through a Supro Model 24 like
this one, it's a groovy little combo just as it sits. Of course, the fact that this model is often rumored to be the famous
lost "Jimmy Page amp"—the "small, blue Supro," as the Zep guitarist has put it—through which he recorded much of
the eviscerating crunch and wail on *Led Zeppelin I* and *II*, certainly adds a little *frisson* to its status. The Model 24 bears
several similarities to the Gretsch 6156 Playboy combo, with its girthsome 6973 output tubes and quirky, ral's-nest
Valco circuitry. But this blue beauty has two independent channels with their own Volume and Tone controls, and the
addition of an intensity control on its great-sounding tremolo. Perhaps more important than any of these, though, is that
its slightly larger cab carries a 12-inch Jensen C12Q speaker, a driver that's primed to make more of this amp's potential
(but sub a Celestion into your own Model 24 and just see what happens!). Inject guitar of choice, get the volume up to
1 o'clock or beyond, and you'll soon believe that this one is another stone in the foundation of great rock tone.

1965 Airline 62-9015A

Hailing from the Montgomery Ward catalog's Airline range, this Twin-size
combo was manufactured by Danelectro, and although it boasts similar
features to the ubiquitous Fender of the era, it has nowhere near the volume
of the mighty Twin or the Twin's smaller 2x12 sibling, the Pro Reverb, for that
matter. Which is not to say it doesn't sound darned nifty. Danelectro, Airline, Silvertone, and the like certainly sold a
lot of amplifiers to players who couldn't afford Fenders, Gibsons, or Ampegs, but Dano founder Nat Daniel never was
one to copy the circuits of bigger names. This Airline, a case in point, has very much its own tone—gritty, snarly, and
raspy when cranked up, a surprisingly effective alternative voice for a broad range of indie-minded rock adventures.
The reverb is rather sproingy and thin, the tremolo perhaps limper than those of several other major amps, and even
with its pair of 6L6GCs, the entire thing only puts out something in the neighborhood of 20 watts, but forget the stats
and just play it a while—the 62-9015A is sure to put a grin on your gob.

Johnny Thunders (right).
Gijsbert Hanekroot/Redferns/Getty Images

1966 Vox Mark VI

Tom Jennings' Vox brand used its success as the backline of the Beatles and several other significant artists to roll out a full line of rock 'n' roll gear in the 1960s, and the Mark series "teardrop" guitars were notable among the throng. These hip, alternatively shaped guitars were successors to the first serious Vox solidbodies, the pentagonal Phantom line of 1962, and looked for a time to be the next big thing on the block, especially when a prototype, and later, production models, were seen in the hands of Rolling Stones guitarist Brian Jones. Later, Johnny Thunders notably played a Vox teardrop during the New York Dolls' appearance on "The Old Grey Whistle Test." A move of production from the U.K. facility in Dartford to Eko in Italy, however, signaled the Vox Mark's early demise, and the company ceased guitar production altogether in 1969. This Mark VI has a bright, wirey tone that you can't resist calling "Fendery," given its narrow single-coil pickups and bolt-on maple neck. Korg launched a reissue of the Mark guitars in the late '90s, but the brief production period of the originals means that vintage examples are thin on the ground. If you can track one down, though, it might be just the thing for that shagadelic British beat-revival combo you've been planning on getting together.

Courtesy Retrofret Vintage Guitars/
www.retrofret.com/photo by George Aslaender

1966 Vox Mark XII

The fledgling success of Vox's 6-string Phantom and Mark VI models helped establish a presence in the guitar market for this company, already a major player in amplification by the mid-1960s. But Vox was arguably slow off the line getting a 12-string into the field. When it arrived in 1965, the Mark XII, for a time, proved one of the cooler electric-12 alternatives and remains a hip choice today. You've got to figure that someone at Vox was kicking themselves, though, over the fact that their most powerful star amp endorsees, the Beatles, were already getting their 12-string jangle from Rickenbacker guitars. Would George Harrison have gone for the Vox Mark XII if he hadn't already had a Rick 360/12 in his hands? Hard to say. This is a good-sounding and easy-playing electric 12, with plenty of ring and chime and good bite for rock 'n' roll riffing, too. It is also rather "Euro-styled," something the Beatles seemed to be moving away from. That said, the guitar's neck, made by Eko in Italy, was one of its strong points, both figuratively and literally. Adapted from the Mark VI neck, it already contained the rigidity necessary to combat added string tension thanks to its double-T reinforcement bar plus an adjustable truss-rod, which Vox boasted of in catalogs and advertisements of the era. If they'd only introduced it two years earlier and gotten it into George's hands.

Courtesy Retrofret Vintage Guitars/ www.retrofret.com/photo by George Aslaender

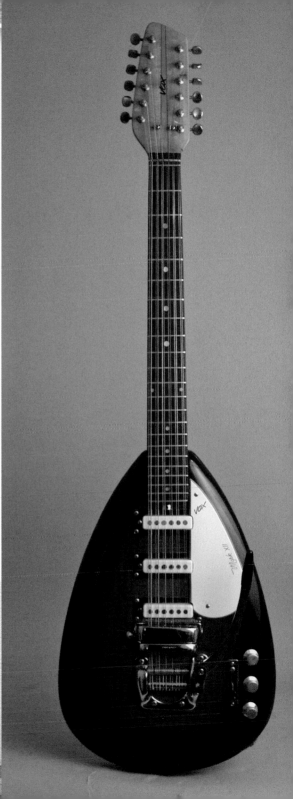

1965 Vox AC50

Virtually sprinting to keep up with the accelerating pace of the Beatles' popularity, Vox developed the first AC50 late in 1963 when designer Dick Denney produced a basic but effective 50-watt tube circuit and paired it with a modified AC30 cabinet with two 12-inch speakers and an added horn. The first AC50s ever produced by Vox were delivered to George Harrison and John Lennon as custom-made, single-channel heads and modified cabs ready just in time for the band's Christmas '63 concerts in Finsbury Park, London (at the same time, Denney concocted the prototype of the AC100, given to Paul McCartney to replace a solid-state Vox T-60 bass amp that wasn't cutting it volume-wise). By 1965, the more common AC50s like this one now had two channels and solid state in place of the early tube rectifier, but they still achieved the bold, punchy, chiming high-headroom tone that the Beatles sought to cut through hordes of screaming girls that were virtually obliterating their live performances. Plugging into this one provides a powerful experience very different from the early breakup that many players today seek from smaller amps, now that a band's stage volume doesn't rely on amp power alone. For all the valiant effort, and although it sounds superb, we might consider Vox's efforts a "failure" of sorts, given that the Beatles abandoned live performance in frustration after 1966—although after a few minutes with this great AC50 you'll declare it a glorious failure indeed.

1965 Vox Pacemaker V-3

The tale of the demise of Vox's original manufacturer, JMI, from the mid- to late 1960s plays like a Greek tragedy, and the "Vox" Pacemaker V-3 of 1965 might be the scene just prior to the denouement. Why the quotation marks? Because this amp wasn't made by the *real* Vox, but by Thomas Organ of California. When JMI proved unable to fill orders for the U.S. market, Thomas Organ was allowed to manufacture its own amps with the Vox logo, and this Pacemaker was one of them. With two Mullard EL84s for around 17 watts, and a Mullard EZ81 rectifier tube, in addition to three Mullard ECC83s in the preamp, it might look outwardly like a JMI-Vox AC15, though there's no fat, juicy EF86 here, and the amp carries only a 10-inch speaker. In and of itself, it's not a bad-sounding little amp, taken as the C-list combo it really is, but it ain't no AC15 either. Still, a fun ride, and a worthy adventure from the "Vox" on the left side of the pond.

1968 Fender Coronado II

Not a "bad" guitar by any means, and a funky alternative by most standards, the thinline Coronado just didn't read much like a Fender at all, other than in its bolt-on neck, 25.5-inch scale length, and six-a-side headstock. If anything, the Coronado perhaps had more in common with many Harmony designs of the '60s than with its Fender brethren, which makes it all the more interesting. Although Fender was one of the guitar world's foremost pickup developers, the company turned to DeArmond, which had supplied countless rival makers' hollowbody electrics, for the single-coil pickups used on the Coronado. Given this construction, this Coronado II also sounds quite a bit more like a Harmony Rocket, for example, than any previous Fender guitar. It has a bright, edgy bite to the tone, but a round, archetypal, hollowbody depth, too. Sustain isn't great, as it rarely is on such guitars, but a certain harmonic girth helps make up for that. The Coronados never quite caught on in their day, and collectability is nowhere on a par with Stratocasters and Telecasters of the same era, but they are fun Fender alternatives nonetheless.

1968 Fender Telecaster

Telecasters from several pre-CBS eras are highly revered by fans of the model: many consider the early "blackguard" examples to be seminal, while the "white-guard" Teles from 1955 to 1957 with lighter blonde finishes and slightly V'd neck profiles certainly have their fans, as do early-'60s rosewood-board Teles. More and more often, however, you seem to stumble upon an opinionated player who will insist that "maple-cap" Telecasters of the early CBS era, from around 1966 to 1968, are among the best Teles Fender ever made. And when one of those players is Brad Paisley, you tend to pay attention. When Fender brought the maple fingerboard option back to the Telecaster in the mid-'60s (first by request only, then as a catalog option), it did so by gluing a separate fillet of maple onto the neck back rather than by carving the one-piece neck used in the '50s. These necks tend to have a profile that feels great in the hand, and as any experienced luthier will tell you, two glued-together pieces of timber tend to be stronger than a single slab, so they are also extremely stable. The rest of these Teles tended to be pretty classy, too, never suffering from the enlarged headstock syndrome that struck the post-CBS Stratocaster. All in all, a classy route to the twang.

Late-1960s Guild F-212

BOOKENDS/SIMON & GARFUNKEL

Guild landed its first 12-string flat-tops, the smaller F-212 and F-312, in 1963 right at the zenith of the folk boom, then blasted forward with the larger, more deluxe maple-bodied F-412 and rosewood-bodied F-512 some five years later. Still, for many performers, the F-212 makes a more comfortable performer, and still puts out an impressively full-voiced sound. With their 17-inch-wide bodies and $1\frac{13}{16}$-inch width at the nut, the "jumbo" versions—while they sounded great, and certainly pounded out the volume—required some effort to play. Nifty F-212s like this little beauty, though, offer plenty of 12-string jangle and chime, and the great value of a vintage Guild acoustic. Paul Simon, Tim Buckley, Howlin' Wolf, and even John Denver became closely associated with great Guild 12-strings, and guitars like this one helped carry the folk movement boldly into another decade, creating one niche in which Guild, for a change, presented a worthy rival to bigger acoustic names like Gibson and Martin.

Gordon Lightfoot
The Way I Feel

HOWLIN' WOLF
THE REAL FOLK BLUES

goodbye and

TIM BUCKLEY

1967 Framus 5/115 Fret Jet

Founded in Bavaria by Fred Wilfer just after the end of World War II, German maker Framus (a contraction of *Frankische Musikindustrie*) rose rather quickly to prominence in Europe and was making inroads into the United States by the mid-1960s. The funky Strato solidbody models, many of which seek to outdo Fender's Jaguar in the switching department, make fun finds today, as does this groovy, gizmo-encrusted 5/115 Fret Jet thinline model. Loaded with three of Framus' characteristically narrow single-coil pickups and a basic vibrato tailpiece that works surprisingly well, the Fret Jet has an upper-horn pickup-selector and tone switches to tap more sonic variety than you're ever likely to need from a single guitar—but hey, it was the '60s, and more was almost universally seen as better . . . by the marketing men, at least. The neck has Framus' notoriously thin profile and a "zero fret" with steel holes-through nut and string retainer. Despite the significant quirk quotient, both electronically and constructionally, the Fret Jet is a pretty easy player and sounds damn nifty pumped through a good amp.

1966 Supro S6651 Big Star

This Supro S6651 Big Star combo from around 1966 is hard to beat for shiny, bright retro-kitchen styling, and being a Valco product, it has its own meaty, gritty, and extremely individual tone, too. Even with a pair of 6L6GCs and two 12-inch Jensen C12N ceramic-magnet speakers, this Supro isn't all that loud, probably putting out 30 watts at most riding downhill on a freshly waxed board. What matters, though, are the way those 30 watts are achieved and the fact that Valco's twist on tube-amp circuitry never sounds quite like anything else. The output tubes are cathode-biased with no negative feedback, a configuration that Fender hadn't used, for example, for more than ten years, and the low-ish plate voltages of around 370VDC keep things juicy and round, with a plummy midrange. Though atmospheric, the reverb isn't the lushest you'll find, but the tremolo is choppy and bold, and the two together make for real retro rock 'n' roll heaven. Hell, when an amp looks this cool you almost don't even need to plug it in—but you will want to, make no mistake.

Amp and photos courtesy Brad Klukow

Vox Tone Bender

Every self-respecting music-electronics manufacturer had to offer a fuzz box in the 1960s, and the Tone Bender was Vox's esteemed unit. The British fuzz-box scene of the '60s was an incestuous one, and accurately tracing the roots of any particular rendition of the near-ubiquitous Tone Bender is a tricky venture. Some early Tone Benders were made for Vox in the U.K. by the Sola Sound company, whose own rendition of the pedal actually predates Vox's. But the best-known Vox Tone Bender is the version manufactured by Jen Electronica in Italy—right alongside the Vox V846 Wah—from around 1966 until the mid-'70s. The Vox Tone Bender was beloved for its razory treble, a factor that aided the cutting power much in demand in British rock in the late '60s, and was generally a less dense and muddy fuzz than the Dallas-Arbiter Fuzz Face. Jeff Beck, Jimmy Page, and Mick Ronson, as well as many others, used various renditions of Tone Bender pedals at times, although the circuits tended to evolve sporadically and any single variation tended to sound somewhat different from another. Still, it's classic fuzz whatever breed you encounter.

1967 Vox Guitar Organ

Drop in on the instrument most loudly declared to be "the next big thing" from decade to decade, and you're likely to conclude that many guitar makers' greatest efforts went into converting guitarists into keyboard players. The Vox Guitar Organ of the mid-'60s was one such notable endeavor. Shaped like a Vox Phantom and playable as a standard guitar, the Guitar Organ was equipped with electronics to produce the sound of Vox's then-popular Continental Organ, all at the hands of a single guitarist. Each fret contained six individual resistors, one for each string, which sensed string pressure and triggered an organ tone, governable from the instrument's extensive onboard control section. Even this simple description hints that there might be a slight chasm between theory and practice, and indeed there was: Vox Guitar Organs were highly prone to fault and failure and, in the end, didn't prove worth the hassle to become a viable product. Still, it's kinda freaky to be able to produce that cheesy, grating '60s organ tone while appearing to play the guitar, and this thing remains an impressively misfired effort at whiz-bang gadgetry.

Courtesy Dean Ellis Kohler/www.deanelliskohler.com

1967 Vox V1141 Super Beatle

After signing an oddly unfavorable contract in 1965 that would ultimately contribute to its downfall, Vox's British parent company, JMI, allowed Thomas Organ of California to "manufacture Vox amps for the USA if JMI couldn't fulfill the demand." This self-fulfilling prophesy saw Organ soon flooding the States with largely solid-state Vox models that generally confused Beatle-crazed players by sounding little like their British tube counterparts, but which did actually sound rather nifty in their own regard. The flagship of these was the V1141 Super Beatle, a transistorized 120-watt monster that the Beatles' themselves used for much of their final U.S. tour of 1966. Although the line would outwardly appear to have been purely the result of a cynical market grab, Organ actually put a lot of thought into the development of the Super Beatle and the rest of the solid-state line, commissioning a gifted engineer named Sava Jacobsen to clone the AC30 tone in a solid-state circuit. In addition to its reverb and tremolo effects, the V1141 Super Beatle had a built-in fuzz circuit that sounded pretty nasty but extremely groovy in the right circumstances and blasted it all through a matching upright cab with a pair of alnico Celestion 12-inch speakers and a Goodmans Midax horn.

1967 Mosrite Joe Maphis Double-Neck

We might think of the double-neck guitar as the domain of stadium rockers of the 1970s: Jimmy Page astraddle the stage in front of a pair of raging full stacks or Alex Lifeson cranking out the prog with Rush. Plenty of multi-neck guitars were made for country artists, though (the 6-string guitar and electric mando combination in particular often proved popular in that neck of the woods), including this Mosrite artist model, a 6/12 made for country showman Joe Maphis (who, yes, also had a Mosrite six/mando). Rather than the fat humbucker rock of the more familiar Gibson double-neck, the Mosrite's P-90-like single coils give a gritty snarl to the 6-string neck, and some slightly raspy, raw, Rickenbacker-styled jangle to the 12-string. Sonically, sure, it could do country, or a slightly more garage-leaning rock 'n' roll, or even soulful funk in the hands of an artist like Sugar Bonner, who frequently used a Joe Maphis Double-Neck with the Ohio Players in the 1970s. In the end, although it is originally a child of the '60s—again, like Gibson's rendition—it is very much a product of '70s bluster and show and looked great on a stage where that counted for something, even if the extra neck wasn't always a necessity.

Fender Vibratone Cabinet

The Leslie rotating speaker cabinet became a popular psychedelic guitar coloration in the mid-'60s, though having been made for use with Hammond organ rather than guitar and configured as such regarding its amplification and connections, it could be a prized bugger to optimize for the old 6-string. Enter Fender's Vibratone, a rotating speaker cabinet designed specifically for use with guitar. The Vibratone, built under license from Leslie and essentially identical to the Leslie 16, eliminated the upper rotary horn that was rather superfluous to the guitar's frequency range and connected between guitar amp and speaker, so no separate amplification was required. A crossover within the unit let a portion of the signal pass through to the amplifier's own speaker or a standard extension speaker cab, while the Vibratone particularly transmitted the midrange from its own internal 10-inch speaker, which was modulated by a rotating drum. The unit's footswitch offered Fast/Slow and On/Off. However cumbersome a cabinet of this size might be to carry and use, the sound really can't be replaced by a solid-state simulation. Fired up and whirling, the Vibratone fills a room with lush, Doppler-effect-modulated, multidimensional sound and can become extremely addictive once it gets its hooks into you.

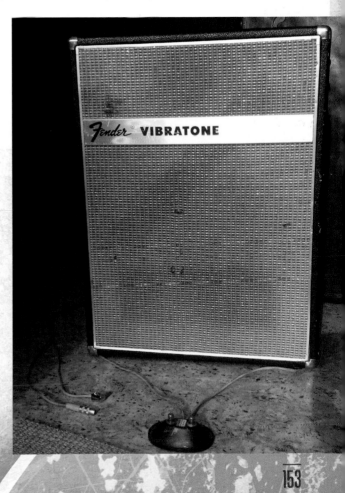

Fender B-Bender Telecaster

While working together on studio sessions around Los Angeles in the mid-1960s, guitarists Clarence White and drummer Gene Parsons, both future members of the Byrds, collaborated on a complex yet ingenious device designed to make White's Fender Telecaster sound like a pedal-steel guitar, and a legendary aftermarket modification was born. Parsons, who had worked in his father's machine shop as a young man, translated White's desires into a spring-loaded, gear-and-pulley type of mechanism that fit into an extensive route in the back of the guitar's body, and was activated by downward pressure on the guitar neck, which pulled the neck-end strap button and relayed the action to a pin that bent the B string up a tone or semi-tone, as desired. This might seem like a lot of work just to bend one string—and it can take some work to accustom yourself to the technique—but the result, when blended seamlessly with a fluid playing style that now requires no pause for traditional finger bending, can really be quite sensational. Clarence White was, unsurprisingly, the master of this technique, but others have applied it with great results, including Marty Stuart, who purchased White's original B-Bender Tele several years after his 1973 death. According to the folks at Fretted Americana, all evidence indicates that the example seen here is a unique one-off built in the 1960s by Chuck Morgan, a friend of Parsons and White.

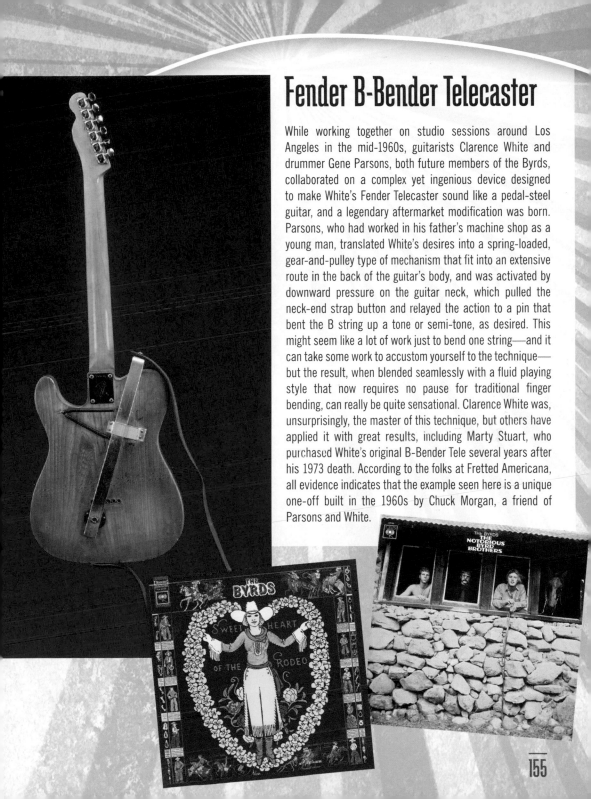

Courtesy Outline Press Limited

Zemaitis Electric

Although his guitars made music in the hands of more major artists of the classic-rock era than those of any other European maker, Tony Zemaitis never became a household name like Leo Fender. The stars who lined up on the waiting list for his creations certainly knew who he was, though, and valued what he could do for both their stage presence and their tone. Tony was born Antanus Casimere Zemaitis in London in 1935 and showed an interest in building and playing guitars early in his lifetime. He played on the London blues scene of the early '60s before achieving his success as a maker and actually first made a name for himself with his 12-string acoustics rather than the intricately adorned metal- and pearl-faced electrics for which he became famous. We know the look of the Zemaitis electric from its use by Ronnie Wood, Keith Richards, Marc Bolan, James Honeyman-Scott, and several others, but anyone who has laid hands on one will tell you that they are also great-playing, superb-sounding instruments into which a lot of thought and craftsmanship has gone, despite the obvious decorative excesses of many of them. Zemaitis retired from guitar making in 2000 and passed away in 2002. His instruments have become increasingly collectible since that time.

1967–1968 Dallas-Arbiter Fuzz Face

The Fuzz Face might not have been the first fuzz pedal on the block, but it was certainly early enough to be regarded as seminal by any standards. Regardless, its use by everyone from Jimi Hendrix to Eric Johnson has helped make it a classic. Arbiter introduced the pedal in 1966. The company, Dallas-Arbiter by 1967, manufactured the pedal until the mid-1970s, first using germanium transistors then silicon. For most, the former are the ones to drool over. Plug into this example, and that soft, chewy, slightly spitty fuzz with a fat bottom and sweet, smooth highs tells you exactly why. Like most early fuzzes, these are relatively simple circuits: a mere handful of components populates the innards, but it's the type, and of course the configuration, of these bits and pieces that makes all the difference. Fuzz Face fanatics tend to rave about the early NKT275 transistors, although the AC128s can sound sublime, too. Since germanium transistors were highly inconsistent, though, and weren't always adequately tested in production, individual Fuzz Faces from any one batch can still sound extremely different. Ah, the fun of the vintage stompbox hunt!

Roger Mayer Octavia

Roger Mayer built his first few Octavia pedals as custom units for several major guitarists on the London scene of the late '60s, most famously Jimi Hendrix, but never put the pedal into commercial production, or even protected his intellectual rights to the name. While other companies later produced their rendition of the effect, Mayer didn't bring his own to market until the early 1980s. With the scarcity of original late-'60s Roger Mayer Octavias in mind, this beast remains one of the most basic—yet dramatic, and potentially nasty—stompboxes known to guitardom. By creating a simulated octave-doubling tone, with some hairy fuzz behind it, the Octavia adds what can range from a vocal and flutey to a demonic and menacing effect. Monophonic, single-note runs are its forte (and it often seems to track neck pickups best), and chords, even of just two notes, can send it into utter freakout. Which means you will give it a try, just to hear what happens.

1967 Guild Starfire V

Clearly developed as a rival to Gibson's popular ES-335, Guild's Starfire V (and similar IV and VI models) presents a few crucial differences from the Kalamazoo semi-hollow and has won some fans as a result. Outwardly, this Starfire does look extremely similar to an ES-335: the double-cutaway, thinline-archtop body clearly follows Gibson's lead but is different enough to avoid being an outright copy. Note that the neck attachment is made a few frets shorter than on the Gibson. And less easily discerned than that, a poke around inside the Starfire V reveals a differently configured laminated center block for feedback reduction rather than the solid center block found on the ES-335. All of these ingredients, combined with Guild's slightly narrower, weaker, and brighter humbucking pickups, result in quite a different voice. The Starfire V has some hollowbody depth to it, certainly, but plenty of bite and jangle, too, making it great at gnarly blues or grinding rock 'n' roll, but also some snappy country twang through a clean amp. A Starfire was purportedly Robben Ford's first good electric guitar, Lightning Hopkins preferred this semi, and Buddy Guy frequently did his thing on one before becoming virtually exclusive to his Fender Stratocaster. Cool guitars, and a great alternative on the vintage market.

1970 Micro-Frets Stage II

Although the Micro-Frets name is not widely known, the company, based in Fredrick, Maryland, built some of the more interesting and original electric guitars of the late 1960s and early 1970s. A semi-hollow maple body and bolt-on maple neck with rosewood fingerboard offer a fairly basic foundation, but the company really shot for the moon in the hardware department. The in-house vibrato system was known as a Calibrato unit and was a floating construction with an easy, smooth action that offered individual adjustment of string tension in an effort to balance the down-bend of pitch when the bar was depressed. At the other end, the company's patented Micro-Nut prefigured the Buzz Feiten system, but in a more complex way, providing six independently adjustable segments for fine-tuning intonation at the headstock end. Furthermore, controls on the archetypal models such as this Stage II were mostly recessed within the two-tiered pickguard. But how did it all sound? Well, pretty good, with a clear, crisp tone from two wide single-coil pickups that earned it endorsements from Carl Perkins, among others.

Counterfeit Fender "GI Amp"

It's hard to imagine in an age when you can look at anything instantly on the Internet that anyone would set out to make what is really a rather high-tech copy of a major product and let it come out looking so incredibly *unlike* the original item. Yet so many of the details of this Korean Fender copy from around 1967—the shape of the chassis, the tube layout, the control features—are so Fender-like you have to assume the builder got a good look at a black-face combo at one time or another. They even went to the trouble of printing Fender labels to stick on the power transformer core for anyone who looked inside. This is one of a breed of amplifiers often referred to as "GI amps" (similarly, there were also "GI guitars"), knockoffs made in Asia and sold to unsuspecting U.S. soldiers stationed in Vietnam, presumably with a little pay to burn and a hankering for some good old American rock 'n' roll tone. For all that, plug in, fire it up, and it actually sounds . . . well, rather *bad*—harsh, lifeless, and anemic. But a good try, eh? Pity the poor GI who dragged it home.

1967–1969 Vox V846 Wah

The first wah-wah pedal was invented by Thomas Organ engineer Brad Plunkett in 1965 to imitate the muted trumpet wah-wah technique of Clyde McCoy and was named after that horn player as a result. Since Vox parent company JMI was in partnership with Thomas Organ for amp distribution (and later, manufacture) in North America at the time, the Californians shared the circuit with the British—resulting in a fork in the road that would eventually bring the world two wah-wahs roughly based on the same circuit: the Vox Wah and the Thomas Organ Cry Baby. After a brief production run in JMI's facility in Dartford, Kent, the manufacture of the Vox V846 Wah was moved to the famous Jen Electronica in Italy, and it was here that the hip chrome-treadle wahs favored by the likes of Jimi Hendrix and Eric Clapton were produced. Many wah fans will tell you it all comes down to that fabled Fasel inductor in the circuit, the component most responsible for a wah-wah pedal's voice. Either way, the plaintive, singing tone of this pedal is truly legendary.

1968 Hiwatt Custom 50 DR504

The Custom 100 DR103 was the big boy of the range, but let's warm up to the mighty power of Hiwatt by plugging into the 50-watt Custom 50 DR504 first, which uses the same circuit and is even built onto the same chassis, minus two of the EL34s from the 100-watter's full quad. Even so, in good condition with a freshly biased pair of NOS Mullard EL34s, the DR504 will

Amp and photos courtesy Victor Mason/Mojave Ampworks

easily blast past 60 watts. Whatever the rating, though, these vintage Hiwatts just feel huge sonically, and despite a control panel and general overall look that might make them appear to have been Marshall wannabes, they are very much an original design. Hiwatt founder Dave Reeves was working at Arbiter's Sound City ampworks in the mid-

1960s when he developed the notion to build a better amp. Applying meticulous workmanship, top-grade components, and original circuits designed for maximum punch and dynamics, he gave birth to the Hiwatt range shortly before this amp was made—and arena-rock was never the same again. Pete Townshend's earth-shaking sound with The Who in the late '60s and early '70s is the best example of what Hiwatt can do, but several other stars made it their amp of choice, too. Could it be yours?

1968 Marshall JMP50

Now this is what we think of when someone mentions "that Marshall sound." In the grand scheme of things, the "Plexi" amps—so named for their gold-backed Plexiglas control panels—of 1966 to 1969 were not all that much different from the earlier JTM amps of 1962–1966, or at least less different than, say, a tweed Fender Bassman of the late '50s or a blonde Bassman of the early '60s. Nevertheless, a few significant tweaks accounted for a tectonic shift in tonal signature. Add 'em up, and the move to EL34 tubes from 5881s and KT66s, hotter B+ voltages applied to those tubes, brighter voicing of the second channel, firmer filtering in the power supply, and a few other component and application changes signaled what was essentially an entirely new sound in rock amplification. When rammed through a closed-back cab with four warm, cracklin' Celestion G12M "greenback" speakers, this amp virtually defines the sound of classic rock and has provided lead tones for several of the most influential players in the history of the music (either in its 50-watt form, as here, or with two more EL34s as the 100-watt Super Lead). Plexi, when nothing but a Marshall will do.

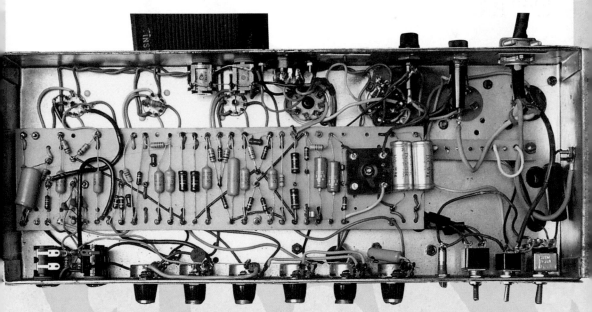

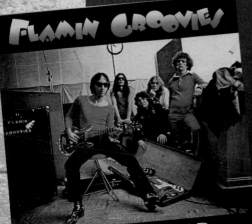

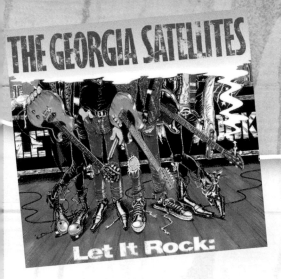

Ampeg Dan Armstrong

Ampeg's see-through Dan Armstrong model was produced for just a little over a year in 1968 and 1969, suffering poor sales figures from its status as more of a show guitar than one to embrace and play regularly. Keith Richards was one notable exception, of course, and the Rolling Stones were already major Ampeg amplifier endorsees when he grabbed an early model and rocked it live in the late '60s and early '70s, but other than this vote of confidence, the Dan Armstrong model has attained far more acclaim as a vintage instrument than it did at its original release. Designed for Ampeg by New York–based guitar tech Dan Armstrong, perhaps best known as the inventor of a line of small effects boxes, the guitar's body was carved from solid Lucite and housed a pickup made by Bill Lawrence. Six available pickup types easily slid in and out of position for swapping. Solid of tone *and* build, these guitars are also heavy on the strap, another factor that likely inhibited sales— but what price that *wow* factor, eh?

Greg Ginn of Black Flag. Frank Mullen/WireImage/Getty Images

1968 Kustom K-200

From the producers of the beloved solid-state tuck 'n' roll amps of the late '60s, the K-200 electric guitar was arguably a more virtuous product from Kustom. Still, it never quite caught on. Maybe a few odd little touches like the unreasonably thin neck or the zero-fret with cumbersome slotted metal string guide squelched its appeal somewhat. Otherwise, these are solid, stylish, hip-sounding, and overall groovy concoctions that deserve their day in the spotlight. There is clearly some Rickenbacker inspiration going on here, as well as a pair of those great DeArmond Model 200 pickups, in use at Kustom a full decade after Gretsch dropped them from the Duo Jet and 6120! Other high-end hardware, such as a Bigsby vibrato and Kluson tuners, as well as generally good build quality, show us that Kustom head honcho Bud Ross was aiming to compete with the big boys. Sure, he lost, but the K-200 remains a fun find today and is a surprisingly able performer, too, with a sturdy, meaty twang that could stand in for other, more expensive vintage models.

The Solid-State Sound
Kustom
(((100)))
New Solid-State Energizer

The Mellow Sound
ROSS INC.
CHANUTE, KANSAS
of Space Age Design

1968 Kustom 100 1-15L-2

Solid-state technology garners little love when found in a vintage guitar amplifier, but Kustom's tuck 'n' roll creations of the late 1960s and early '70s are among the few that just about any guitarist will drool over now and then. The lack of tube circuitry didn't stop many a great artist from endorsing these groovy amps; they were a big part of John Fogerty's sound with Credence Clearwater Revival, and more recently, Tom Petty's guitarist Mike Campbell, usually a Vox addict, turned to a vintage Kustom for much of his recording needs on the Heartbreakers' *Echo* album. Back in the day, funk, soul, and R&B artists were using them all over the shop, and barely would an episode of *Soul Train* or *Don Kirshner's Rock Concert* pass without a backline of Kustom amps in evidence. This groovily dated stack bops out a bold, punchy tone that remains sweet and clear while clean, if a little fizzy and nasty when overdriven hard, and dishes up one of the most ominous tremolo effects of its era. You just know there's a corner of your music room dying to sport a metalflake style monster like this one!

1969 Fender Stratocaster

For all the fuss that's made of pre-CBS Stratocasters, it's worth remembering that one of the greatest Stratsmiths of all time, Jimi Hendrix, played post-CBS Strats through much of his career. Reverse snobs will try to tell you that Hendrix discerned some magic in the large-headstock, late-'60s Strat, but he also played small-headstock pre-CBS Stratocasters early on. In truth, not a lot of fuss was being made of the pre- or post-CBS issue at that time, and the most viable accounts confirm that for Hendrix, a Strat was a Strat. That said, a good 1969 Stratocaster captures the Hendrix aura beautifully while still offering many specs that link it to preferable details of the pre-CBS era. These guitars had the enlarged headstocks but had yet to take on the three-bolt "tilt-neck" attachment and bullet-head truss-rod adjustment nut that are seen by many as demarcations of Fender's downward slide in the '70s. Also, until late 1971 the Stratocaster retained the original vintage-style vibrato bridge, which was tonally superior in several ways to what followed. So, still a great Strat by any reckoning, and you can just listen to Jimi if you have any doubts.

1969 Marshall Major

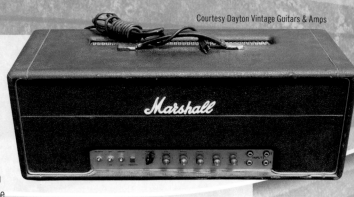

You want big vintage tone? I mean *really* big vintage tone? The Marshall Major gets you there in a way that few players (or sound men) are likely to ever have experienced in this day and age. Produced by Marshall from 1967 to around 1975 in a kind of "Well, take *that* then!" fashion, the Major ripped 200 watts from a quad of stonking KT88 output tubes to produce the massive volumes that a handful of top touring acts demanded in the day. Plug in, crank up, and it's definitely still Marshall, but Marshall with even more gut-thump than usual, the added low-end girth and high-end glimmer of the powerful KT88, and the kind of SPLs that few live scenarios can, or want to, handle in this day and age. For a leading example of the tone, look to Mick Ronson's Bowie-era work, when he coupled his Les Paul Custom with a big Major stack dubbed "the Pig" to squeeze out the heady signature licks for Ziggy Stardust's glam-rock extravaganzas. If you ever get the chance, bring your earplugs—or stand far, far away.

Late-1960s Thomas Organ Cry Baby Wah Wah

The original Cry Baby was essentially the American-market rendition of the Vox Wah, using an evolution of Thomas Organ's original Clyde McCoy circuit and housed in a different enclosure. Early examples employed the same red Fasel inductor found in the most prized Vox Wahs; later units carried TDK inductors and can still sound great, though they are somewhat less desirable. Its origins indicate that the Cry Baby should sound rather similar to the Vox, although the pedal's design gives it a slightly shorter travel and minor circuit variations give it a sweeter, more fluid sound compared to the Vox's vowelly, singing wail. Since they were plentiful—and never top of the vintage desirability list—vintage Cry Baby Wahs can still be had for fairly reasonable money and usually put back into good working order for relatively little outlay, thanks to the availability of good replacement parts. If you prefer to go vintage rather than reissue for your effects needs, the original pre-Dunlop Cry Baby might be a unit worth tracking down.

cry baby

1968 Rickenbacker Transonic TS100

Speaking of the few solid-state guitar amps that any self-respecting guitarist would consider plugging into—mammoth transistorized Ricky monolith, anyone? Having graced the U.S. tours of Led Zeppelin, the Jeff Beck Group, and Steppenwolf in the late 1960s, the Rickenbacker Transonic should have been enshrined in an athenaeum of rock, yet this wild line of hulking solid-state amplifiers has all but vanished from memory, other than in the collections of a few more esoteric amp-o-philes. The fact that Jimmy Page and John Paul Jones left most of their Transonics in the United States upon returning to England at tour's end in 1969 might imply something, yet most players who have had the chance to jack into a Transonic will tell you that they can sound strikingly good, though often with the caveat of "for a transistor amp." One hundred watts of potentially hard-clipping power gives these giants plenty of oomph, and onboard Tremolo, Reverb, and Fuzz-Tortion—along with tone switches for settings named Hollow, Mellow, and Pierce—make the Transonic a one-stop psychedelic sonic freak show.

Late-1960s Melobar

So popular was the lap-steel guitar during the Hawaiian music craze of the early twentieth century that you could dedicate an entire book to those instruments. Designed to be worn as a standard electric guitar—"disguised" as one, you might even say—the Melobar was created in the early '60s by Walter Smith of Sweet, Idaho, to put the slide player back into the action on stage. The most common models were wooden instruments with an angled "block" body core and neck that put the fretboard in vertical playing position, all mounted on a guitar-shaped blank that was worn on a strap, like a traditional electric guitar. While the instrument never replaced the lap steel entirely (maybe a lot of steel players didn't *want* to stand up), it did find its way into the hands of some major slide aficionados, including Bonnie Raitt, Ry Cooder, and David Lindley. Playing this fine example is no easier for the standard guitarist than playing a lap steel, unless you're already familiar with slide technique and open tunings, but at least you've got a lot better chance of duck walking with the Melobar strapped on than when seated at an old Fender Stringmaster.

Courtesy Outline Press Limited

Univox Uni-Vibe

The Uni-Vibe was a four-stage analog phaser designed by Fumio Mieda and manufactured by Shin-Ei of Japan for just a few years in the late '60s and early '70s—and, although it sounded pretty darn cool at the foot of any competent guitarist, the fact that it was another of a small number of notable "Hendrix-approved" pedals forever sealed its place in guitar Valhalla. This slightly cumbersome unit

was actually not first intended as a guitar effect but as a compact transistorized simulation of a Leslie rotating speaker cabinet for organ players. Its warm, swirling sound is positively delightful when applied to guitar, though—preferably with a little overdrive thrown in for good measure—and it's hard to imagine it used in any other way. The heart of the Uni-Vibe is found in the four lamp/photoresistor units that make up the phasing stages of the device. The sound can't easily be replicated by chip-based effects circuits. Fortunately, several contemporary makers have taken their best shot at approximating the real deal, with impressive results. Plug in, and get your swirl on.

Travis Bean TB1000

The eponymous guitars made by Travis Bean in Sun Valley, California, between 1974 and 1979 were—though short-lived—among the most successful aluminum-necked constructions, if not the very first to try to pierce the market. As others who had experimented with metal construction before him, Bean reasoned that an aluminum neck and central body block would remain more stable than one made of wood and therefore form a core that was more resistant to the detrimental forces of string tension. Behind a solid, robust-feeling instrument with a likeable simplicity in its rounded slab body and basic appointments, the TB1000 certainly lives up to that hope. With the strings anchored at the back of the neck block's aluminum core before passing over the bridge, this guitar has rather different resonant characteristics of its own, too, exhibiting a smoothly edgy zing and outstanding sustain. The cold feel of the aluminum neck's back was among the chief criticisms of the design, and Travis Bean ultimately found it difficult to gain a lasting foothold in the traditional market, but his efforts remain a hip and adventurous detour on the electric guitar's journey.

1969 Gibson Les Paul Personal

The Les Paul Custom and Les Paul Model (but, rather puzzlingly, no humbucker-loaded Standard) finally returned to the Gibson catalog in 1968 in their pseudo '56 and '57 guises, respectively, but *this* one truly gets personal. It seems that in luring Les Paul back to the fold, Gibson agreed to bring out a rendition of the guitar that the artist himself was playing at the time. Les Paul being ever the tinkerer, this model turned out to be, well, rather eccentric. Mounted on the three-piece mahogany/maple/mahogany body is a pair of oblong low-impedance pickups, of which Les Paul (the man) was a very vocal fan, in addition to an XLR mic jack with associated Volume control on the top edge, where Les Paul (again, the man) liked to mount his vocal mic for mobility. The neck carried the low frets known from the "fretless wonder" Customs of the '50s, and the entire concoction tended to weigh a veritable ton. Despite (or perhaps because of) all this, the Les Paul Personal actual sounds . . . well, rather odd. Not bad by any means, but also nothing like the Les Paul of legend. Still, a slice of Gibson history.

Late-1960s Jordan Boss Tone

From the hallowed annals of "cheap-ass gear that sounds mystifyingly magical" comes the Jordan Boss Tone, possibly one of the most poorly made pieces of musical electronics to ever achieve such iconic status. The fuzz circuit within the Boss Tone's plastic casing was a clever little creation, with an unusually biting, nasal sound that was entirely unforgettable, but there's no way you could expect that textured box to survive any serious tour—or more than the mildest stage antics, really—and the board within often suffered an early demise as a result. Developed in 1966 and properly released in 1967, the square-ish unit had a plug on the back to ram it straight into your guitar (good luck with your Strat's recessed jack) and a jack on the bottom for your guitar cord, with two trim pots on top for Volume and Attack (a.k.a. fuzz). It was part of a wave that saw every electronics manufacturer producing a fuzz box of its own, although Jordan's had more veracity than most, and remains a favorite of many players to this day. The Boss Tone's legacy is arguably best honored in a number of surviving homages from contemporary effects makers, who almost invariably repackage the circuit in a sturdier floor unit and add some much-needed low-end oomph to the sound besides. Dan Auerbach of the Black Keys has been known to use a rehoused Jordan unit.

172

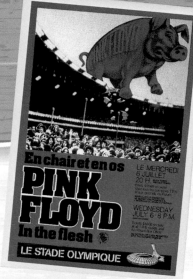

Early-1970s Maestro Rover RO-1

Truly an odd duck of rotating-speaker design, the Rover RO-1 is an extremely cool-sounding piece of gear regardless, and a rare and prized collectible in the effects world besides. Rather than follow the more traditional format of the rotating speaker (i.e., a square-ish cabinet with a rotor or drum mounted on the vertical plane), this wacky unit flipped it all on its ear, and conjured some hip psychedelic sounds as a result. The circular Rover measures 19 inches in diameter and 9 inches high (stand excluded), and produces its Doppler-inducing rotary-speaker effect by means of a 6-inch speaker inside a plastic enclosure that spins within the corrugated drum. While Roto-Vibes and their modern clones, and even many phaser and chorus pedals, seek to reproduce a sound that has its roots in this type of motion-induced warble, there's nothing like hearing the real thing and virtually feeling the three-dimensional sound as it bounces around you. The Rover was a particular favorite of Pink Floyd's David Gilmour, for one.

Ovation Adamas

The signature round, composite-fiberglass back of the Ovation guitar was the brainchild of the company's founder, Charles Kaman, an aeronautical engineer who was also an avid jazz guitarist. Using technology adapted from that employed in helicopter blades, Kaman developed a guitar body that would enhance volume and projection and resist wood's natural instabilities. While many Ovation guitars have carried more traditional wood soundboards, the top-of-the-line Adamas model has a thin carbon-graphite top with elaborately carved wood bridge and headstock, not to mention ornamental leaves around its twenty-two variously sized upper-bout sound holes. Its acoustic tone is bold, clear, and full, yet the plugged-in tone is part of what lured many major artists to the brand early on and helped Ovation virtually corner the electric-acoustic market in the 1970s when few major makers included pickups in their acoustic flat-tops. Glen Campbell, Larry Coryell, Paul McCartney, Adrian Legg, Charlie Byrd, and several others were drawn to Ovation's easy path to amplified acoustic tone and helped gain acceptance for the round-back in the surprisingly square world of the guitar.

Bernabé Classical

After bringing new heights of quality and efficiency to the renowned Ramírez workshop in Madrid, Spain, Paulino Bernabé set out on his own in 1969 to build hand-made classic guitars for the performing professional musician. Even if you have never dabbled in the true classical style, it's worth wrapping your hands around a top-notch instrument like this one if and when the opportunity arises. Rather than being merely "soft" or "mellow" like the nylon-string folk guitars on which many of us learned our first campfire chords, this Bernabé is lively, bold, and succulent with surprising body and projection, two of this skilled luthier's goals for creating guitars worthy of the concert hall. Refusing to settle on any fixed standards, Bernabé, later working alongside his son (another Paulino), has continually refined his technique, improved his bracing patterns for better resonance and volume, and brought a number of unusual and exotic tonewoods to his building palette. Far more than just a nylon-string guitar, this is truly a classical concert instrument with a voice as refined and individual as that of any prized cello or violin.

Early-1970s
Fender Thinline Telecaster

Seth Lover was one of the true geniuses of pickup development, and we tend to think of him as purely a Gibson designer. There, he helped to create both the single-coil Alnico V (a.k.a. "staple") pickup used on the 1954 Les Paul Custom and the famed PAF humbucker that followed. After leaving Gibson in 1967, Lover was hired by Fender and developed the first humbucking pickup used by the California guitar maker, previously so strongly associated with single-coil pickups. These new pickups, known as the Wide Range Humbuckers, first appeared on the revamped Telecaster Thinline of late 1971 and, soon after, on the Telecaster Custom and Deluxe models. Despite having the same inventor, the only real tie between the Fender humbucker and the Gibson is, well, the inventor. Despite its overwound coils, the Fender unit was made with unusual threaded cunife magnet pole pieces for a bright, clear sound, maintaining an air of Fender chime amid the bluster. As a result, this Telecaster Thinline can grind and wail through a cranked Marshall, yet still give some twang and jangle through a Twin Reverb. All that, and it's a window on a new generation of Fender guitars.

Fender TELECASTER® THINLINE
(P/N 12-3000)

Ref	Part Number	Description
1	010204 000	Neck, Maple, Tilt, w/hard
2	010179 000	Body, All Finishes
3	010187 000	Humbucking Pick-Up (pac
4	011243 000	Pickguard (Black)
4	015578 000	Screw, Pickguard
5	017053 000	3-Way Selector Switch
5	019448 000	Knob, 3-Way Switch
6	013366 000	Volume Knob
7	013364 000	Tone Knob
8	021956 000	Phone Jack
8	010355 060	Retainer Jack Assembly
8	010383 070	Jack Ferrule
8	016436 000	Washer, Control/Jack
8	016352 000	Nut, Control/Jack
9	010223 080	Bridge Cover (Chrome)
10	012344 000	Strap Button
10	016188 000	Screw, Bridge Plate/Strap Butto
11	083675 000	Bone Nut (Neck)
11	010286 000	Nut, Truss Rod (Bullet)
13	053694 000	Patent Head (Keys)
13	012229 000	Bushings, Patent Head
13	011357 000	Screw, Patent Head, String Guid
14	010389 000	String Guide (Neck)
14	011358 000	Screw, String Guide ¾"
14	016881 000	Spacer, String Guide

SHEET NO. 24-0142 (F/GF)

1970 Marshall Model 1959 Super Lead

Mention "Marshall full stack" and *this* is what most people are talking about. Back in the day, when PA systems proved too feeble to translate musicians' dreams to sonic reality and stage volumes tended to be louder than the apocalypse in a hurricane, anyone who was anyone really had to have a 100-watt full stack to be heard. Jimi Hendrix, Eric Clapton, Jimmy Page, Paul Kossoff . . . this is how they rolled. Just

Amp and photo courtesy Paul Moskwa/PM Blues

plug into this ominous affair and crank the knob north, and you too will begin to feel an inkling of the power and otherworldliness they must have felt when raging before the fury of more than 100 watts of tube power through eight pumping Celestion speakers. These "metal panel" Marshalls of the early '70s weren't much different from the Plexis of the late '60s, other than a few spec and component changes and, frequently, slightly hotter operating voltages. And while the Plexis are raved about, *these* are more often than not the amps that laid the foundations of that enduring Brit-rock tone. It's as if you can still hear them ringing in your ears . . . and if you ever owned one, chances are you can.

Early-1970s Fender Blender

The Fender brand isn't widely associated with fuzz—other than as the name on the headstock of the guitar that Jimi Hendrix most often plugged into his Fuzz Face—but this latecomer to the party did its best to make up for that. The Fender Blender is an extreme and powerful fuzz box with the addition of a tone boost and, in later units, an added octave effect to boot. Housed in a large, two-stomp-switch, four-knob box, this unit gives a thick, sick, and densely hairy fuzz with bucket loads of gain that is not the least bit transparent and not for the faint of heart. Bringing it in on anything other than the most basic power-chord rhythm work can wreak havoc on any tune, but give it

some driving single-note leads and it will soar. Recorded examples of the Fender Blender sound include Robin Trower's occasional use in the '70s and Billy Corgan's purported reliance on the pedal for some of the more extreme guitar tones on the Smashing Pumpkins' *Gish* album.

Electro-Harmonix Big Muff

Electro-Harmonix was launched in 1968 with the release of the LPB1 Power Booster, but the Big Muff Pi, unveiled two years later, is undoubtedly the company's best-known pedal. Without delving into the origins of the pedal's name (the π on the front is fooling no one), this thick, hairy, brick wall of a fuzz became a standard for American rockers of the '70s and helped establish the fortunes of a company that went on to become one of the effects world's most adventurous and, for a time, the United States' biggest. E-H founder Mike Matthews went to great lengths to keep the brand going in the mid-'80s after aggressive external efforts toward unionization drove his original New York City–based incarnation to bankruptcy in 1982. An army-green rendition of the Big Muff was produced in Russia in 1990, following Matthews' adventures founding the Sovtek tube brand in the late '80s, and the fuzz box returned in its most popular mid-'70s incarnation as one of the first reissues of the revitalized Electro-Harmonix when he brought the company back to New York City later in the '90s. If you don't already own a Big Muff, you owe it to yourself to try one.

Ibanez Model 2351

Plenty of Japanese copies of the 1970s are advertised as "lawsuit" guitars in an effort to emphasize their supposed high degree of likeness to the originals on which they were based, yet relatively few lawsuits have actually been filed against Asian copyists. One of the most successful of the '70s, however, was Ibanez, which cut its teeth by directly aping models made by Gibson and to some extent Fender. This Model 2351 from the mid-'70s, clearly a copy of Gibson's Les Paul, put the fright into plenty of U.S. makers, Gibson among them, by displaying how confident Japan's FujiGen Gakki factory was becoming at making serious contenders in the market. Pick this one up and plug it in, and perhaps it doesn't quite feel or sound like a good Gibson, but the U.S. company's quality was sliding steadily through the '70s anyway, and the fact that an Asian company could even come close was a scary thing. In the summer of 1977, Gibson owner Norlin filed a federal lawsuit to stop Ibanez owner Hoshino Gakki and its U.S. distributor, Elger, from using its trademarked headstock design and logo font. Soon after, Ibanez achieved even greater success with myriad original designs of its own.

1971 Orange Graphic Overdrive GRO100

The future was bright back in swinging London at the end of the 1960s, and for many a wide-flared rocker, the future looked Orange. After trying to establish the Orange brand as an all-in-one music publishing, recording, and agency presence in a London shop front in 1968, Cliff Cooper soon found he could make money more quickly by supplying the high-powered gear that guitarists were craving in the form of well-endowed tube amps wrapped in, what else, orange Tolex. The GRO100 generated more than 100 watts from a quartet of EL34s; the "Graphic" in its name denoted the fact that its controls were defined by small graphics rather than words, while the "Overdrive" told you that, yes, this amp was devoted to *overdrive*. Two stages of gain ramp up the simple preamp stage pretty quickly, and with just a Loudness control and no gain-plus-master pairing, this thing gets loud *fast*. But hey, that's what you needed to cut through back in the day. Throaty, hairy, and just a little bit nasty, it's not a particularly refined tone, but it sure helped the likes of Peter Green of Fleetwood Mac and Marc Bolan of T. Rex be heard in grand style.

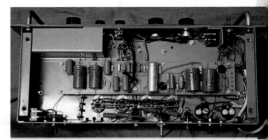

Early-1970s Pignose

Any guitarist of a certain age will vividly recall the time when the petite and obnoxious Pignose promised to take over the world of guitar amplification—and failed, but not without trying. This 3-watt, 9x6x4-inch warthog invented in 1969 by Richard Edlund and Wayne Kimball as a portable practice amp was brought into full production around 1973. Practice amp gave way to studio wunderkind, however, after Frank Zappa, Eric Clapton, Joe Walsh, and others were purported to have obtained their crazy-dirty lead tones from closely miked Pignose amps, and the product was widely marketed as a savior of the studio. If it doesn't quite equal the bountiful tone of your cranked AC30, tweed Deluxe, or JTM45, the Pignose does at least make an effective and distinctive tone, and it sure offers a lot of mustard for its $79 price tag ("same price as in the '70s!") and six AA battery power complement. Plug in, crank that little piggy nose, and let the dirt begin.

Courtesy Southside Guitars/
www.southsideguitars.com

MXR Phase 90

Founded in Rochester, New York, in 1972, MXR Innovations was an early leader in the American effects-pedal market and made a name for itself on the strength of several solid and good-sounding units. The Phase 90, however, one of MXR's first and most popular pedals, possibly made the greatest impact of all of them. This lush-sounding but ultra-simple pedal, carrying just a single knob for Speed and an on-off stomp switch, was a near-instant hit. Its bubbly, liquid tone caught guitarists' attention in a big way throughout the 1970s, and everyone from Jimmy Page to Keith Richards to Edward Van Halen to Mick Jones of the Clash used a Phase 90 prominently live and on record. Part of the beauty of the Phase 90 seems to be its ability to sound great in either clean or distorted tones, with a fuzz or overdrive pedal placed either before or after it, with varying but equally viable results. Less dramatic than more complex phasers, perhaps, but unfailingly musical, it's a timeless gem.

Musitronics Mu-Tron III

Put your hands together, ladies and gentleman, for what might very well be the funkiest pedal of all time. If the Mu-Tron III had only ever been responsible for the auto-wah'd clav tone on Stevie Wonder's "Higher Ground," it would have assured its place in effects-pedal history—and that's not even a guitar application—but this groove inducer became further certified in its use by a plethora of '70s funk merchants. The Mu-Tron III was the first product released by Musitronics, founded in 1972 by former Guild engineer Aaron Newman and electrical designer Mike Biegel. The pedal's success helped the company hit the ground running. In fact, it was first marketed heavily to jazz players and was taken up by the likes of Larry Coryell, Pat Martino, and Herb Ellis, while also becoming a major component of

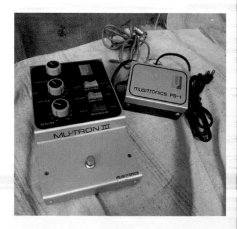

Grateful Dead guitarist Jerry Garcia's sound. Plug this one in to see what all the fuss is about, and even the most straight-assed players will soon experience irrepressible funk-booty thanks to that infectious auto-wah (a.k.a. envelope filter, a.k.a. envelope follower) sound. Dig?

Mid-1970s WEM Dominator MkIII

Sure, the wedge-fronted MkI of the late 1950s, the predecessor to this squarer combo, might earn most of the adulation, but for sheer unexpected tonal bliss where you might least expect it, it really does pay to plug into one of the later WEM Dominators at least once in your life (and, as cheap as many still are, to then buy the damn thing). WEM founder Charlie Watkins was making and marketing amplifiers, as well as guitars and accessories, under his own name even before Vox and Marshall entered the game, and changed his brand identity to the three-letter acronym WEM in the mid-'60s because he liked the look, and success, of the similarly three-lettered Vox range. The Dominator was long his flagship range and provided surprisingly stout, juicy tone to countless players who couldn't spring for the A-list amps of the '60s and '70s. This one is a sweetheart of a churning, chiming, crunchy, EL84-flavored beauty, despite its rather homely looks, and a killer little club and recording amp in every respect.

Morley RWV

Although the company is probably best known for its industrial-looking chromed wah pedals of the 1970s, Morley actually evolved out of a previous company that first made its name with an ingenious, if rather strange effect designed in the 1960s and licensed to Fender and others. Brothers Marvin and Raymond Lubow founded Tel-Ray Electronics in Burbank, California, and patented a design for an echo effect that worked by writing the guitar signal in electrostatic oil on a rotating drum. The resultant sound was far from pure, pristine delay, and had warm, liquid tones that sound more like a combination of tremolo, vibrato, and echo. When Tel-Ray evolved into Morley in the early '70s, the Lubows repackaged this patented technology into a few new designs, including the mammoth EVO-1 Echo Volume pedal, and this freakish RWV (for "rotating wah volume"). Morley ads boasted "one 5-way unit does the work of as much as $1,000 or more [of] accessories," although some of these five-way sounds are, of course, combinations of features. Regardless, the rotating effect is itself a trippy take on the Leslie effect, and adding wah-wah to the brew takes it right over the moon.

Benedetto La Cremona

Master acoustic archtop luthier Robert Benedetto has been making instruments by hand since 1968 and enhanced his skills early on by going back to the old traditions, making more than fifty violin-family instruments. Although the bulk of his work is custom-order, the La Cremona was his first "standardized" model, of sorts. Introduced in 1972, it represents a marriage of tradition and modernity, the latter seen in an almost total lack of unnecessary and non-wood adornment in the inlay-free fingerboard, ebony tailpiece, and sleek, narrow pickguard. Whether it's the dearth of inorganic materials or Benedetto's sheer skill, the La Cremona issues a sublime acoustic tone. Where so many archtops—even those of a high quality—seem rather muted, dull, and dark, this guitar rings with a zing and clarity above the overarching richness and depth. Many artists, of necessity, install floating pickups on their archtops for club performance, but it's almost a shame to bolt any dead weight to this beauty. Benedetto players like Chuck Wayne, Jimmy Bruno, Kenny Burrell, and Bucky Pizzarelli have often exhibited the pure sonic beauty of their guitars by miking them in the studio rather than amplifying them through a magnetic pickup.

Courtesy Outline Press Limited

MXR Distortion+

In a business where the marketing trend was to lean wild and funky, both with names and visuals, MXR was resolutely serious and professional from the start. If the others were making toy boxes to tickle the toes of the hippies, MXR would aim for the hardworking professional musician, or so the company's approach would have us believe. To that end, MXR effects were housed in sturdy, compact, brick-like metal boxes with simple color schemes and sedate graphics. Founded in 1972 in Rochester, New York, MXR's first hit was the Phase 90, but the Distortion+ steamed in a close second in 1973, and became pretty much the standard for overdrive pedals at the time, a good few years before the Ibanez Tube Screamer and Boss SD-1 hit the scene. In reality, this pedal probably should have been called the Distortion−, given that it really isn't a "distortion" pedal as such, or not by today's standards anyway (even in '73 it sounded far less distorted than a heavy fuzz pedal); instead it issues a smooth, warm, pliable overdrive that helps push an amp into tubey clipping. And that's just the way we like it.

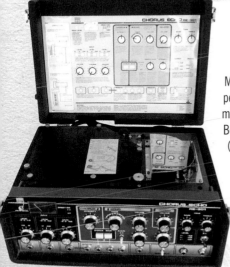

Roland Chorus Echo RE-301

Music electronics giant Roland, parent company to the massive Boss pedal line, released several formative effects in its own right in the early to mid-'70s, and the Space Echo is arguably one of the most, well, effective. Beloved of many guitarists, the feature-packed Chorus Echo RE-301 (Roland also offered the Space Echo RE-101 and RE-201 models) was the top of the line for a time, designed to be a studio-quality multi-effect unit, an application at which it excelled. In addition to a juicy solid-state analog tape echo, available at variable speeds, depths, and repeat rates, the RE-301 gives a decent reverb (perhaps its least-loved effect, actually), as well as an early rendition of the chorus effect that would become a Roland and Boss staple loaded into a wide range of pedals and amps alike. While the Maestro Echoplex was the echo of the '60s, the Chorus Echo was generally the echo of the '70s, and it remains, as often as not, the preferred analog echo of today.

1977 Mesa/Boogie Mark 1

After hot-rodding some 200 Fender Princeton Reverb amps in the late 1960s and into the early '70s, Mesa founder Randall Smith started building his cascading-gain circuit from the ground up in a new range of amps around late '71 or early '72, and the Boogie was born. This cute yet fearsome little 1x12 combo set new standards for achieving singing lead tones at less-than-stack volumes, and by the mid '70s, everyone who was anyone had to have one. By the time Keith Richards was personally ordering six for himself over the phone in 1978, Boogies were already on stage with Carlos Santana, Frank Zappa, Wishbone Ash, Joe Walsh, Pete Townshend, the Kinks, and many others. The saturated overdrive sizzle of cascading gain might be nothing new today, when near countless makers use it in their "lead" channels, but plug into this archaic-seeming little beast and you are quickly reminded of what a sensation it must have been to play when it was the only trick on the block. Hit a note, stand in just the right place, and it will still be sustaining by breakfast time.

Dan Armstrong Orange Squeezer

Dan Armstrong marketed his range of cube-shaped effects units as "Sound Modifiers" rather than pedals because, well, they *weren't* pedals; they plugged straight into the guitar via the built-in jack on the back of the box. And therein, perhaps, lies the only weakness in these clever, sturdy, and good-sounding effects, of which the Orange Squeezer compressor retains the most tangible legacy. Dan Armstrong ran an extremely successful guitar shop in New York City in the 1960s (where his son, noted pickup maker Kent Armstrong, got his start) but packed up for London in the early '70s to pursue other opportunities. Among these, the line of diminutive and colorfully named Sound Modifiers—developed with fellow expat, electrical engineer George Merriman, and manufactured under the Musitronics umbrella—is perhaps best remembered. This Orange Squeezer, like others in the line, carries only a mini-toggle On/Off switch and an output jack, but its preset sound is extremely well judged right out of the box and yields a tasty squash that juices up your guitar tone just right.

Foxx Fuzz Wah Volume Machine

A relatively short-lived brand of the '70s, Foxx is possibly best remembered for the electrostatically fuzz-flocked casings that housed many of its effects—and occasionally gummed up the potentiometers and circuits when the fuzz began to shed and work its way inside. The pedals were designed by Steve Ridinger, who was in his late teens when he founded the company in 1970; Foxx closed its doors in 1975 in the face of increased competition from other makers and, it would seem, poor sales for its newer units. The bright-red Fuzz Wah Volume Machine (later released in black, too) was one of the company's staples, and presented itself as a do-it-all effects wizard for the early-'70s rocker. The wah sound was funky and quacky and really quite good by any standard, and it offered the bonus of a volume pedal when disengaged. Slep on the stomp switch mounted above the rocker pedal for a thick, meaty fuzz tone that rolls from warm and fat to bright and edgy. A classic in its own right—which is perhaps why a newly revitalized Foxx has reissued it, along with a host of other pedals.

1975 Park Lead 50

The Park story makes an interesting sidebar to the history of Marshall, and several Park amps make great alternatives in EL34-based tone. In the mid-1960s, Jim Marshall signed a 15-year agreement that gave U.K. giant Rose-Morris the exclusive rights to Marshall distribution. To sidestep the limitations of this contract and continue supplying amps to Birmingham music-shop owner Johnny Jones, Marshall initiated the Park line. The amps were made in the same English factory as Marshalls, and early models shared several circuits, though interesting variations soon worked their way into the line. This Lead 50 from the mid-'70s doesn't look or sound quite like any existing Marshall combo, although it is roughly similar to several. Plugging into its Hi input taps two consecutive tube gain stages, not unlike those in the JCM800 preamp, and there's a master Volume to rein it all in as necessary. As such, the Park Lead 50 proves a fast track to classic Marshall-like crunch and grind, with wailing lead tones at the ready when you push it harder. It's a far, far cry from the small transistor practice combos that the Park name would grace two decades later.

1970s Fender Starcaster

If the Coronado line wasn't entirely successful as a rival to Gibson's semi-acoustic market, the Starcaster of the 1970s should have had a better run at it. This bolt-neck semi-acoustic clearly echoed the ES-335 and other similar Gibsons, but it was no direct copy, either. Which is to say, Fender built the Starcaster almost as you would expect Fender to build a semi-acoustic guitar, even if they never had the context of Gibson's iconic efforts. Accordingly, the Starcaster has an all-maple neck with a three-screw attachment and bullet-head truss-rod nut, along with a body made from laminated maple with a solid center core and a characteristically Fender-ish offset double-cutaway design, all built to a 25.5-inch scale length. A new bridge design catered to Tele-influenced through-body stringing, and the dual Wide Range Humbuckers came from the Tele lineup, too. Add it all together, and the Starcaster is brighter and twangier than Gibson's semi, but with plenty of girth too, which translates to a biting snarl through a pushed tube amp. The result is a guitar that isn't going to stand in for an ES-335 in any blind test, but which has bags of character in its own right.

Courtesy Guitar Exchange/www.guitarexchangeonline.com

Late-1970s Polytone Mini-Brute

Whether or not there's any inherent reason for it, "jazz tone" has come to mean warm, deep, and round, and after years of jazz guitarists pointing their rigs to that setting, Polytone jumped in to create a little combo that took you straight there. The company was founded in 1968 by accordionist Tommy Gumina (those guys needed amps too), and took off with the Brute model, which aimed to fulfill the needs of function and jazz guitarists and double-bassists with its power, portability, and headroom. By putting it all into a package that you could heft onto the subway for that Uptown gig, however, the smaller Mini-Brute of 1976 essentially became the flagship. Its popularity on the jazz scene made the Mini-Brute the tone of late-'70s and early-'80s electric jazz guitar, and it's still one of the go-to standards today. Of course, your accomplished jazz artist is too busy conjuring slash chords and polyrhythms to worry about replacing and biasing tubes, so that's clearly a bonus, too.

Electro-Harmonix Talking Machine

In the realm of "novelty effects in the extreme," the E-H Talking Machine is definitely in the big race for the biscuit. Yet, there is something oddly endearing about this too, even if it's likely to get little action through the course of your average set. While the best wah-wah pedals of all time had already been created by the late '60s, in most players' estimations, manufacturers forged into the mid-'70s in their efforts to one-up the competition, and the Talking Machine is most likely the result of that quack contest. Built like a large-bodied wah, the Talking Machine, in E-H's own words, was developed "from advanced research in speech synthesis." In short, rock the treadle to the desired position and its "critically-tuned resonant filtering of instrument input" produces the vowel series A-E-I-O-U. In use, it's just as weird as that description might imply, and while it proves a fun funk machine for a while, there remains the question of generating some consonants to truly get this pedal talking.

Tycobrahe Pedalflanger

Nearly every self-respecting effects-pedal manufacturer had a flanger in their lineup by the end of the '70s, but the Tycobrahe Pedalflanger is widely considered the first flanger on the market, and many still feel it is the best sounding. Released early in 1976, this rocker-pedal device had external controls for Spread and Intensity, governing the main aspects of the effect, as well as a treadle for manual control of the effect's sweep. A host of internal trim pots accessed other parameters, however, and needed to be set correctly for optimum performance. A flanger, used anywhere toward the extreme of abuse, can be a cold, grating, and off-putting effect, but the Pedalflanger is generally rated as extremely smooth and organic. As a result, it makes a great bed for more musical modulation effects, including chorus, flanging, vibrato, and rotary-speaker simulation, rather than a "special effect" slathered on top of your tone. The rarity of this pedal from the short-lived Tycobrahe company makes originals highly prized, although Chicago Iron has put considerable R&D into its own rendition of the Pedalflanger, which is highly regarded by many guitarists.

Late-1970s Ibanez GB-10 George Benson Model

It's a testament to Ibanez's rapidly elevating status in the late 1970s that the maker could not only land an endorsee the caliber of George Benson, but could also build a guitar of a quality that would suit such an artist. Hot on the heels of his crossover pop and R&B success, Benson was the most successful jazz guitarist of the day. Schooled in swing and bebop, he had played other great American jazzboxes on his way up, but Ibanez captured his ideal performance guitar in the shape of downsized, full hollowbody with a spruce archtop and maple back and sides. Pearl and abalone block markers and a custom "GB" pearl headstock inlay gave the model a deluxe look in line with the great archtops of years past, while dual floating mini-humbuckers mounted to the edge of the bound tortoiseshell pickguard impressively copped their tone, too. While this guitar won't match the acoustic sound of a golden-era Gibson L-5 or Epiphone Emperor, it nails that warm, rich jazz tone when plugged in, and its breezy playability was just the thing the fleet-fingered bopper was looking for.

Late-1970s Ibanez Iceman IC210

One of the more original early Japanese guitar designs, the Ibanez Iceman hit Western markets in 1978. (The Greco company handled the same guitar from the FujiGen factory for the Japanese markets, where it was dubbed the Mirage.) The Iceman had its roots in an earlier Ibanez Artist 2663 model. The slightly offset, angular shape with its "bottle opener" lower horn would find most fame in the hands of Kiss guitarist Paul Stanley, who made it his main weapon throughout the end of the decade. Although the Iceman was a major departure from Ibanez's earlier Gibson copies, it still had a little Kalamazoo at its core: at a distance, its Explorer influence was obvious, and something in the block inlays and the gloss-black finish of Stanley's fave version also spoke to the Les Paul Custom. Either way, it rocked supremely and showed that its owner was not bound by musical tradition, which was equally important back in the day. Original examples are quite collectable, and several reissues have kept the spirit alive.

Paul Stanley. Michael Ochs Archives/Getty Images

Courtesy Cutline Press Limited

Heil Talk Box

Other lower-powered and/or homemade talk boxes existed before it, but the Heil Talk Box, developed in the early '70s by Bob Heil, was the first commercially produced unit with the power to cut it on the big concert stage—where it fast became an item in that decade of arena rock. Not an "effect pedal" in the common sense of the term, but really a compact speaker (a high-powered horn driver with horn removed, in this case) with a tube attached, the Talk Box was first heard prominently in Joe Walsh's "Rocky Mountain Way" and Rufus & Chaka Khan's "Tell Me Something Good" but probably most famously appeared on Peter Frampton's live versions of "Do You Feel Like I Do" and "Show Me The Way," released a couple years later. As dramatic as it sounds, the Heil Talk Box is one of the simplest effects going. Wired between guitar amp and speaker, a stomp of the on switch redirects the amplified guitar signal to the Talk Box driver and into the mouth tube, where the sound is shaped by the player's oral gesticulations and broadcast via a standard vocal mic. While overuse can descend into the realm of novelty, if judiciously applied the Talk Box is a great way to grab some attention on stage.

THE INCREDIBLE
'TALK BOX'

- CREATES fantastic 'WAH' type vowel sounds as heard from Joe Walsh, Stevie Wonder, John Kaye & Jeff Beck.

- Easy to use with ANY guitar, synthesizer or bass.

- Built-in footswitch allows by-pass feature for regular sound.

- Durable fiberglass floor module complete with all jacks & switches.

- Features the great HEIL HD800 power driver for best response.

Professional Musicians Cost $149.00

AVAILABLE from

HEIL SOUND

HEIL INDUSTRIAL BLVD.
MARISSA, ILL. 62257
618-295-3000

DO YOU FEEL LIKE I DO?

Late-1970s Alembic Series 1

Dial back to the early 1970s, and Alembic's electronically advanced guitars crafted from exotic "hippie sandwich" wood combinations foretold a bold future of custom electric guitar making—if one that wouldn't entirely come to fruition on the mass market. Alembic was founded in the San Francisco Bay Area in 1969 by husband-and-wife team Ron and Susan Wickersham (with partners Rick Turner and Bob Matthews) as a company devoted to improving the Grateful Dead's live and recorded sound. By the early '70s, their efforts had extended to building custom guitars of the ilk that Dead frontman Jerry Garcia preferred. The Series I and its brethren were born of that effort. The first thing you notice upon strapping on this Series I is that it is *heavy*, the result of all those laminated hardwoods. The second is that it feels pretty darn slick with its through-neck construction eliminating the traditional neck heel and its rounded body contours giving it a sensual heft in the hand. The third is that its electronics are quite unlike anything else out there. Via the onboard active electronics, the two single-coil pickups are extremely sensitive (that's a hum-canceling dummy coil between them) with a broad frequency range and detailed articulation, all of which translates to an extremely high-fidelity playing experience. Freaky stuff.

Hamer Studio

Formed in the mid-1970s by Paul Hamer and Jol Dantzig, Hamer quickly established a reputation for high-quality, Gibson-esque, U.S.-made electric guitars that remains strong to this day. The Studio has long been one of the company's cornerstone models and to some extent evolved out of the early Sunburst model, which differed in a few details, such as its rather incongruous yet tone-enhancing Fender-like through-body bridge. The Studio isn't necessarily a "studio guitar," but it furthers the effort to upstage the Gibson template with a more traditional Tune-o-matic bridge and stop-bar tailpiece and generally aims straight at the hot-rodded, double-cutaway Les Paul territory. And, to be fair, it hits a bull's-eye in the process. This guitar is meaty and thick through a good tube amp, with heaps of cutting power and willing sustain. The handy control positions make pickup switching and volume changes for both positions an easy right-hand maneuver. For all this, the Studio is a surprisingly good buy on the used market.

Both courtesy Outline Press Limited

199

Yamaha SG2000

From near-novelties to high-quality professional guitars, Yamaha rose quickly in the musical instrument trade from the late 1960s to the late 1970s, and the SG2000 was the guitar that told the world that this Japanese company had truly arrived in the rock arena. Look at the clunky, rather Italianate efforts of just a few years before, and the leap in both manufacturing quality and general functionality is indeed impressive. But Yamaha clearly put its mind to producing a serious solidbody, and the world responded with open arms. Designed from the ground up as a "Les Paul beater," the SG2000 was made with an integral neck and body core—referred to as a "through neck"—made from layers of mahogany and maple, with a multipiece mahogany and maple body, an ebony fingerboard, a bridge mounted to a solid brass sustain block, and several other refinements. Dig into this one, and it shows you how successful the effort truly was, issuing a bold, ringing voice, good definition with meaty punch through an overdriven amp, and superb sustain.

Courtesy Outline Press Limited

Jackson Randy Rhoads Model

Grover Jackson virtually invented the "droopy headstock" guitar that would become the staple of countless heavy rockers and launched the breed in grand style with one of the hottest young players of the day. Just a couple years after purchasing Charvel guitars in 1978, Jackson crossed paths with Ozzy Osbourne guitarist Randy Rhoads and built the rising star a few Flying V–inspired instruments to which he affixed his own name rather than the Charvel brand. The Randy Rhoads Model settled into standard production in 1983 and became a staple of hair-metal shredmeisters of the era. A quick whip round this one's pointy corners reveals a guitar that was built for speed, and that leans you toward slash-and-burn rock antics—whatever you try to throw at it. The neck is thin and sleek, the action barely hovers above the jumbo frets, and the Floyd Rose vibrato unit drops you to subsonic depths and back again with nary a flutter the tuning stability. Randy Rhoads is gone, sadly, but the shred lives on.

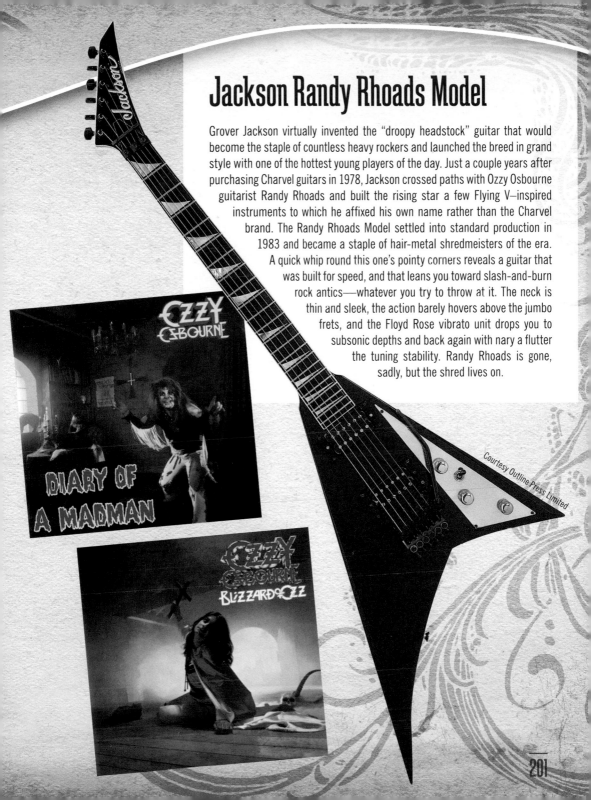

Courtesy Outline Press, Limited

Electro-Harmonix Small Clone

A partner in size, look, and general ethos to the extremely popular Small Stone phaser, Electro-Harmonix's Small Clone chorus pedal has likely inscribed itself more indelibly on the consciousness of semi-contemporary music thanks to Kurt Cobain's use of the effect on Nirvana's seminal "Smells Like Teen Spirit" and elsewhere. Like many of the smaller E-H pedals, the Small Clone simply did the job, and did it well. Released in the late 1970s, this simple analog chorus had just one knob for Rate (speed) and a switch to change the Depth level. But so dialed-in was the sound that you really didn't need a lot more, unless you were looking for spacey extremes. The circuit issued a soothing, watery chorus that did a great job of livening up potentially dull clean tones (the virtue that probably helped chorus pedals catch on so well in the era of many sterile-sounding late-'70s and early-'80s amps) but sounded particularly bubbly and thick when used with distortion. Indeed, Kurt Cobain might have come off like he didn't put a moment's thought into his rig, but he knew an infectious sound when he heard one.

A/DA Flanger

Magazine ads for the A/DA Flanger, released in 1977, called it "the most advanced flanger available today," and perhaps for once in the realm of music electronics, the marketing department's claims were fully justified. At $200 in '77, plus $40 for the optional foot controller, it didn't come cheap, but if flanger was your sound, the A/DA offered a tempting package. Controls for Threshold, Manual, Range, Speed, and Enhance governed a sweet, lush analog circuit, while a switch for even/odd harmonic emphasis considerably increased the package's versatility. The Flanger's extremely wide sweep range, from 0.1 to 25 seconds, was far more extreme than that of most rivals, or you could take charge of the sweep yourself by connecting the optional Control Pedal A. Fans of the original claim that the earlier units using the Reticon SAD1024 "bucket brigade" chip are more desirable, but later examples with the Matsushita MN3010 are still pretty darn impressive.

Ibanez Tube Screamer TS808

The ubiquitous overdrive pedal might seem a standard today, but in the late 1970s, when a booster or fuzz provided the usual means of kicking a clean amp into breakup, the Tube Screamer seemed a revelation. Very possibly the most used and copied overdrive pedal, the TS808 of 1979–1981 (as well as the TS9 of 1981–1985) is beloved for its juicy midrange and natural, tube-like breakup. Well, at least it sounded natural to us back in the day, when few other options existed. Today, many players consider the Tube Screamer somewhat midrange-heavy and low-end-light, and not entirely transparent at that (criticisms that have inspired a wealth of mods), but put a good one between guitar and amp, setting the latter just to the edge of breakup, then stomp that switch for a quick reminder of how playable and versatile this pedal remains. This little green box has probably landed on more pedal boards over the years than any other single effects pedal—including that of Stevie Ray Vaughn in its TS9 and TS10 incarnations—and that is something in itself.

Larrivée L-09

Jean Larrivée has risen from building acoustic guitars in his home in Toronto, Canada, in the late 1960s to being one of the most prolific makers in North America today. After an apprenticeship with Edgar Mönch, Larrivée initially specialized in classical guitars in the style of his mentor, but soon saw the marketing sense in moving into steel-string flat-tops as well. This intensive training in the classical style, however, instilled an originality of both look and construction that remains central to several Larrivée guitars to this day. This L-09 is a superbly playable flat-top with a rich, lithe tone that benefits from several details of the Larrivée approach. Symmetrical parabolic X-bracing undoubtedly influences the Canadian Sitka spruce top's vibrational characteristics and helps produce a bold steel-string performer in a guitar that, at first glance, might appear to be a nylon-string classical in disguise. Cosmetic details like the abalone sound hole rosette, Canadian maple body binding, and African ebony fingerboard and bridge are icing on the cake.

Paul Natkin/WireImage/Getty Images

Gallagher Doc Watson Model

As Gallagher's foremost endorsee, Doc Watson was rewarded with this small maker's first signature model in 1974, and the ace flatpicker undoubtedly helped broaden the popularity of these Tennessee flat-top boxes throughout the worlds of bluegrass and country music. Like Watson's own playing, Gallagher's signature dreadnought is known to be a fleet, nimble performer with a strong, complex voice. It's impressive that Gallagher not only made such inroads into scenes so dominated by Martin and Gibson when the newcomer arrived in 1965 (back before independent luthiers were as valued as they are today), but quickly compiled a long waiting list as well. And while Gallagher's dreadnoughts, as well as its smaller fingerstyle model, clearly bear traces of Martin's influence, they also offer the small-shop craftsmanship and attention to detail that plenty of players have come to value. Founder J. W. Gallagher passed the business along to his son Don upon his retirement in 1976, and Don's son Stephen is now in the family business, too. Still located in Wartrace, Tennessee, Gallagher builds approximately 75 guitars a year, still entirely by hand.

Electro-Harmonix Memory Man Deluxe

The Big Muff might be the best known of all Electro-Harmonix pedals, but the Memory Man Deluxe is very likely the most successful in terms of sonic virtue and player acclaim. Several compact analog delay units arrived in the late '70s to save guitarists from the rigors of lugging a clunky electromechanical tape delay on the road, but the Memory Man Deluxe (and its slightly more affordable Standard sibling) seemed to best embody the tone and feel of tape echo and offer the well-judged control and added features that made it a useful creation in its own right. Original units used the then-new "bucket brigade" chips to replicate and delay the guitar signal, all in analog, resulting in a rich, warm, slightly furry echo tone that proved to be extremely appealing to guitarists' ears. Level, Blend, Feedback, and Delay controls offered governance of all essential aspects of the effect, while a great bonus, your choice of analog Chorus or Vibrato (according to the front-panel switch) could be added as desired. Still extremely desirable, and still considered one of the best-sounding echo units for guitar, bar none.

Electro-Harmonix Electric Mistress

Courtesy Southside Guitars/
www.southsideguitars.com

The seductively named Electric Mistress flanger brought extreme modulation to the feet of waiting guitarists in the sturdy, functional form that the New York–based company was fast becoming known for at the time of the unit's release in 1976. Never mind that the new analog flanger, possibly the hottest and most exotic effect in the late '60s to mid-'70s, cost nearly as much as a good used Stratocaster. You needed this thing if you were going to sound at all "with it" back in the day—even if overuse could leave you sounding distinctly "without it" in no time flat. Used subtly, the Electric Mistress provides musical, harmonically rich flanging that graces your guitar tone with shimmering motion. Used *in extremis*, it lashes out notchy extremes and severe oscillation that bludgeon your tone with robotic modulation excess . . . which, certainly, might be exactly what you're looking for. Classic examples include David Gilmour's occasional use of the effect as well as its up-front application on the intro to Heart's hit "Barracuda."

Boss Super Overdrive SD-1

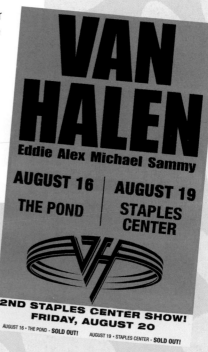

If a guitarist wasn't getting a helping hand from an Ibanez Tube Screamer to goose his amp into breakup in the late '70s and early '80s, it's a safe bet he or she was getting there with the aid of a Boss Super Overdrive SD-1 pedal instead. This popular Boss box offered a smooth yet ever so slightly jagged, asymmetrical, medium-gain overdrive with well-balanced frequency retention, and it sounded best partnered with an edge-of-breakup tube amp rather than as a distortion generator in its own right. Again, much like the Tube Screamer. Much is made of Edward Van Halen's use of a browned-out Marshall 50-watter to produce his signature singing tone and sustain, but the Titan of Tap also included an SD-1 in his rig almost from the start. Many players today might feel that newer renditions of the omnipresent overdrive pedal are more transparent, more powerful, more balanced, or all of the above, but this humble Boss is still an impressive performer. Subtle and solid, the SD-1 remains a tangible illustration of what a good overdrive does best: help your real tone poke through, rather than poking its own head above the fray.

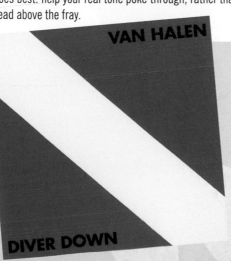

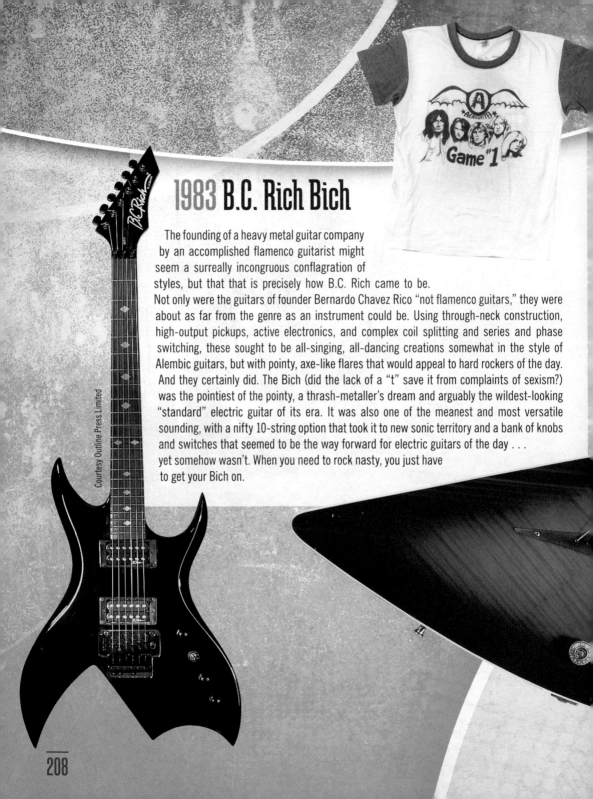

1983 B.C. Rich Bich

The founding of a heavy metal guitar company by an accomplished flamenco guitarist might seem a surreally incongruous conflagration of styles, but that that is precisely how B.C. Rich came to be. Not only were the guitars of founder Bernardo Chavez Rico "not flamenco guitars," they were about as far from the genre as an instrument could be. Using through-neck construction, high-output pickups, active electronics, and complex coil splitting and series and phase switching, these sought to be all-singing, all-dancing creations somewhat in the style of Alembic guitars, but with pointy, axe-like flares that would appeal to hard rockers of the day. And they certainly did. The Bich (did the lack of a "t" save it from complaints of sexism?) was the pointiest of the pointy, a thrash-metaller's dream and arguably the wildest-looking "standard" electric guitar of its era. It was also one of the meanest and most versatile sounding, with a nifty 10-string option that took it to new sonic territory and a bank of knobs and switches that seemed to be the way forward for electric guitars of the day . . . yet somehow wasn't. When you need to rock nasty, you just have to get your Bich on.

Courtesy Outline Press Limited

1985 Dean Z

Illinois native Dean Zelinsky founded Dean Guitars in 1976 when he was still in his late teens, and his instruments gained prominence surprisingly quickly. Designs were carved from the wilder branches of the Gibson tree and aimed resolutely at the harder rockers on the scene. This Z was clearly influenced by the Big G's Explorer model but offered a bound, figured maple top and other refinements of construction and tone that some players might have felt they weren't getting from Gibson's guitars of the era. High-output humbuckers and a weighty disposition give this Z a gutsy voice, and it really demands a cranked JCM800 or other high-gain stack to do its thing properly. The success of this one, plus its partners the V (guess the shape) and ML (kinda LP-meets-Explorer), brought several prominent artists to the Dean camp. Uli John Roth, Michael Angelo Batio, Bret Michaels, Leslie West, Michael Schenker, and Dave Mustaine are among notables on that roster today.

Rick Turner Model 1

Rick Turner has a long and illustrious history in electric guitar making, yet relatively few of the uninitiated are likely to recognize his work, despite having seen this guitar in the hands of one of the world's most successful artists. Turner was an original partner in Alembic but left the company in the late '70s and soon released his seminal Model 1, a minimalistic guitar designed, in part, to suit the needs of then–Fleetwood Mac frontman Lindsey Buckingham. The virtually amorphous-bodied guitar carries a single magnetic humbucking pickup near the neck position, mounted on a round plate that can be rotated to adjust its tonal response. Onboard electronics offer a considerable gain boost and broad EQ tweaking as desired, as well as coil splitting for single-coil tones. Part of the Model 1's appeal for Buckingham might have been the space it affords for his fingerstyle playing, although the guitar's thick yet crisp tone also suited the Fleetwood Mac sound perfectly, and it has remained one of the guitarist's favorites over the years, as well as having been taken up by newer sensation John Mayer.

Giffin Model T

Why "Model T"? We're not entirely sure, but perhaps it's because this simple, solid performance machine echoes Henry Ford's design ethos—although it's certainly available in colors other than black. Segueing smoothly from cars to guitars, the Model T is influenced very much by the Gibson Les Paul Junior template, tonally at least, but Giffin redraws the blueprint for a more inventively shaped guitar that still packs that no-nonsense rock 'n' roll punch yet offers nuanced versatility where you might least expect to find it. Working in his shop under the arches of a bridge crossing the River Thames, Roger Giffin first made his name repairing, then building, guitars for several stars on the late-1960s London scene. Upon moving to the U.S. West Coast in the late 1970s, Giffin brought along his pioneering designs and uncompromising craftsmanship and soon built a following among discerning American guitarists. The Model T is the most basic in a line of hand-made electrics that runs toward the posh and exclusive, yet it's fun to be reminded now and then how exciting it can be to play a simple guitar rendered flawlessly by a great luthier.

Early-1980s Yamaha SA2200

While Yamaha's solidbody SG2000 represented a significant departure from Gibson's legendary carved-top, single-cutaway Les Paul, the SA2200 cut closer to the seminal semi-acoustic ES-335 and became a true sleeper classic in the process. Studied in detail, the SA2200 is an excellent lesson in how a guitar that outwardly appears to ape an existing classic design can, through several minute refinements, take on a quality and character all its own. The consistency and quality of Yamaha's best Japanese luthiers give this guitar a confidence and solidity in the hand that instantly declares its intentions, while the figured top, multi-bound body and headstock, floral crest pearl headstock inlay, and pearl split-block markers in an ebony fingerboard show the rest of the world that it intends to look good while sounding great, with added versatility from the dual humbuckers' individually switchable tapped coils. The SA2200's versatility—something with which we can, to some extent, credit the entire ES-335 breed—has made it a favorite of several first-call L.A. and Nashville session players.

Steinberger GL-2

Another instrument that seemed to promise "the future of the electric guitar" upon its release in 1983, Steinberger's GL guitar followed its big brother, the L-2 bass of a couple years before, as well as the similarly configured basses that designer Ned Steinberger built for Spector in the late '70s. Usually referred to as "headless," these guitars are virtually "bodyless" too, or minimal of body at best, with revolutionary low-profile tuners at the butt-end of the body and the strings anchored just past the nut. While we might view it as the archetypal "log" construction (the natural evolution of Les Paul's prototype, without the Epiphone wings bolted on), the GL actually has a hollow one-piece neck and body made from resin-fiber composite with a removable body top that enables access of the active, low-impedance EMG pickups and electronics. Perhaps the greatest surprise upon plugging in one of these is that it doesn't sound drastically *unlike* a traditional, wood-bodied (and full-headed) electric guitar, the EMGs notwithstanding. Crystalline and chiming through a clean amp, yet with plenty of grind when you crank things a little, it's a great all-around rock guitar, and the clever TransTrem whammy system on the GL-2 post-'84 makes it even more versatile.

Pro Co Rat

Founded in Kalamazoo, Michigan, in 1970, Pro Co made a name for itself as a manufacturer of guitar cables, DI boxes, and other non-sound-generating guitar accessories until engineering director Scott Burnham drew up his design for this over-the-top distortion pedal. Released in 1979, the Rat was the first successful, genuine heavy-rock distortion pedal, and while it might not sound quite as heavy today as it did at the time—compared to all else available in the twenty-first century—it remains an extremely popular noisemaker. The Rat's circuit displays some similarities to the MXR Distortion+ that preceded it (actually more an overdrive than a distortion box) but with a few crucial changes to up the filth factor. Among these are the use of harder-edged silicon diodes in place of the MXR's germanium, and a low-value resistor that drives the opamp harder than those in conventional overdrive pedals of the day. The result is a smooth but heavy distortion, with good low-end weight and a characteristic high-frequency howl when cranked. 'Nuff said.

Ross Compressor

Destined for also-ran status in the field of music electronics if not for the retroactive achievements of this gray squash box, Ross was mainly a manufacturer of budget pedals, four-track port-a-studio cassette machines, and other bits and pieces in the 1980s. Enter the thick, juicy, ultra-sustaining tone that Phish guitarist Trey Anastasio originally achieved with the help of an old Ross Compressor, and boom—these things go whatever was the early-1990s equivalent of viral. The Ross Compressor was essentially an update of MXR's Dyna Comp and seemed to offer a slightly more delectable squash than the original, with plenty of sustain to boot. With just Sustain and Level controls and an On/Off switch, it's a doddle to use, and like many good compressors, it becomes more of an addictive "always on" tone enhancer after some use rather than an "effect" as such. Prices for original examples soared skyward for a time, although an accelerating line in reproductions (and updates) from a range of boutique makers in the late 1990s and after seemed to calm the vintage market slightly.

Courtesy Rumble Seat Music/www.rumbleseatmusic.com

Marshall JCM800

For many players, Marshall's glory years spanned the 1960s and early '70s, but the later JCM800 was a modern classic in its own right and virtually defined the sound of rock guitar for several years in the 1980s. The amp was designed as a high-gain alternative to the models that had preceded it, intended to work its best in conjunction with its master Volume control, enabling a player to craft massive crunch and lead tones at less-than-flat-out volumes. Although it's more "medium gain" by today's incendiary standards, the humble JCM800 still provides a fast track to tumescent contemporary rock tones that remain distinctly Marshall. Despite the foot-switchable rhythm and lead channels, evolved front-panel styling, and bonus features such as an FX loop and reverb, the JCM800 still has something of an old-school Marshall vibe to it, and through a good 4x12 cab (go with Greenbacks, G12H-30s, or G12-65s rather than the G12-70s in the matching cabs of the era, if you can), this amp should provide all the juicy rock bluster you desire, with more versatility than a vintage alternative.

1982 Dumble Overdrive Special

Alexander Dumble's creations are among the most hallowed in ampdom, and the smooth, thick, creamy overdrive he has packed into designs such as this Overdrive Special have virtually spawned an industry of imitators. Dumble built the first Overdrive Special in 1972—following what is often described as a heavily modified Fender template, with particular consideration for preamp gain staging as well as build and component quality—and has continued to manufacture them more or less steadily in his workshop in Southern California by custom order only ever since. Mere mortals like us are likely to know the sound best from the playing of Robben Ford, Larry Carlton, Sonny Landreth, and a few other major names who ply their trade on a Dumble, but those who have been fortunate enough to plug into one in person report a range of ecstatic reactions, most of which fall into the "blown away" camp. For all the superlatives, the Overtone Special is a simple enough amp in use: dial in the Volume control to set your initial gain level, tweak distortion content further with the Overdrive Level and Ratio knob set EQ to taste, and the Master to put the output where you need it. Feel it moving you yet? Great! That'll be $40,000 please.

Amp and photo courtesy Bruce Sandler/Guitar Exchange

Roland GR-300 Guitar Synthesizer

Guitar synthesizers have become more elaborate and more versatile, but many players interested in the field will tell you that Roland's GR-300 was the first really competent, relatively affordable, commercially produced guitar synth to hit the market—and that it is still a cool-sounding unit by any standards. Where earlier units such as the GR-500 of 1978 and the GR-100 of 1980 had some difficulty tracking notes accurately, forcing the guitarist to heavily adapt his or her playing style, the GR-300's six individual voltage-controlled oscillators (VCOs, that is, one per string) provided much-improved control over the attack and decay of each note. Pitch control, vibrato, hexa-fuzz, envelope attack, and other functions provided excellent rudimentary analog synth sounds, many of which were accessible from the GR-300's floor-controller unit's five footswitches, and helped the synth's creative potential appeal to adventurous players such as Robert Fripp and Andy Summers. To top it off, the three controller options made by Japan's Fujigen Gaki factory, which made guitars for Ibanez and others, were all perfectly good instruments in their own right.

Boss Chorus Ensemble CE-1

The analog chorus was a ubiquitous effect in popular music by the early '80s, with countless makers churning out their own rendition of this modulation device, and the Boss Chorus Ensemble CE-1 is often considered the granddaddy of them all. Released early in 1976 before the signature slope-front Boss housing with rubber-tread switch became the standard, this big unit was housed in a hammer-finish box similar to some of parent-company Roland's effects, with plenty of room for two stomp switches and related control knobs. The buttons gave you On/Off and Vibrato/Chorus (a holdover from Uni-Vibe—based effects); further slide switches provided High/Low speed and power; and knobs controlled Level, Chorus Intensity, and Vibrato Depth, with stereo output when desired. While the unit is probably best known for its subtly warm and watery chorus sound, it also does a pretty nifty faux-Leslie when desired, and thanks to the onboard Level control, a rarity on a chorus pedal, it's easy to dial the correct amount of signal drive into the circuit when used in a chain with either clean or overdriven tones. By many estimations, the finest-sounding chorus pedal ever built.

Chapman Stick

Emmett Chapman invented his Stick in the early 1970s as the ideal vehicle for the "free hands" playing method the jazz guitarist had devised a few years before, which involves tapping the fretboard with the fingertips of both hands to sound strings rather than fretting and plucking in the conventional manner. The seminal design has ten strings and is best known in the playing of Tony Levin, longtime Peter Gabriel sideman. Its range runs the gamut from the bass' low to the guitar's high. Traditional tuning, if you can call it that, goes low E, A, D, G, C, although the bass strings progress *upward*—that is, the reverse of those on a standard bass guitar, from highest pitched string at the top to the lowest pitched at the middle of the tapboard; the treble strings run conventionally downward, tuned F#, B, E, A, D. As you can imagine, it takes the standard guitarist a little time to get the hang of the Stick—which is usually played with the left hand approaching the board from underneath and the right hand from above—but in no time you'll be blowing out thundering glissando bass runs and arpeggiated chord forms . . . or not. But you'll sure have fun trying.

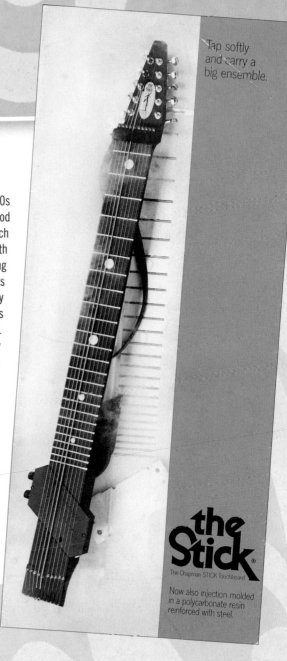

Tap softly and carry a big ensemble.

the Stick®

The Chapman STICK Touchboard

Now also injection molded in a polycarbonate resin reinforced with steel.

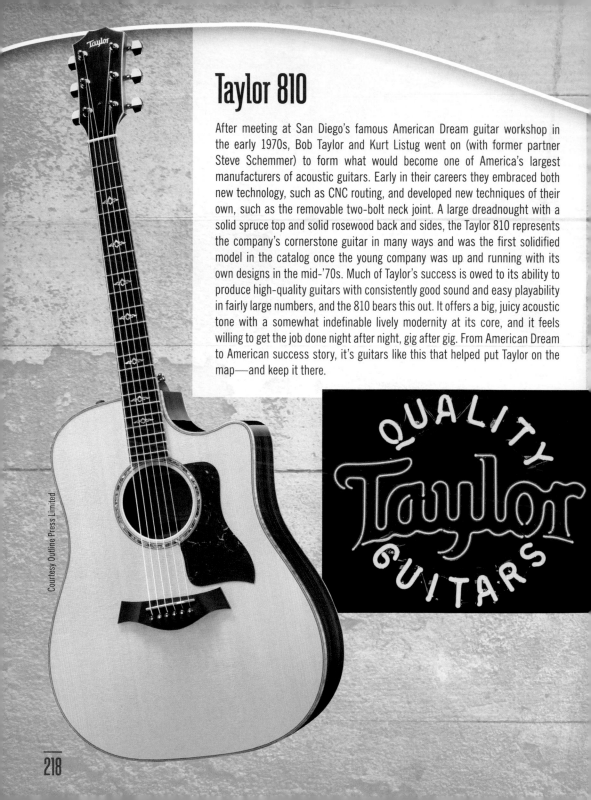

Taylor 810

After meeting at San Diego's famous American Dream guitar workshop in the early 1970s, Bob Taylor and Kurt Listug went on (with former partner Steve Schemmer) to form what would become one of America's largest manufacturers of acoustic guitars. Early in their careers they embraced both new technology, such as CNC routing, and developed new techniques of their own, such as the removable two-bolt neck joint. A large dreadnought with a solid spruce top and solid rosewood back and sides, the Taylor 810 represents the company's cornerstone guitar in many ways and was the first solidified model in the catalog once the young company was up and running with its own designs in the mid-'70s. Much of Taylor's success is owed to its ability to produce high-quality guitars with consistently good sound and easy playability in fairly large numbers, and the 810 bears this out. It offers a big, juicy acoustic tone with a somewhat indefinable lively modernity at its core, and it feels willing to get the job done night after night, gig after gig. From American Dream to American success story, it's guitars like this that helped put Taylor on the map—and keep it there.

Courtesy Outline Press Limited

Contreras Carlevaro

The world of the classical guitar might seem staid, conservative, and, well, classical, yet several adventurous builders have made strides to advance the art form, occasionally through radical design work. Spanish maker Manuel Contreras was among the most respected of such makers and, before his death in 1994, developed several revolutionary techniques for increasing the volume of the instrument, as well as other improvements. The Carlevaro, first built for Uruguayan guitarist Abel Carlevaro in 1983, is curved only on the treble side of the waist and is built with a second "floating" back that resonates in sympathy with the guitar's soundboard while also preventing the player's contact with the back from dampening the top's vibrations. The result is a deep, bold, and surprisingly loud classical guitar with excellent clarity and note definition. After Contreras' death, his work was carried on by his son, Pablo, who changed his name to Manuel II and has maintained the family tradition for experimentation and innovation.

PRS Custom 22

As a young hopeful, Paul Reed Smith might have landed his first major endorsee, Carlos Santana, largely through sheer tenacity. But he made his name in the guitar market with unfettered skill, impressive attention to detail, and a drive for consistency and unfailingly high standards at a time when U.S. guitar manufacturing was well into perhaps its worst decline ever. For his hard work, Smith was rewarded in the late '80s or so by becoming the first new American maker to genuinely stand alongside the likes of Fender and Gibson—and even to outgun them in the quality stakes, in the eyes (and hands . . . and ears. . .) of many players. Strap on one of

his flagship models like this Custom 22, and you quickly discern its confidence as well as its stylistic versatility. In creating a Gibson-Fender hybrid of sorts—25-inch scale, set-neck mahogany construction with figured maple top, updated Strat-style vibrato, humbuckers with useful coil-split switching—Smith landed upon a format that really could do a little of anything, and touring guitarists latched on by the boatload. Great-playing, great-looking, great-sounding, and with a vibrato that "won't go out of tune"—as originally requested by Santana himself—PRS guitars represent an achievement not to be dismissed.

Peavey Classic 30

Rarely (if ever) considered as romantic or as lust-worthy as the classic American amp manufacturers that made their names in the guitar world of the 1950s and '60s, Peavey has nevertheless been a solid, dependable supplier for several decades—and one that has filled the needs of myriad working guitarists. Every player should plug into a humble Classic 30 at least once in his or her lifetime and take it for a spin, not simply because it has been proven to be the only combo needed by countless hard-gigging players, but simply because these ubiquitous beasts can really sound pretty darn good. Four EL84s and a traditional Treble-Middle-Bass tone stack will take the Classic 30 into Vox territory when desired, but somehow there's also something inherently American about this amp, and with its reverb circuit (not the lushest, but functional), footswitchable clean and lead channels, and boost control, there's surprising versatility on tap, too. Hard to sneeze at for something in the $300–$400 range on the used market.

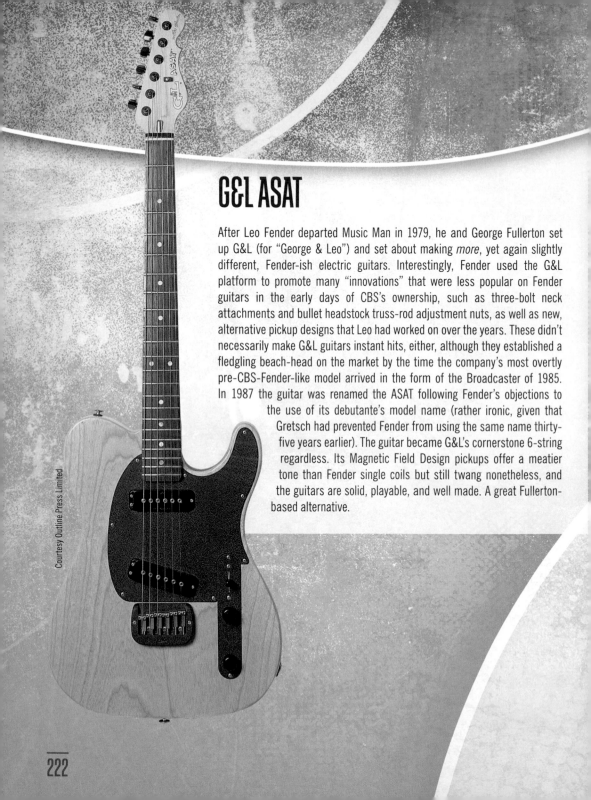

G&L ASAT

After Leo Fender departed Music Man in 1979, he and George Fullerton set up G&L (for "George & Leo") and set about making *more*, yet again slightly different, Fender-ish electric guitars. Interestingly, Fender used the G&L platform to promote many "innovations" that were less popular on Fender guitars in the early days of CBS's ownership, such as three-bolt neck attachments and bullet headstock truss-rod adjustment nuts, as well as new, alternative pickup designs that Leo had worked on over the years. These didn't necessarily make G&L guitars instant hits, either, although they established a fledgling beach-head on the market by the time the company's most overtly pre-CBS-Fender-like model arrived in the form of the Broadcaster of 1985. In 1987 the guitar was renamed the ASAT following Fender's objections to the use of its debutante's model name (rather ironic, given that Gretsch had prevented Fender from using the same name thirty-five years earlier). The guitar became G&L's cornerstone 6-string regardless. Its Magnetic Field Design pickups offer a meatier tone than Fender single coils but still twang nonetheless, and the guitars are solid, playable, and well made. A great Fullerton-based alternative.

Tom Anderson T Classic

The Tom Anderson guitar line has expanded to encompass several models based on existing classics, as well as a handful of entirely original designs, but the company probably best forged its reputation building updates of the solidbody that started it all in the first place. Anderson's T Classic has been the first choice of many great artists who dig the vibe and tone of Fender's seminal slab but seek a little more elegance of feel and refinement of voice. Using a tight-fitting neck joint and carefully selected woods, Anderson claims to get as much resonance and sustain out of a bolt-neck guitar as any set-neck maker can achieve with glue. An outstanding attention to detail also results in a neck that feels sleeker and speedier than you're likely to find on many original vintage Teles. In-house pickups add more punch and breadth, while chopping down the traditional bridge plate and mounting the pickup straight into the wood offer a slightly rounder tone from that setting with less of the characteristically nasal "honk." It might not be for the absolute purist, perhaps, but plenty of top-notch Nashville studio aces have chosen to do their thing with Anderson's variation on the theme, and this elegant T-style is one sweet, smooth ride for sure.

Mid-1980s Roland JC-120 Jazz Chorus

In the late '60s, proponents proclaimed solid-state amplification "the technology of the future," and according to the preferences of many guitarists, they were entirely correct. Which is to say, for most who took to solid state, it wouldn't prove the technology of choice until *several years* into the future, namely, when the Roland JC-120 Jazz Chorus finally arrived in the early 1980s. This big, powerful, clean guitar combo with plenty of tricks up its sleeve would prove one of the few viable solid-state options amid a world that still preferred tube technology, and it ended up on stage and in studio behind Andy Summers of the Police, Bob Mould of Hüsker Dü and Sugar, Kevin Shields of My Bloody Valentine, Robert Fripp and Adrian Belew of King Crimson, and many other major players. The stellar, burnished-chrome, clean tones are the JC-120's primary draw, but plenty of guitarists make great use of the true-stereo chorus, tremolo, and pseudo-rotary effects, too. The amp's built-in distortion effect is nothing to write home about, but a lot of the pedalheads who tend to use JC-120s craft their own overdrive tones from effects pedals, so most ignore this shortcoming.

Amp and photo courtesy Matte Henderson

1986 Trainwreck Express

If you just aren't a Dumble dude, chances are you go silly for a Trainwreck. The late Ken Fischer's rather rustic, wood-cabbed creations form the other branch of the dual-forked best-of-the-best branch in the family tree of rarified boutique tube amps. Fischer concocted the Express for guitarists who wanted something in the Marshall vein but with more gain, improved dynamics, and exponentially more refined touch sensitivity. The circuit cops little from the Marshall Plexi other than the basic topology of the three-knob tone stack, but the ensuing crunch-to-wail that hits the unsuspecting quartet of EL34s yields an instant Brit-rock-on-steroids tone that, with perhaps a little nudging in the right direction, feels like it's about ready to play itself. A humble creator, Fischer was one of relatively few amp makers whose talents truly justified the "guru" tag that was often applied to him. His work has graced the performances of guitar stars such as Mark Knopfler and Brad Paisley, as well as others lucky enough to access these rare beasts. More's the shame this gentleman didn't stick around long enough to build a few for the rest of us.

Lowden O-25

One of the most respected names in European flat-tops, Lowden has forged a reputation for both quality and originality and earned some major artist endorsements in the process, including fingerstyle wizard Pierre Bensusan and singer/songwriter David Gray. George Lowden started making guitars in Northern Ireland in the mid-'70s and, less than a decade later, was turning out more than 200 instruments a year with help from a small (but soon expanding) staff. The O model (for "Original Series Jumbo") is his flagship, with a grand size and a body style that only slightly resembles Gibson's vintage Super Jumbo and more than enough originality to mark it as clearly something else. Even through his rapidly escalating popularity, Lowden eschewed CNC work for handcrafting and insisted on ancient luthier techniques such as hand-split braces, rather than sawn, for their supposedly superior tone. Whatever magic is behind it, this O-25's balanced tone and muscular voice indicate Lowden has been doing something right.

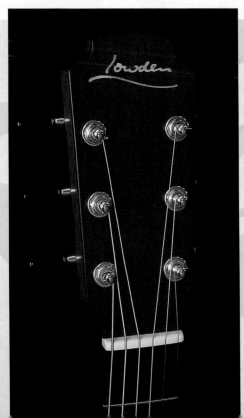

Franklin OM

Nick Kukich named his Franklin guitars for the Michigan town where he started his work, before moving to Sandpoint, Idaho, then Seattle, Washington, then Portland, Oregon, and finally to a small river town in mid-Missouri. Sometimes built by Kukich alone, sometimes by a team of luthiers that has included different people over the years (Steve Anderson, to name one), Franklin guitars are known for their superb tone and consistently high quality. The Franklin OM roughly follows the line of Martin's OM model and offers the strong, clear voice that these guitars are known for. Tasteful touches such as a marquetry back stripe and herringbone purfling dress it up, though Franklin's OM is known as a tone machine first and foremost and has been played by John Renbourn, among others. Guitarist Stefan Grossman's interest in a jumbo-sized guitar that Kukich had designed after an old Prairie State guitar years ago led to the release of a jumbo model that is another Franklin cornerstone, a belter of a music maker that has also made waves in the flat-top community.

Chandler Tube Driver

Rather esoteric and far less often seen than an Ibanez Tube Screamer or a Fulltone Full-Drive 2, the Tube Driver—in whatever incarnation—is nevertheless a modern classic of the overdrive world. The Tube Driver was invented by electronics hobbyist and Hammond organ fanatic Brent Butler in the mid-1970s after he conscripted the innards of his dad's old Westinghouse tube stereo to create a DIY Leslie overdrive sound. After selling a few handmade units to guitarist pals and then producing them by custom order under the Butronics name, Butler eventually marketed the more common—and somewhat evolved—Chandler Tube Driver from 1985 to 1989, the pedal that gained fame for its use by Texas guitarist Eric Johnson. Carrying a single 12AX7 dual-triode preamp tube and controls for Tube Drive, Hi and Lo EQ, and Out Level, the Tube Driver is a fast track to juicy tube-amp overdrive without necessarily cranking said tube amp into the stratosphere. Although when you do, the whole shebang sounds even better.

Boss Super Feedbacker & Distortion DF-2

Talk about a one-stop noise machine in a box! The Boss Super Feedbacker & Distortion, or DF-2, was released in 1984 by way of, well, giving the guitarist heavy distortion and feedback from a single box. High-gain, hard-clipping distortion offers a heavy crunch factor and good body, determined via the Level, Tone, and Distortion knobs. Hit a note and step on this pedal's switch a second time and hold it, and the DF-2 sustains the signal into harmonic feedback for as long as you hold down the pedal. How groovy is that? The fourth knob, labeled Feedback Over Tone, determines the overtone at which the feedback occurs, so you can even fine-tune the sound on the fly, if you're quick and clever. All in all, if feedback is your game, this is a nifty way of achieving it, even at less-than-mind-melting volumes. The only downside might be that you don't get a natural decay of the feedbacked note—it ends the moment you lift your toe from the pedal. Still, we can't have it all.

Mesa/Boogie V-Twin

Looking to nail that cascading-gain Mesa/Boogie preamp tone in an entirely different amplifier? The most obvious way to get it might be to inject the Mesa/Boogie V-Twin pedal. Developed by the famous California amp company in the early 1990s, this pedal carries two 12AX7 preamp tubes and compacts the guts of the archetypal preamp of the Boogie Mark series. Dual footswitches access crunch and high-gain lead modes, and there are control knobs for Gain, Master, Bass, Mid, Treble, and Presence. The entire thing is housed in the rugged chromed tread-plate that fronts many of the later Mesa Rectifier Series amplifiers. Will your Epiphone Valve Junior sound exactly like a Boogie Mark IIB with this chunky steel pedal in front of it? Well, probably not, but you will induce no end of succulent, sizzly, saturated overdrive, most likely experience near-endless singing sustain, and hopefully walk away with a big smile on your face regardless. Often that is more than enough.

Late-1980s Ernie Ball Silhouette

Leo Fender started the company that would become Music Man with two former Fender employees in 1971 and introduced a handful of Fender-ish electric guitars in the mid-'70s once his noncompete clause with CBS had expired. The most successful Music Man design, however, arrived nearly a decade after Leo had moved on to found G&L and after Ernie Ball had bought up the company. The Silhouette was one of the first U.S.-made, Fender-ish, non-Fender guitars to gain wide acceptance among players and critics alike, and Keith Richards' uptake didn't hurt the instrument's status much, either. Clearly very Strat-like in build and tone, with a bolt-on maple neck, three single-coil pickups (one or two humbuckers optional), and a solid alder body with offset double cutaways, the Silhouette is also more compact than the seminal Fender—despite sharing its 25.5-inch scale length—and has an ergonomic feel that plenty of players still dig.

1990s Olson SJ

Minnesota-based James Olson was near the front of a major wave of small-shop acoustic guitar makers when he hit the scene in 1977, and his work remains among the most respected, the choice of James Taylor, Leo Kottke, Phil Keaggy, and others. The SJ, for "Small Jumbo" (seemingly a contradiction in terms, but the shape bears it out), is his signature model of sorts. About the size of a Martin 000, but with the overtly rounded bouts of Gibson's Super Jumbo, this model is popular with contemporary fingerstyle players in particular. Whether strummed or picked, Olson's consummate skill shines through in the broad, earthy tones and impressive projection of this medium-bodied flat-top. Although he also uses good German, Adirondack, and Sitka spruce for his tops, Olson is fond of crafting soundboards from cedar, which offers a consistently rich and more immediately "broken in" sound. He frequently features Brazilian rosewood, too, when available, not only for backs and sides, but also for binding, decorative trim, and headstock facings. Whatever goes into their aesthetics, whether simple workhorses or elaborate showpieces, Olson's flat-tops remain uncompromisingly sweet performers.

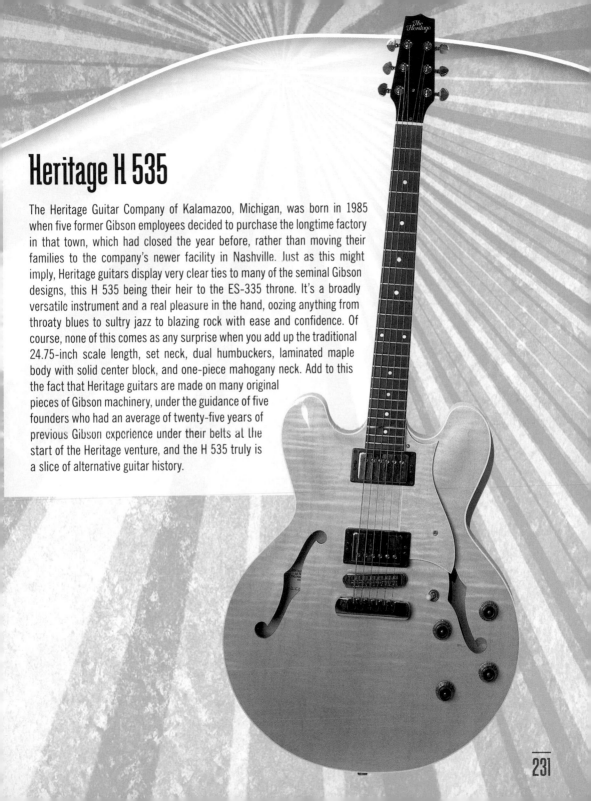

Heritage H 535

The Heritage Guitar Company of Kalamazoo, Michigan, was born in 1985 when five former Gibson employees decided to purchase the longtime factory in that town, which had closed the year before, rather than moving their families to the company's newer facility in Nashville. Just as this might imply, Heritage guitars display very clear ties to many of the seminal Gibson designs, this H 535 being their heir to the ES-335 throne. It's a broadly versatile instrument and a real pleasure in the hand, oozing anything from throaty blues to sultry jazz to blazing rock with ease and confidence. Of course, none of this comes as any surprise when you add up the traditional 24.75-inch scale length, set neck, dual humbuckers, laminated maple body with solid center block, and one-piece mahogany neck. Add to this the fact that Heritage guitars are made on many original pieces of Gibson machinery, under the guidance of five founders who had an average of twenty-five years of previous Gibson experience under their belts at the start of the Heritage venture, and the H 535 truly is a slice of alternative guitar history.

1990 Soldano Super Lead Overdrive SLO-100

Soldano has been making a big noise in high-gain circles ever since Michael J. Soldano released his first Super Lead Overdrive (SLO-100) in 1987. Eric Clapton, Mark Knopfler, George Lynch, Gary Moore, Vivian Campbell, Lou Reed, Joe Satriani, and many others have been drawn to the fold. Even if some have moved on, the SLO-100 has remained a modern classic and the first choice of many professional players seeking wailing lead tones and chunky, thick body. The easiest way to describe the tone and feel of the SLO is, perhaps, to think Mesa/Boogie crossed with Marshall crossed with Fender. The output stage comprises a quartet of 6L6GCs, although the EQ stage perhaps leans more British than American, while the clean and lead tones fall somewhere in between. Regardless, this is very much a font of the "modern California rock sound," a tone machine that is unabashedly contemporary rather than retro-leaning. For singing sustain, meaty low-end *woomph*, and a voice as big as the Sierra Mountains, you still can't go wrong with the mighty SLO.

Amp courtesy Keith Welchel/photos Robin Lane

Fender Vibro-King

After some dark years and the company's near implosion in the early to mid-'80s, Fender was a little slow getting its amp line back on track while focusing their efforts on bringing the guitars back up to scratch. But when it did get some quality tube amps up and running in 1993, a new set of Custom Amp Shop models led the charge, with the Vibro-King garnering especially high acclaim. Aesthetically, the Vibro-King—like its partner, the Tone-Master—looked to the blonde Tolex amps of the early '60s with richly contrasting oxblood grille cloth. The preamp and output stages follow the basic brown, blonde, and black-face topologies too, but these are bookended by the drippingly luscious retro effects of a full three-knob Fender Reverb Unit bolted into the front end, with tube-powered, bias-modulating vibrato adding its deep throb to the back end. As such, this sweet 50-watter is very much the "vintage Fender that never was" and offers a great encapsulation of the company's trademark sound, which makes it a delightfully versatile platform for a wide range of musical styles.

1990 Matchless DC30

After teaming up in California in the late 1980s, Mark Sampson and Rick Perrotta, following the latter's desire to "build an AC30 that wouldn't break," put their heads together to design and build the DC30, and a true modern classic was born. With one channel based loosely on the EF86 pentode preamp of the Vox AC15 (and earliest AC30s) and another based on the Top Boost channel of the AC30, the DC30 2x12 combo, HC30 head, and SC30 1x12 combo offer a useful range of British-toned voices. From the thick, meaty, and easily overdriven pentode to the chiming, glassy, blooming Top Boost tones, it's all here, but it's rendered as so much more through the overengineering, rigorous component quality and outstanding build standards of the Matchless chassis. Some players find these amps rather bright and cutting for solo playing in the basement or home music room, but they are designed as professional performance tools, and up on stage or in the studio amid a full band mix, they display a marriage of harmonic richness and never-gonna'-lose-you cutting power that few amps can, well, match.

Early-1990s Peavey 5150

Ever wonder what it feels like to tap the girth, harmonic saturation, and singing sustain employed by leading shred-rockers of the 1990s and harness it to your own semidestructive purposes? Plug into a Peavey 5150 and find out. This amp was designed by Peavey in close cooperation with Edward Van Halen in the early '90s in an effort to put the rock virtuoso's signature "cranked and Variac'd" Marshall Plexi tone into a contemporary head with footswitchable clean and lead channels. Many EVH-tone chasers consider the effort a sterling success, and it has been a first choice of many shred heads in the two decades since it came out. Most raves fall on the Lead Channel, which is a singing, wailing, raging good time for any player who likes to dabble in fleet-fingered heavy rock stylings, with a harmonic bloom and juicy harmonic saturation that can make it feel even bigger than its 120-watt rating. The Rhythm Channel isn't to be discounted, either, and yields gutsy chunk when rolled up just beyond the purely clean zone. Van Halen took his endorsement elsewhere in 2004 (and now heads his own 5150 brand, having retained the rights to that name), at which point Peavey morphed the amp into the 6505 model.

235

1991 Charvel Surfcaster

Charvel started out in the 1970s offering the parts to build complete guitars and modify existing instruments. The Surfcaster, which debuted in 1991, is one of the company's more distinctive non-shred-oriented guitars, treading a different path entirely from the pointy headstocks that traditionally wear the brand. Two alnico-magnet lipstick-tube pickups, à la many Danelectro and Silvertone models, present a sparkling-clean jangle, while the routed semi-hollow ash body with laminated maple top lends a little more depth and resonance to the brew than we are used to hearing from vintage guitars that carried these pickups. While the whole shebang just begs you to go blast out some punk-infused surf twang, this Surfcaster also excels at snarly garage rock and jangly indie styles, and it can even do convincing country in a pinch. All that, and it truly was at the forefront of a large and slowly cresting retro-design wave that still hasn't broken.

Courtesy Outline Press Limited

Steve Vai. Mick Hutson/Redferns/Getty Images

1990s Ibanez JEM7

Shredder extraordinaire Steve Vai collaborated with Ibanez to create the new JEM signature model, and this guitar and its offshoots have remained among the most popular and successful high-performance rock axes ever since. If you've never played a "super strat" of this caliber, it's quite an experience—although a high-gain amp and the appropriate playing style help make it the real deal. The JEM is all about the low action, fast neck, powerful tone, and subterranean whammy capabilities required by today's top shredders, and you might be surprised what fun it is to kick these über-playable elements into overdrive, even if you're usually one for moody, clean jazz inversions or country twang. Ram all that unfeasibly easy action and DiMarzio-powered goodness into enough sizzle and sustain at the amp end, and you'll soon get an inkling of how these players achieve the blinding speeds that are de rigueur for the genre, even if you aren't quite there yourself. When you're finished, you can carry it all home with the nifty hand grip cut right into the body.

Courtesy Outline Press Limited

D'Aquisto Solo

The literal and figurative heir to legendary archtop maker John D'Angelico, James D'Aquisto apprenticed with the New York luthier for several years before purchasing the workshop upon D'Angelico's death in 1964 and beginning his own career as master builder by finishing ten D'Angelicos that had been left in states of partial completion. After his early, unsurprisingly D'Angelico-inspired beginnings, however, D'Aquisto developed the art form considerably, virtually redrawing the blueprint of the archtop acoustic guitar in regard to bracing, sound-hole structure, bridge construction, and several other features before passing away in 1995. The Solo is probably most representative of these advances in his later years. With no superfluous adornments and an absolute minimum of metal parts, it is designed to be one unified, resonating, sound-enhancing unit, and it rewards the effort richly when played. From its elliptical sound holes to its ingeniously simple bridge (carved from a single block of ebony, with slot-in saddle piece) to its integral minimalistic pickguard, it displays the genius of a maker who was willing to turn from tradition and reinvent the form from scratch.

Smallman Classical

Working for most of his career in the small town of Glen Innes deep in the Australian bush, Greg Smallman has pioneered some of the most significant innovations of the modern classical guitar and, in the process, has earned the endorsements of concert artists such as John Williams, David Tannenbaum, Carlos Bonell, Thibault Cauvin, and several others. By extrapolating what he remembered of building model balsawood-and-paper airplanes as a boy—namely the way the fine latticework frame supported the outer shell of the aircraft—Smallman developed an extremely light yet incredibly strong latticework bracing system made from carbon fiber, which allows a thinner and superbly resonant soundboard to be used atop the guitar's body. As a result, this Smallman classical guitar is unabashedly lively and detailed, with a sonic girth that belies its otherwise rather traditional size and shape. Now based in Esperance in Western Australia, Greg Smallman and his sons, Damon and Kym, continue to craft some of the most desirable classical guitars available today.

Courtesy Outline Press Limited

Fender Prosonic

Another product of the Custom Amp Shop, which brought us the Vibro-King a couple years before, the Prosonic was a creative and extremely versatile contemporary tube amp design from Fender that never quite achieved the success it was due. Cosmetics gave a nod to classic '60s combos but took it all a step or two toward leftfield with seafoam green and lizard-skin Tolex options. Inside the chassis is where it all took shape, though, with a bold and versatile circuit that should have been the answer to many a modern guitarist's dreams. Channel switching provides the option of classic cleans or adaptable cascading-gain lead tones, both of which can be tilted from Fender to Vox according to your setting of the bias switch. Generating from 30 to 50 watts from a pair of 5881 output tubes (6L6 equivalents) according to Class A or Class AB setting, the Prosonic roars with a thick, meaty lead voice that belies its compact 2x10 cabinet. Despite its deletion from the line in 2001 after a run of just six years, the Prosonic remains a desirable find with players in the know.

Dunlop Rotovibe

After establishing itself mainly in guitar accessories—capos, picks, slides—the Jim Dunlop company has carved out an extremely successful niche in buying up the rights to the names of vintage pedals and marketing their own reissues of each. While the company's current-issue Fuzz Face and Cry Baby Wah Wah (including several variations of each) certainly fall into this category, the Rotovibe does not. Instead, this wah-style pedal contains a circuit intended to emulate a rotating speaker effect, something akin to the original Univox Uni-Vibe, and offers selectable chorus and vibrato effects, with on-the-fly speed control via the unit's rocker treadle. The Rotovibe's strength lies, perhaps, in its relative subtlety, at least compared to heavy-handed modulation effects such as flanging. Within a distorted guitar tone, as it is so often used by the likes of Zakk Wylde, Jack White, Jerry Cantrell, and others, the pedal adds a chewy, dynamic swirl to the tone rather than totally enveloping it.

Fender Custom Shop
1956 Heavy Relic Stratocaster

Having unveiled its first Vintage Reissue Stratocaster and Telecaster back in 1982, Fender caught up in the mid-'90s with the fact that many players liked to have these guitars pre-abused. Some of the first distressed guitars were allegedly made for Keith Richards, who said he'd feel better playing them on tour if they had some wear on them, but the official Custom Shop Relic series was born soon after and evolved into a full-time machine lineup with guitars in three different stages of wear. This 1956 Heavy Relic Stratocaster is an example of the highest aging level of the range, and its siblings the Closet Classic and NOS models were each respectively less pre-worn. Take this cosmetically distressed reissue in hand, and you quickly see why the range proved so popular. There is something instantly welcoming—so easily "bond-with-able"—about these relic-finished Fenders. And the Custom Shop's excellent work with the rest of the build makes them supremely playable and superbly toneful instruments to boot. For vibe, looks, mojo, and that extra "is that *really* a . . . ?" factor, these are pretty tough to beat.

Courtesy Fender Musical Instruments Corporation

Crowther Hot Cake

New Zealand drummer-turned-effects builder Paul Crowther strayed from his throne behind the skins for the band Split Enz for a time in the late '70s to tinker with electronics, and the eventual result became one of the most beloved Tube Screamer alternatives ever produced. The Hot Cake overdrive is a rugged, compact unit with controls for Gain, Level, and Presence and is adored for its natural, tubey-sounding tone. Like many other overdrives, this one sounds best into a good tube amp set at the edge of breakup, and does go into thrashy gain levels, but will get a little hotter than some when cranked. Since Crowther produced these essentially as a one-man shop for a time, Hot Cakes are semi-rare pedals, virtually the stuff of myth and legend in some corners, although they have become more plentiful in recent years. The choice of guitarists in the Melvins, Sonic Youth, Oasis, and Pavement, it's definitely one for the annals of overdrive.

Fulltone Full-Drive 2

One of the foremost names in the boutique pedal business, and one of the early successes, Fulltone was founded by Mike Fuller in 1994, shortly after he won *Guitar Player* magazine's "Ultimate Guitarist" competition, a cutting contest giving exposure to relatively unknown local and regional artists. A fuzz pedal was among Fuller's first offerings, but the Full-Drive 2 soon became the company's cornerstone. Derived from the popular Tube Screamer circuit, the Full-Drive 2 was given more gain, fatter lows, and far broader drive and tone ranges than the original Ibanez standard. In addition, the pedal includes a bonus channel with a Boost switch to help you push your solo into overdrive above and beyond your preset rhythm tone, a real boon for many gigging guitarists. These features, and the pedal's punchy, asymmetrical overdrive tone, helped make it something close to a new standard in the world of OD pedals, and the Full-Drive 2 has found its way onto several professional pedalboards as a result.

Marshall ShredMaster

ShredMaster! What more could a thrash-metal wannabe ask for in a distortion pedal? Well, maybe a lot more gain, and some gut-busting low-end thump. In fact, the ShredMaster, introduced as part of a range of U.K.-made Marshall pedals in chunky black steel enclosures in the early 1990s, isn't entirely up to shred, death-, black- or nü-metal tones by contemporary standards, but it offers an approximation of Marshall-stack classic-metal tone in analog pedal form. Which, for many players, is a great thing. The ShredMaster earned iconic status at the hands—or, rather, feet—of Radiohead guitarist Jonny Greenwood, primarily on the band's breakthrough hit "Creep," where it kicks in for that guitar-check *gchkkk, gchkkk* sound before the heavy power-chord romp in the chorus then in said power-chord romp itself, but he has used it on plenty of other tracks as well. With a three-knob Tone selection in addition to its Gain and Volume controls, it allows you to craft your EQ to taste but always seems to excel at a thumpy scooped-mids sound, which is perhaps its forte.

Mid-1990s Parker Fly Artist

When it hit the scene in the mid-1990s, Ken Parker's Fly Artist model exhibited more innovation and originality than all but a very few guitars that had gone before, and this without looking *all* that wildly different from our traditional template of the "electric guitar." The Fly Artist is made from a body core of solid carved spruce and a neck core of solid poplar, both encased in a super-rigid glass and carbon fiber epoxy outer shell, which also forms the fingerboard. Two DiMarzio humbuckers provide traditional electric guitar tones while piezo pickups built into the bridge saddles produce acoustic-like tones, which can be used independently or blended with the magnetic pickups. Also, Parker's clever flat-spring vibrato provides a smooth, consistent action and has an adjustment wheel to set the tension as you like it. Put it all together, and it's an extremely light yet full and rich-sounding electric with an extremely broad sonic palette and a smooth, easy-playing feel. Impressive as it is, the Fly Artist never blasted completely into the mainstream, yet it has become a favorite of many adventurous players.

Courtesy Outline Press Limited

Klon Centaur

Ah, the fabled Klon Centaur, known to many as the mysterious box of tone tricks that simply makes your guitar and amp sound better, without really ever fully defining its intentions. Bill Finnegan and the Klon company's one and only product, the Centaur hit the scene around 1994 and has maintained its air of enigma ever since by slathering the circuit within the pedal in thick epoxy (not that the effort has prevented all determined copyists). Although it never really says so, the Centaur, with its simple Gain, Treble, and Output controls, is essentially a low-gain overdrive pedal designed to make an already good-sounding tube amp sound better. Used right, it does so in spades and becomes one of those virtually transparent yet addictive effects that is extremely hard to switch off. Juicier overtones, larger apparent sonic size, greater dynamics, improved responsiveness—all are yours when you step on that Klon. Of course, they come at a price, too: used examples tend to sell in the $800 to $900 range, and the original design ceased production late in 2009.

Roger Mayer Vision Wah

Although he was around at the birth of the pedal boom to hand-wire pedals for Jimi Hendrix and others on the London music scene of the late 1960s, Roger Mayer has nevertheless remained one of the more adventurous pedal makers working today, and he seems to continually strive to improve not only his own designs, but also the format of the effects pedal in general. Mayer's Vision Wah is an effort to redraw the blueprint by stripping away virtually everything involved in the construction of the vintage rendition of the wah—its more problematic aspects in particular—and redesigning it with cutting-edge materials and technology. The Vison Wah's F1 carbon-fiber composite rocker pedal sits at a lower profile, making the entire unit more comfortable and natural to play, and instead of a potentiometer, the effect is activated by a noncontact electronic position sensor. Four pushbuttons offer sixteen frequency range combinations, and there are controls for Volume and Blend, as well as for Wah Sweep and Rocker Feel. How does it sound? "Bloody great," as Roger might put it.

Froggy Bottom H12

Michael Millard began building Froggy Bottom guitars in New York City in 1970, while still the shop foreman for Gurian Guitars, and moved his operation to New Hampshire before settling in Vermont in 1985. Now boasting a master finisher and four builders, including partner Andy Mueller, Froggy Bottom continues to make its flat-top acoustic guitars entirely by hand, using traditional techniques. Some 100 to 120 guitars are made each year, entirely to custom order, in three grades of trim that include Standard, Deluxe, and Limited. While the range includes a variety of body sizes, this H12 is very much at the core of the Froggy Bottom style. A traditional fingerstyle acoustic, it has a 000-sized "H" body with a twelfth-fret neck joint for a surprisingly rich, luscious tone out of a rather diminutive guitar. The H12 offers a voice and feel that are instant proof of the care that has gone into its manufacture. Elegant touches such as multicolored wood marquetry, abalone inlays, and carefully wrought binding add elegance of appearance to the H12's sublime tone, and the abalone frog profile on the headstock marks it as a distinct creation in the flat-top world.

Courtesy Froggy Bottom Guitars

Bourgeois D-150

Dana Bourgeois set out to build guitars full time shortly after leaving college and worked with Martin, Gibson, and PRS before properly establishing Bourgeois Guitars. The Maine-based luthier is known for the fine craftsmanship and high-quality tonewoods used in his flat-tops, which have become the favorites of a select circle of Nashville virtuosi, consummate picker Bryan Sutton and bluegrass artist Ricky Skaggs among them. Bourgeois' use of prized Adirondack spruce and solid Brazilian rosewood back and sides in this D-150 dreadnought results in an unsurprisingly superlative tone: it presents the clarity and articulation needed for speedy flatpicked bluegrass runs, with a lush tone that is utterly enticing. The maker's skill obviously aids matters, too, with Bourgeois' particular techniques for hand-selecting tap-tested woods and carving his unique single-scalloped X bracing clearly helping matters. In 2000, Bourgeois joined forces with a group of business investors to form Pantheon Guitars, which now exclusively represents his instruments.

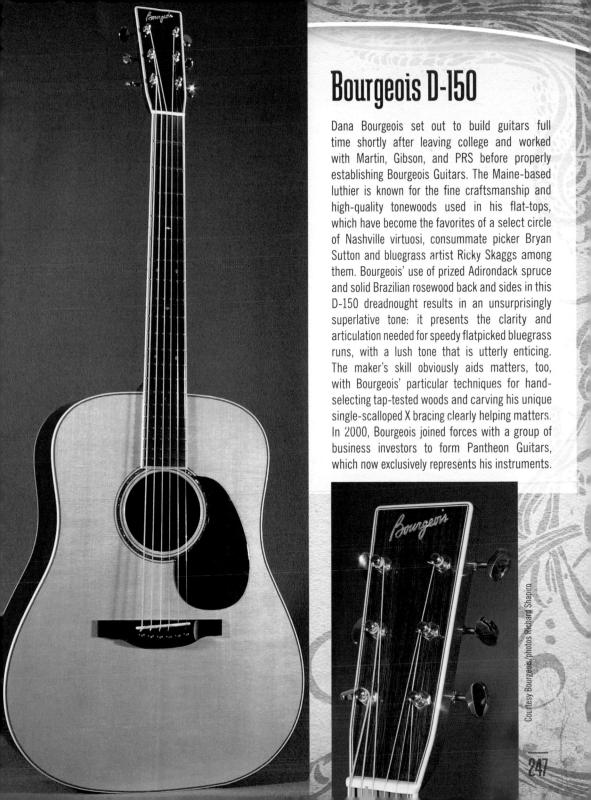

Santa Cruz H13

The H13 was one of the earliest models conceived by Santa Cruz Guitars founder Richard Hoover. First released back in 1978 and then reissued in 2006, the H13 sums up the beauty of Santa Cruz guitars et al while also carrying a few interesting design quirks. Not intended as the taunt to triskaidekaphobics that the model name might imply, the H13 (originally just model H) was Hoover's homage to the legendary Gibson Nick Lucas model of the 1920s, which at times was made with an odd 13th-fret neck joint. The slight repositioning of the guitar's bridge to deeper within the lower bout of the guitar that comes along with this neck joint gives the H13 a bounteous, blooming warmth for a relatively small-bodied flat-top. Although much of that might also come from the H13's unusually deep body (for its size, particularly, at a full $4\frac{13}{16}$ inches at the tail block), the use of scalloped and tapered X bracing, or simply the maker's acclaimed skills. Whatever the case, it's a fun guitar to play and a great example of what this California maker can do.

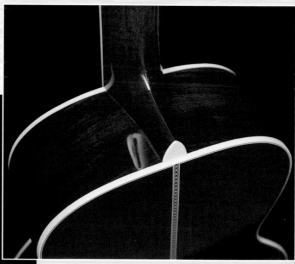

Ruck Classical

One of America's foremost classical guitar makers, Robert Ruck has evolved from the very traditional baby steps of his learning years in the mid-1960s to embrace innovation and originality in their broadest senses while still delivering guitars that are inherently classical. Although Ruck uses several modern tools in the early stages of his work, the completion and fine points of the instrument involve a very intuitive process and include a meditation-like "visualization" of the ultimate sound of the guitar through every step of its construction. The effort has clearly paid off, bringing artists such as Sharon Isbin, Celin and Pepe Romero, Carlos Barbosa-Lima, Manuel Barrueco, and several others to the Ruck fold and forcing the luthier to close his waiting list indefinitely due to high demand. The ongoing evolution of Ruck's building style includes the addition of acoustic ports in the body sides on both sides of the neck joint to present an accurate sonic dispersal to the performer and the occasional use of composite tops and backs made with two different wood types to enhance resonant characteristics.

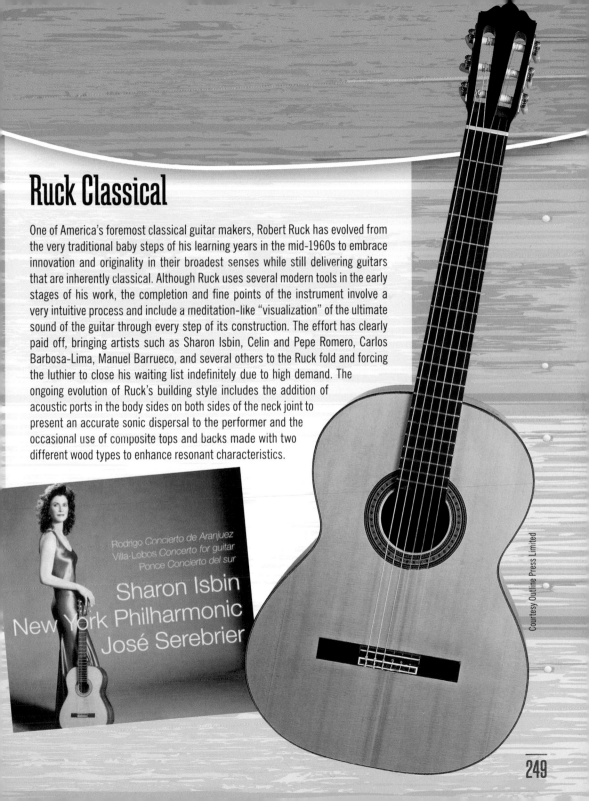

Rodrigo *Concierto de Aranjuez*
Villa-Lobos *Concerto for guitar*
Ponce *Concierto del sur*

Sharon Isbin
New York Philharmonic
José Serebrier

Courtesy Outline Press Limited

Suhr Classic

The consummate craftsman, John Suhr is perhaps best known for what we might call the "California hot rod"—a skillful update on an archetypal form otherwise known as the "superstrat," a guitar that has become a standard for the shredder and the West Coast studio ace alike. Suhr's Classic blends elements of the familiar offset double-cutaway styling and three-pickup versatility with several refinements. Top-notch pickups (often with a humbucker in the bridge position for easy rockin'), superbly crafted tonewoods, and advanced hardware components such as contemporary vibrato systems and efficient locking tuners all elevate the Classic way beyond the mere "updated S-type," making it the optimum performance tool for many demanding professional guitarists. Strap on this fine Suhr, and as much as it impresses with its power, versatility, and smooth playability, it also proves instructive in reminding us just how impressive Leo Fender's own template was in the first place and how a few clever updates can really make it soar.

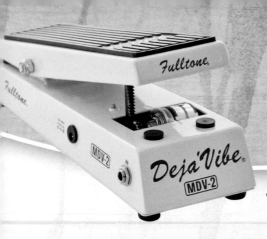

Fulltone Deja-Vibe 2

As with the company's popular dual-channel overdrive pedal, the Full-Drive 2, Fulltone rather quickly upgraded the circuit of its original Uni-Vibe impersonator of 1996 to the "2" model, and the results encapsulated, for many players, the finest easily available modern rendition of that addictive Jimi-certified sound. Rather than providing a separate effects circuit and speed-control pedal, as did Univox's original Uni-Vibe, the Deja-Vibe 2 incorporated the whole shebang into a single unit that looks like a standard wah-wah with a sidecar appended to it. Simple rotary controls for Intensity and Speed (the rocker treadle), and switches for Chorus/Vibrato and Vintage/Modern (the former a little warmer, the latter more hi-fi), tap everything a player needs to hear from a 'vibe—and keep it all simple for stage use. The best part, though, is that the light-cell circuit uses essentially the same technology as the original for a rich, juicy sound that takes you from bubbling, watery chorus to gentle pitch-wavering "true vibrato," and it does it well enough to have enticed original Uni-Vibe artist Robin Trower to use the Fulltone.

Hughes & Kettner Tube Rotosphere

On home turf in Germany, Hughes & Kettner has a long and good-standing reputation as a maker of solidly performing tube amplifiers. In the United States, the company is probably best known for its tube-loaded pedals, the Tube Rotosphere in particular. Released in the early 1990s (and upgraded to the MkII version in 2003), the Rotosphere doesn't aim to reproduce the Uni-Vibe sounds that so many other 'vibe pedals shoot for; rather, it guns straight for the Leslie-style rotary-speaker tones that the Uni-Vibe sought to put into compact form in the first place and does it successfully enough that several reputable artists have joined the party. With Drive, Output, and Rotor Balance knobs, stomp switches for Bypass, Breaker, and Slow/Fast (the latter the Leslie's two usable functions), and a switch for guitar or keyboard input level, it's a versatile unit that goes a long way toward emulating that infectious Doppler-fueled sound. Sonic features include independently whirling bass and treble "rotors," as well as that authentic gradual buildup and slowdown experienced from a Leslie cabinet between speed settings.

Reverend Slingshot

Before segueing exclusively into a line of quality import guitars around 2006 and 2007, Joe Naylor's Reverend company built guitars and basses at the brand's HQ in Michigan, putting nearly 5,000 solid, toneful, U.S.-made instruments onto the market at extremely good prices. The Slingshot was one of the more popular of a creative and colorful range, offering a blend of Fender twang and Gibson muscle in an extremely appealing package. Naylor's designs took some cues from Danelectro guitars of old, and he often used Formica tops and backs over semi-hollow constructions with solid-wood cores. But U.S.-made Reverends exude a quality that surpasses most Danos (cool as Danos are), with well-carved and extremely playable necks, solid hardware, and excellent pickups. This one offers enough snarl and attitude for most any breed of sub-metal rock you might want to aim it at—and Reverend's P-90s were always favorites of many players—while excelling at rockabilly and rowdier country styles. Yet it's nuanced enough for pop and classic blues, too. The brand's imported guitars continue a tradition of good, utilitarian instruments in clever designs, but there's something special about the U.S.-made Revs of old.

Budda Twinmaster

Amp designer Jeff Bober has been hailed as "the godfather of the low-watt revolution," and the Bober-designed Budda Twinmaster, first released in 1995, provides substantial grounds to back up this claim. Like so many dual-EL84 1x12 amps out there, the Twinmaster clearly springs from Vox's loins but nevertheless emerges with a tone all its own, which is simultaneously edgier and more contemporary while maintaining vintage-styled depth and purity at the same time. Controls are limited to Volume, Bass, and Treble, but the dual inputs—Normal Gain and High Gain— tap two distinct degrees of sizzle, the latter offering a fast track to that cranked tube tone in the more usable form that a smaller 15-watter often provides these days. Dig in, and the Twinmaster yields a chewy, sweetly saturated overdrive with an easy, touch-sensitive playability, yet it all cleans up beautifully when you wind down the guitar's Volume control. Show it a Telecaster for toothsome alt-country twang 'n' grind or a Les Paul for fat classic rock or grunge, and bring in any range of pedals to convert this plug-and-play beauty to a surprisingly versatile sonic foundation. Fun stuff, through and through.

Z. Vex Fuzz Factory

Minnesota-based effects manufacturer Z. Vex, founded by the estimable Zachary Vex, has several wild and woolly pedals on offer, but the Fuzz Factory is undoubtedly the flag-bearer of the line. Vex's effects business was born out of the former recording engineer's efforts to dig up a new income stream during a time of slowing studio business in the early '90s, and the Fuzz Factory was born out of his curiosity to discover what would happen if he built a fuzz with a control to govern virtually every governable aspect of an otherwise inherently simple fuzz circuit. As a result, this compact and groovy hand-painted box takes you from smooth and creamy, to thick and hairy, to thin and raspy, to battery-about-to-die spitty at the turn of a few knobs, and has proved to be a powerful and creative sound-shaper for more than a few guitarists. The nature of the beast is that it can take some fiddling to find your own favorite tones, but from classic fuzz shapes to radical noise sculptures, there's a whole lot of sound lurking in this thing.

Courtesy Z. Vex Effects

Carr Rambler

One of the first amps designed by Steve Carr of Pittsboro, North Carolina, the Carr Rambler aims to be sort of a "grown up Deluxe Reverb," achieving the lovably utilitarian tone of Fender's seminal 1x12 combo, but with a bigger low-end response, greater headroom, and overall a more *deluxe* interpretation of the Deluxe. Most who have played one would agree that it achieves all this and more. The Rambler's tonal splendor owes a lot to Carr's carefully tweaked, hand-wired, point-to-point circuit, but by using a pair of larger 6L6 output tubes in a cathode-biased circuit, he's able to give the combo a full 28 watts of output power (switchable to 14 in triode mode) while also attaining a strong hint of the Class A shimmer that the Vox format was better known for. Carr also gave his Rambler great-sounding tube reverb and tremolo circuits at a time when few boutique makers were offering these vintage standards, so this stout 1x12 combo really is an all-you-need solution for the gigging guitarist who likes an easy grab 'n' go package.

PRS McCarty

It's a comment on Paul Reed Smith's integrity that he would dabble with a formula that was already extremely successful and come out with a distinctive new voice and feel in the process—one familiarly "classic" yet simultaneously fresh. With consultation from Ted McCarty, Gibson president from 1950 to 1966 and co-designer of the Les Paul alongside the guitar's namesake, Smith tweaked his standard formula in several ways in order to produce a guitar that sounded more like the classic set-neck, dual-humbucker Gibson solidbody. The resultant McCarty model was an instant hit and has remained a PRS staple since its introduction in 1994. The McCarty, aided by a stonking deep-set neck joint and a more Les Paul–leaning construction overall, noticeably dispenses with PRS' trademark five-way switch and its resultant single-coil-like tonal options for a simple three-way toggle and thick, creamy humbucker tones. Adept at anything from contemporary jazz to wailing classic rock to rich, throaty rock solo excursions, the McCarty has made fans of several major players and established itself almost immediately as another PRS classic.

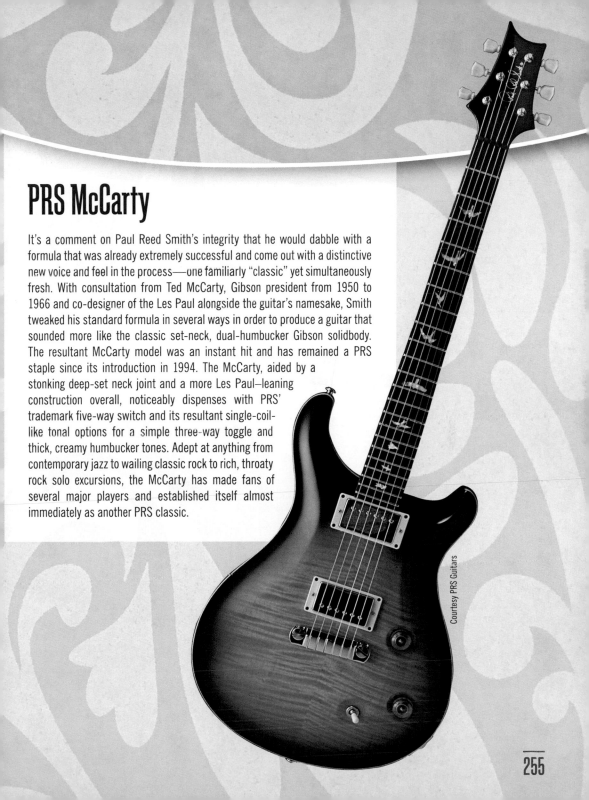

Courtesy PRS Guitars

Foxrox Captain Coconut

While still a young mixing console quality-control technician for Crest Audio in the mid-1980s, Foxrox founder Dave Fox had the opportunity to design Crest's reissue of the Dallas-Arbiter Fuzz Face, as Crest had absorbed Dallas Music Industries and the Fuzz Face name some years before. After founding his own pedal business in 1992, working initially out of his New Jersey home, Fox put his Hendrix love to further use by banding together the wondrous Captain Coconut pedal in cooperation with Mike Piera of Analog Man. Really a discrete analog multi-effects unit of sorts, the Captain Coconut combines octave, fuzz, and vibe effects (Foxrox's Octave, FuzzFoot, and Provibe) into one box, making it a fast track to that psychedelic Woodstock sound of 1969. With nine control knobs to access the individual effect parameters and three stomp switches, one for independent on/off of each segment, this truly is the analog Luddite's answer to the all-encompassing digital multi-effects floor unit and really could be the only pedal that plenty of guitarists need.

Lovetone Meatball

Like many a classic pedal—or modern classic, in this case—the Meatball was the product of close cooperation between one inspired guitarist and one dedicated engineer. In 1994, Vlad Naslas tasked Dan Coggins with building an envelope follower "with the most knobs ever," and after weeks of building and tweaking during Coggins' downtime during nightshifts as a BBC studio engineer, the Meatball was born. The pedal became the debutante release of the London-based Lovetone company, subsequently established by Naslas and Coggins to market their creations, which later included further extreme tone twisters such as the Wobulator tremolo and Doppelganger rotary/phaser effect. The Meatball has become the

Holy Grail for many true lovers of envelope followers/trigger filters (a.k.a. auto-wahs) though this pedal is really so much more. That complement of "most knobs ever" includes controls for Sensitivity, Attack, Decay, Colour, Intensity, and Blend. There are also four switches to access various modes, two controller-pedal inputs, and an effects loop. In addition to superbly P-Funky wah voices, more creative control settings can take the Meatball into genuine analog synth territory. Definitely a meal on its own.

Way Huge Swollen Pickle

Before closing shop in 1999 to work for digital amp modeling company Line 6, Jeorge Tripps earned enormous respect for his Way Huge pedal line, of which none was quite so beloved as the frog-green Swollen Pickle fuzz pedal. Described by Tripps as a "'70s-style fuzz that goes from mild crunch to Armageddon," this was a modern fuzz that attained some degree of collectibility before Jim Dunlop bought up the Way Huge name and lineup and reissued the MkII version, which in itself has helped original examples to retain a status of their own. In addition to the standard gain and output controls (dubbed Sustain and Loudness here), the Swollen Pickle carried a Filter knob that accessed a range of bandpass-filter tones, taking you from smooth to whacked-out and screechy (MkII reissues add knobs labeled Scoop and Crunch for further versatility). On the strength of this green meanie, and other favorites such as the Ringworm modulator and Red Llama overdrive, Way Huge pedals found their way onto the boards of players such as Matthew Sweet, Dean Wareham, and Joe Bonamassa.

Collings D2H

After dropping out of med school in the mid-1970s to pursue his love of guitars, Bill Collings moved from Ohio to Texas—first Houston, later Austin—and proceeded in the grueling work of establishing himself as a respected small-shop luthier. Some three and a half decades later he is all that and more. The flat-tops that were Collings' stock in trade early on are widely regarded as being among the world's finest, and the archtops, mandolins, ukuleles, and electrics into which he has expanded all have stellar reputations, too. Sticking with "plain old flat-tops," Collings builds a wide variety of styles, from OMs to 00s and 000s to the cute subparlor Baby short scale, but dreadnoughts like this D2H probably remain his best-known lines. By applying great artistry to classic ingredients such as spruce tops and East Indian rosewood backs and sides, Collings retains the rhythm-cannon projection and thundering bass that bring the dreadnought to many string-band settings while attaining a surprising clarity and treble cut, too, making it an extremely able soloing instrument. All in all, a prime incarnation of a seminal breed.

Andy Manson Magpie

Since building his first instrument in 1967—an odd teardrop-shaped guitar with a 30-inch scale, purely for his own use—Britain's Andy Manson has become one of the most respected acoustic guitar makers in Europe and even the world. Manson has built guitars, from traditional to avant-garde, for Jimmy Page and John Paul Jones of Led Zeppelin, Jethro Tull main man Ian Anderson, Andy Summers, Mike Oldfield, and many others. Working for most of his career in his shop in the county of Devon in England's West Country before a recent relocation to Portugal, Manson has never shied away from extreme custom-order instruments or radically experimental ventures. Compared to Page's triple-neck acoustic or Jones' triple-neck bass, though, the Magpie is a relatively conventional flat-top, though one that bears the hallmarks of Manson's unique creative personality—and has the superb playability and sublime tone to show for it. It's a timeless testament to the talents of a maker who really deserves far wider recognition.

Courtesy Andy Manson

Manzer Pikasso

Although our featured instrument here might imply a tendency toward the avant-garde, Canadian luthier Linda Manzer has forged a reputation for building more traditional yet high-end flat-top, archtop, and classical guitars and has plied her trade for several big-name artists. After apprenticeships with Canada's Jean Larrivée and New York's James D'Aquisto, Manzer set up shop on her own in 1978 and was soon recognized as one of North America's most skilled makers. The Pikasso, clearly named for its odd resemblance to one of Picasso's famed portraits, was custom-made for jazz star Pat Metheny at his simple request to make a guitar with as many strings as possible. The result—perhaps truly playable only by a virtuoso like Metheny himself—includes three different sets of harp-style drone strings as well as a traditional, fretted six-string neck, for a total of forty-two strings. As ungainly as this might seem, Manzer crafts it all into a work of modern art and instills elegance amid the potentially awkward plethora of strings, bridges, and tuners.

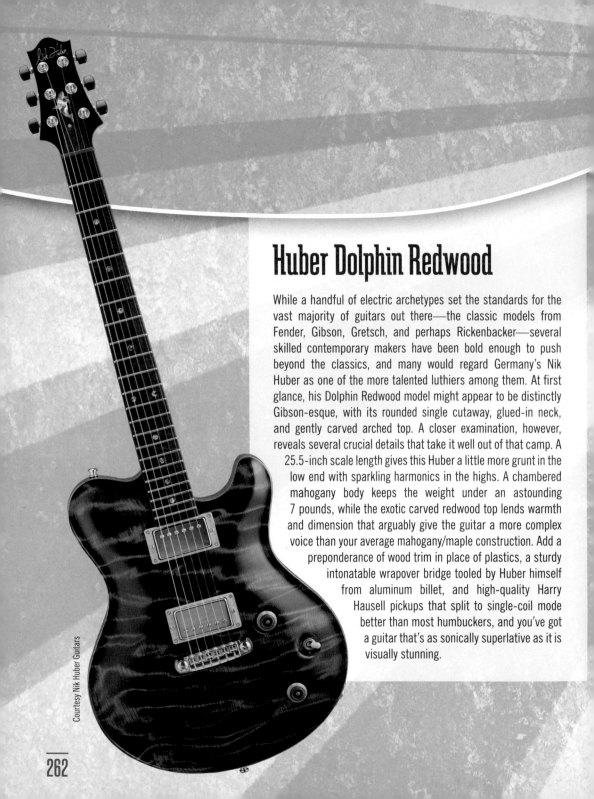

Huber Dolphin Redwood

While a handful of electric archetypes set the standards for the vast majority of guitars out there—the classic models from Fender, Gibson, Gretsch, and perhaps Rickenbacker—several skilled contemporary makers have been bold enough to push beyond the classics, and many would regard Germany's Nik Huber as one of the more talented luthiers among them. At first glance, his Dolphin Redwood model might appear to be distinctly Gibson-esque, with its rounded single cutaway, glued-in neck, and gently carved arched top. A closer examination, however, reveals several crucial details that take it well out of that camp. A 25.5-inch scale length gives this Huber a little more grunt in the low end with sparkling harmonics in the highs. A chambered mahogany body keeps the weight under an astounding 7 pounds, while the exotic carved redwood top lends warmth and dimension that arguably give the guitar a more complex voice than your average mahogany/maple construction. Add a preponderance of wood trim in place of plastics, a sturdy intonatable wrapover bridge tooled by Huber himself from aluminum billet, and high-quality Harry Hausell pickups that split to single-coil mode better than most humbuckers, and you've got a guitar that's as sonically superlative as it is visually stunning.

Courtesy Nik Huber Guitars

Courtesy TopHat

2000 TopHat Club Royale

Although the brand is less well known than some others amid the boutique crowd, TopHat, founded by Brian Gerhardt, is enormously respected by those who know it. The company's bestselling model, the Club Royale, is also perhaps one of the most versatile non-channel-switching amps on the market—giving up chunky Marshall, chiming Vox, or snappy Fender at the twist of a few dials—as well as excellent value in a hand-wired, made-in-the-USA tube amp. As an eternal tone chaser himself, Gerhardt is not afraid to change the product in pursuit of his own personal tone quest, and the Club Royale has evolved through several iterations since its arrival on the scene in the early 1990s. Basic specs have remained largely the same since around 2000, though, with a few component and circuit tweaks as exceptions: Volume, Treble, Mid, Bass, Cut, and Master controls govern three 12AX7s in the preamp and a pair of EL84 output tubes for around 20 watts of power, with an extremely useful three-way Boost switch to add thicker or fatter gain to the brew. From classic rock, to indie, to country, to blues, the humble Club Royale can handle it all and ride home in the front seat of your Mini Cooper without complaint.

Z. Vex Seek Wah

What sick tone freak would combine a tremolo, wah-wah, and sequencer into one effects pedal? Why, the demented creative Zachary Vex, that's who! Following the success of his Fuzz Factory and Super Hard On booster pedals, this Minnesota effects maker rolled out a series of far more adventurous offerings, with the Seek Wah of the late 1990s being among the more sublime. Still housed in his compact "hobby box" with hand-painted

Courtesy Z. Vex Effects

graphics from J. Myrold, the Seek Wah carries eight individual subminiature filter-frequency knobs—one for each pulse position, with accompanying LED—along with a speed knob and a three-way mini-toggle to set it for four, eight, or six pulses (in that order). Essentially, you tune each pulse position to the triggered-wah-style frequency of your choice, select your speed and pattern, and the little fella runs away with your guitar signal, bleeping and blooping through its tremelo'd wah sequence like there's no tomorrow. The sonic result of all this runs from sweetly hypnotic techno-style pulses to haunting freq-tweaked arpeggios—and makes the Seek Wah a nifty way to spice up your aural arsenal.

Martin DXMAE

With all the great newer Martin flat-tops out there made from solid traditional tonewoods, why dip into this entry-level dreadnought constructed from wood alternatives? Well, partly to prove a point, just as Martin has proved its own point about new approaches to guitar manufacture in the effort of conserving endangered wood species. Introduced in the early 2000s the introductory DX model is manufactured with a top made from spruce-grained high-pressure laminate (HPL) and mahogany-grained HPL back and sides, yet it remains a Martin in every respect. The alternative "particleboard" materials and other cost savings help you bring it in at well under a grand for the buyer, yet take it in hand and strum it with attitude, and the DXMAE rewards with a deep, well-balanced tone that compares extremely well to many all-wood acoustics in a similar price range. It might be difficult to convince some players that a wood alternative such as HPL is the way to go, but you've got to applaud an otherwise traditional guitar company like Martin for making such a bold effort.

Xotic Effects Robotalk

Los Angeles–based Xotic Effects, a division of Prosound Communications, has possibly become best known for its broad range of variously flavored booster pedals, but a passionate cult of players remains devoted to its first pedal, a far more exotic effort released in 1999 called the Robotalk. At the heart of this box lurks a well-tuned envelope filter

(a.k.a. auto wah), but by tacking on a clever arpeggiator, the Xotic boffins take it way past the standard funk machine. Controls for Volume, Rate, Range, and Freq determine the Robotalk's voicing and performance, and footswitches for On/Off and Mode give you on-the-fly accessibility. The pedal is a nifty tone generator when used as a mere envelope follower, producing round, funky auto-wah sounds with plump, musical peaks. Kick it into random arpeggiator mode, though, and it virtually takes on a life of its own, churning out a bleeping, bubbling blend of tremolo and peaking tone filter that totally lives up to its name. Set the robot talking, and you can pretty much just sit back and listen while your band mates carry on with the tune.

Prescription Vibe Unit

As passionate about their Uni-Vibe clones as several boutique effects manufacturers are, you can imagine it might be fun to put them all in the ring together and see which comes out top dog. That's exactly what *Guitar Player* magazine did in a 1996 "Univibe

Courtesy Prescription Electronics Inc.

Shootout," and the Prescription Electronics Vibe Unit was deemed champion. A vibe/chorus effect—four-stage phaser—based on the classic late-'60s photocell circuit, the Vibe Unit carries an On/Off stomp switch, Vibe/Chorus switch, and controls for Volume, Intensity, and Speed, the latter with an enlarged knob you can manipulate with your toe between tunes or even while playing, if you're nimble enough. Plug in, and as you might expect, this box yields a great rendition of that warm, lush, liquid sound, from gentle pulse to emotive swirl to throbbing pulse. Like other great modern vibes, this pedal even enhances your tone with an indefinable added depth when Intensity or Speed knobs are turned to their minimum so no "effect" is perceived. For the total Hendrix mojo, pair it with Prescription's Experience—a three-in-one fuzz, octave, and swell pedal—and go to town.

Analog Man Bi-CompROSSor

Gotta love these modern pedal makers, stuffing two useful effects variations into one pedal, to both expand our sonic horizons *and* save real estate on our ever-crowded pedalboards. Analog Man, otherwise known as Mike Piera, developed a name for himself late in the second millennium for reconceiving classic effects with tweaks and updates for the contemporary guitarist and has earned endorsements from several major players as a result. The Bi-CompROSSor is one of Analog Man's cornerstone pedals, packaging together two of the world's favorite vintage compressors in one nifty box (which is even smaller in the form of his Mini Bi-Comp). Adding an "Attack" knob that the original gray Ross compressor never had to the complement of Sustain and Volume—and the Volume knob that the Dan Armstrong Orange Squeezer lacked, along with stomp switches for On/Off and Ross/OS selection—makes the Bi-CompROSSor extremely versatile, but its choice of two great-sounding compression flavors with less noise and broader ranges than the original really are the icing on the cake.

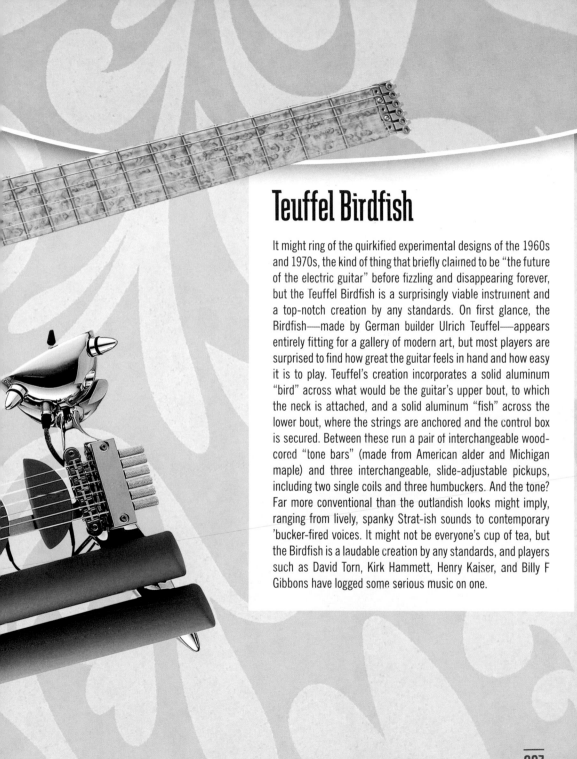

Teuffel Birdfish

It might ring of the quirkified experimental designs of the 1960s and 1970s, the kind of thing that briefly claimed to be "the future of the electric guitar" before fizzling and disappearing forever, but the Teuffel Birdfish is a surprisingly viable instrument and a top-notch creation by any standards. On first glance, the Birdfish—made by German builder Ulrich Teuffel—appears entirely fitting for a gallery of modern art, but most players are surprised to find how great the guitar feels in hand and how easy it is to play. Teuffel's creation incorporates a solid aluminum "bird" across what would be the guitar's upper bout, to which the neck is attached, and a solid aluminum "fish" across the lower bout, where the strings are anchored and the control box is secured. Between these run a pair of interchangeable wood-cored "tone bars" (made from American alder and Michigan maple) and three interchangeable, slide-adjustable pickups, including two single coils and three humbuckers. And the tone? Far more conventional than the outlandish looks might imply, ranging from lively, spanky Strat-ish sounds to contemporary 'bucker-fired voices. It might not be everyone's cup of tea, but the Birdfish is a laudable creation by any standards, and players such as David Torn, Kirk Hammett, Henry Kaiser, and Billy F Gibbons have logged some serious music on one.

Brook Clyst

Located in a reclaimed barn outside the city of Exeter in Devon, England, Brook was founded in 1995 by luthiers Simon Smidmore and Andy Petherick, with guidance from brothers Andy and Hugh Manson. In keeping with the brand name, all of their hand-made guitars are named after rivers and streams in the county of Devon. In another fun nod to the "keep it local" movement, Brook makes an effort to use a range of reclaimed English woods when possible, including sycamore, walnut, yew, and cherry, although they also use plenty of imported traditional and exotic tonewoods. Their line includes a range of body styles, from petite to jumbo, but the hair-above-parlor-size Clyst has always been particularly appealing, as well as exceedingly cute. It's the kind of guitar that makes you want to curl up indoors around a cottage fire for an evening or cart down to the Coach & Horses for a few pints and a spontaneous session. Comfortable and easy to play, it has a surprisingly muscular and well-balanced voice, too, and stretches confidently to stage performance or recording.

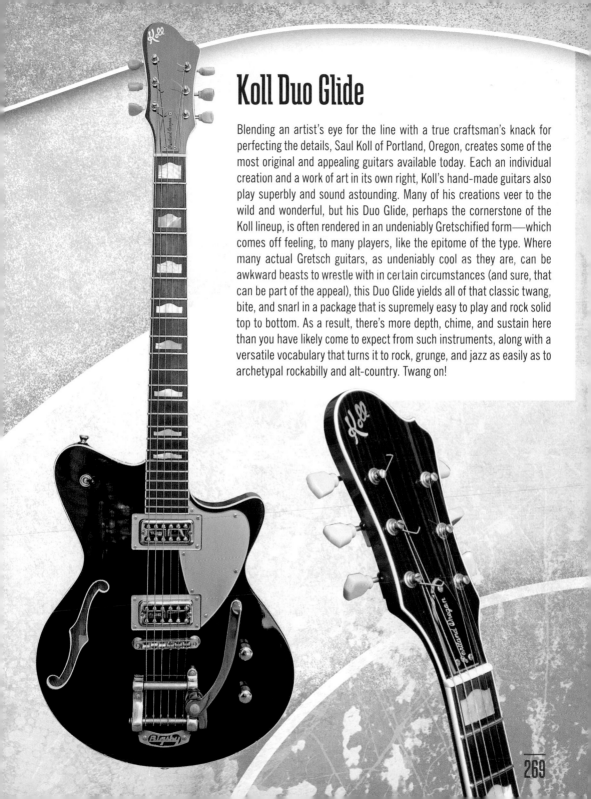

Koll Duo Glide

Blending an artist's eye for the line with a true craftsman's knack for perfecting the details, Saul Koll of Portland, Oregon, creates some of the most original and appealing guitars available today. Each an individual creation and a work of art in its own right, Koll's hand-made guitars also play superbly and sound astounding. Many of his creations veer to the wild and wonderful, but his Duo Glide, perhaps the cornerstone of the Koll lineup, is often rendered in an undeniably Gretschified form—which comes off feeling, to many players, like the epitome of the type. Where many actual Gretsch guitars, as undeniably cool as they are, can be awkward beasts to wrestle with in certain circumstances (and sure, that can be part of the appeal), this Duo Glide yields all of that classic twang, bite, and snarl in a package that is supremely easy to play and rock solid top to bottom. As a result, there's more depth, chime, and sustain here than you have likely come to expect from such instruments, along with a versatile vocabulary that turns it to rock, grunge, and jazz as easily as to archetypal rockabilly and alt-country. Twang on!

Bogner Uberschall Twin Jet

Reinhold Bogner calls his Uberschall an "Armageddon in a box," and it's hard to improve upon that description. The standard Uberschall offers the traditional clean and super-high-gain channels, but the Uberschall Twin Jet dispenses with the clean for a semi-clean to hot-rodded channel along with the defining super-high-gain channel. In the back end, the Uberschall Twin Jet runs four KT88s for a bludgeoning 150-plus watts of tuber power (versus its sibling's 120 watts from four EL34s). But the front end is the public face of this amp's aggression and rage. An ultra-high-gain preamp, ramming stage after stage of 12AX7 goodness one into the other, sets you up for thundering low-end crunch, scorching lead work, insane sustain, and what is virtually an out-of-body experience of tube-generated distortion. A word to the wise: don't approach it with your archtop jazzer or anything with even remotely microphonic pickups. With anything else, hold on tight, and step back *fast*.

Fulltone Clyde Deluxe Wah

Vox Wah or Cry Baby . . . where do you turn if you just can't decide on your favorite flavor of vintage wah-wah? One solution might be to turn elsewhere and consider something like the Fulltone Clyde Deluxe Wah. This pedal expands on Fulltone's original Clyde Wah, which was based on the classic Vox circuit, to add extra features that make a wah-wah more flexible in today's playing environment. In addition to having the original pedal's true-bypass feature to avoid the tone-sucking created by many vintage wahs when supposedly switched "off" (a feature many other contemporary wah-wah makers include these days), the Clyde Deluxe has a 10-step Input Level control, a three-way voicing switch, and a bypassable Booster/Buffer knob, as well as the status light that so many wah-wahs lack ("Is it on? Let's find out. . ."). The Whacked/Jimi/Shaft settings on the voicing switch take you from extreme quack to classic to superfunky, making it three wahs in one, while the Input and Buffer controls help the Clyde Deluxe play well with a wide range of amps and pedal setups. Vintage tones in a do-it-all format make this just about everything a wah-wah fan could require from a single pedal.

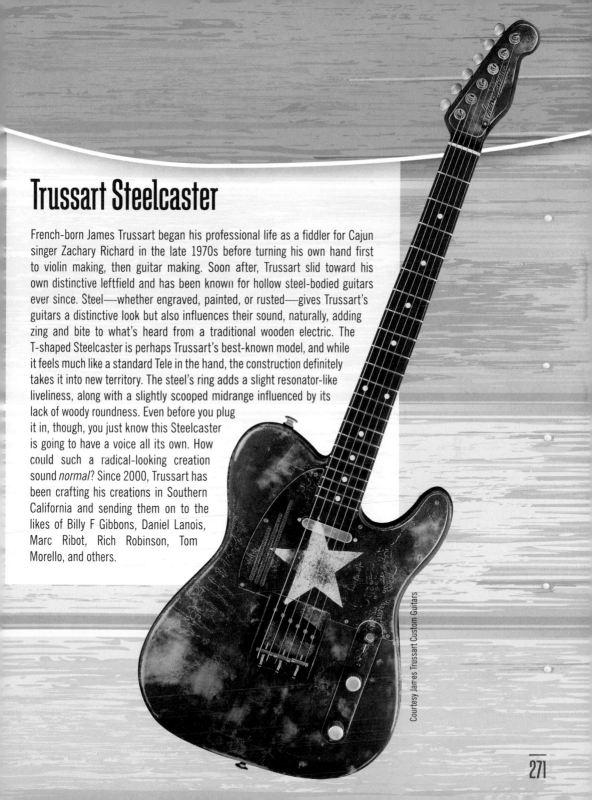

Trussart Steelcaster

French-born James Trussart began his professional life as a fiddler for Cajun singer Zachary Richard in the late 1970s before turning his own hand first to violin making, then guitar making. Soon after, Trussart slid toward his own distinctive leftfield and has been known for hollow steel-bodied guitars ever since. Steel—whether engraved, painted, or rusted—gives Trussart's guitars a distinctive look but also influences their sound, naturally, adding zing and bite to what's heard from a traditional wooden electric. The T-shaped Steelcaster is perhaps Trussart's best-known model, and while it feels much like a standard Tele in the hand, the construction definitely takes it into new territory. The steel's ring adds a slight resonator-like liveliness, along with a slightly scooped midrange influenced by its lack of woody roundness. Even before you plug it in, though, you just know this Steelcaster is going to have a voice all its own. How could such a radical-looking creation sound *normal*? Since 2000, Trussart has been crafting his creations in Southern California and sending them on to the likes of Billy F Gibbons, Daniel Lanois, Marc Ribot, Rich Robinson, Tom Morello, and others.

Courtesy James Trussart Custom Guitars

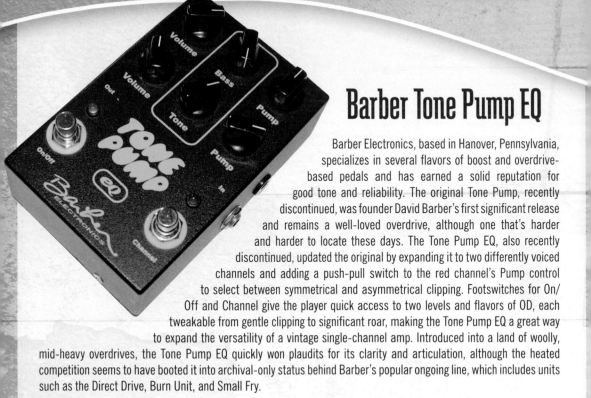

Barber Tone Pump EQ

Barber Electronics, based in Hanover, Pennsylvania, specializes in several flavors of boost and overdrive-based pedals and has earned a solid reputation for good tone and reliability. The original Tone Pump, recently discontinued, was founder David Barber's first significant release and remains a well-loved overdrive, although one that's harder and harder to locate these days. The Tone Pump EQ, also recently discontinued, updated the original by expanding it to two differently voiced channels and adding a push-pull switch to the red channel's Pump control to select between symmetrical and asymmetrical clipping. Footswitches for On/Off and Channel give the player quick access to two levels and flavors of OD, each tweakable from gentle clipping to significant roar, making the Tone Pump EQ a great way to expand the versatility of a vintage single-channel amp. Introduced into a land of woolly, mid-heavy overdrives, the Tone Pump EQ quickly won plaudits for its clarity and articulation, although the heated competition seems to have booted it into archival-only status behind Barber's popular ongoing line, which includes units such as the Direct Drive, Burn Unit, and Small Fry.

Z. Vex Lo-Fi Loop Junky

Courtesy Z. Vex Effects

It doesn't do traditional echo, it doesn't do sound on sound, and really it doesn't put out anything that sounds much like what you put into it in terms of fidelity and frequency range. The Z. Vex Lo-Fi Loop Junky lets you create lo-fi loops, pure and simple, and it might even be considered quite expensive for what it does—but there's a cult of players who simply *love* this pedal, and it's not hard to see why. Simply stomp the Rec footswitch to begin and conclude recording your guitar riff for looping, up to a full 20 seconds, then hit Start to play it at will, infinitely. The Volume and Tone controls might seem self-explanatory, although the latter is more for degrading the tone rather than tweaking it in the traditional sense (and the frequency range is limited to 2.6kHz already, mind you). Depth and Speed knobs work more toward crafting the degree of lo-fidelity heard in your repeats, which tend to result in a warm, fuzzy sound much like a well-played 45 vinyl record. And to think, that mad genius Zachary Vex did it all in a circuit that relies on an analog answering-machine chip. Beautiful stuff.

Campellone Special

In many ways a "youngster" in the field of archtop guitars, Mark Campellone has come to be recognized as one of the more skilled luthiers working today while also offering good value in a market populated by some of the more expensive new acoustic guitars available. From his workshop in Providence, Rhode Island, Campellone crafts archtops that pay homage to the great Gibson, Epiphone, Stromberg, and D'Angelico guitars from an age when jazz was king while employing contemporary techniques to optimize tone, performance, and consistency. Without knowing any of that, though, what is likely to grab you first about this stunning Special is its sheer beauty: elegant inlay work, a custom-designed tailpiece, and an intricate art deco headstock motif with cursive logo all hint that this is something special. Then strum a few chord inversions or pick out a blue run and you quickly *know* it is. Whether played acoustically or amplified for club performance, often through the original DeArmond pickup frequently used on these guitars, the Campellone is a first-class instrument and a modern work of art.

Victoria Reverberato

Housed in a stand-alone box somewhat like that of the original Fender Reverb Unit, the Reverberato is made only by customorder by Victoria Amp Company, best known for its tweed amp reproductions, and even then it is described by owner Mark Baier as "the most labor-intensive product we make." Carrying four 12AX7 preamp tubes, one 12AT7, and a 5Y3 rectifier, the Reverberato's effects are driven by circuits based on the '65 black-face Fender Twin Reverb and the '63 brown-face Concert amp. While the former needs no explanation, the latter is a complex approximation of "true vibrato," which hints at some pitch-changing rather than just volume-fluctuating tremolo, and results in a smooth, warbly, delectable sound that many consider to be the epitome of this breed of effect. Having the two in one box is a real godsend to the vintage-minded player, and if the results cost about the same as a lower-wattage hand-wired 1x12 combo, you need only ask if you really can put a price on superior tone.

Dr Z Carmen Ghia

Outwardly looking somewhat like a no-count practice amp from days gone by, the diminutive Carmen Ghia has gathered a whole shopping list of name-artist users and rave reviews in its time on this planet. Dr Z is one of the most respected, and successful, makers in the boutique amp world, and is headed by Mike Zaite, formerly a GE engineer specializing in high-quality medical instruments. During his transition from corporate tech to mad professor of ampology, Zaite stumbled on a low-wattage Hammond organ reverb amplifier and liked the way it worked for guitar. A few twists and turns later, the Hammond cornerstone had formed the foundation of the little Carmen Ghia, a basic yet surprisingly sumptuous performer. Generating around 18 watts from a pair of EL84s, with a 12AX7 in the preamp and a lower-gain 5751 phase inverter, the Carmen Ghia is refreshingly simple with just a Volume and Tone control, yet its circuit hides some clever quirks not found in other amps on the market. Fire her up, and the depth, clarity, and dynamics this thing has in store are likely to keep you playing all day.

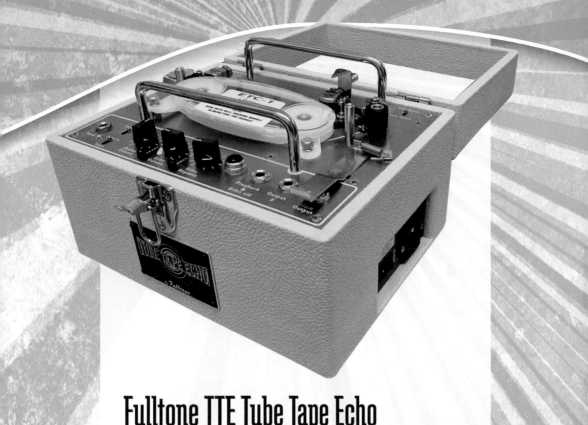

Fulltone TTE Tube Tape Echo

The effects industry might have spent the previous three decades trying to compact the tone of a genuine tape echo into a more portable and robust format, but never mind; Mike Fuller of California's Fulltone knew the original article still sounded better by far and set about re-creating it for the modern guitarist. The result, issued around 2005, was the Fulltone Tube Tape Echo (TTE). Designed primarily in the image of the tube-driven Maestro Echoplex EP-2, but with upgrades in the name of noise reduction and roadworthiness, the TTE offers the incomparable sound of tape-loop echo in a smooth-running and relatively compact package, with the bonus of a juicy tube boost even with echo bypassed, that has proven impressively resistant to breakdown since the time of its release. Of course, the abundance of moving parts here, and the presence of a loop of magnetic recording tape-loop cartridge at the center of it all, means these machines are never maintenance-free. So, with all the good solid-state analog and digital options available, can the TTE really be worth the relative hassle? Use one for a time and you will quickly answer that question for yourself. If echo is a big part of your tone, and you like the warm, rich, retro sound of tape, it's hard to go back once you have experienced the real thing.

GVCG Model "T"

There's just something so cool—and so comfortable—about a well-played, semi-beat-up old electric guitar, and Fenders seem to take to the treatment more than others. Fender has taken to making its own Relic series guitars, of course, but plenty of other makers have stepped in to fill the demand, some of which apply extremely high build standards and an artist's eye for aging and distressing techniques. Many consider Greenwich Village Custom Guitars to be among the best of the breed. Outwardly, this guitar might seem to be "just another broken-in Tele copy," but what the pictures don't show is that GVCG proprietor Jonathan Wilson's skill goes far beyond skin deep. Those who have played a few tend to agree almost universally that these aren't just impressive vintage knockoffs, but that they possess a genuine magic—found in the resonance, depth, complexity, and sheer playability of the instrument—that makes them superb hand-built guitars by any standards. If the real thing is far beyond your means, one of Wilson's GVCG works of art might just be the closest you're likely to get.

Courtesy Jonathan Wilson

Grant James photo, courtesy Jonathan Wilson

Mojave Coyote

Mojave Ampworks head honcho Victor Mason cut his tone teeth running the California vintage amplifier dealership Plexi Palace, and his shop's new production amps show distinctly British sonic leanings. Kicking out 15 watts from a pair of EL84s, the Coyote is the smallest model of the range, but perhaps the most highly acclaimed, too. Mojave's ethos is to take an intelligent, efficient design inspired by classic circuits, build it like it was intended to survive being airdropped into battle, and keep the features down to the simple essentials. The little Coyote, therefore, sports an entirely hand-wired circuit on a tidily laid-out turret board, connecting its top-notch components, military-grade switches and sockets, and Mercury Magnetics transformers with Teflon-coated, silver-plated copper wire, all loaded within a reinforced aluminum chassis. For all this, the front-panel control array is deceptively simple: Treble and Bass volume controls can be blended as desired to craft your own voice from the two discrete preamps, while the Tone control determines high-end content, and Power Dampening (a proprietary tube-voltage regulator) governs output level. The result is a tone that's definitely part Vox, part Marshall, and broader and more versatile than either, with body and low-end thump that belie the Coyote's diminutive size.

Electro-Harmonix POG (Polyphonic Octave Generator)

In addition to producing many fundamental, functional pedals in the 1970s, such as fuzz boxes, phasers, choruses, and delays, Electro-Harmonix was prone to throw practicality out the window now and then and come out with something completely out of left field. That sense of fun and adventure has continued into the company's modern era and exhibits itself in flying colors in the POG, or Polyphonic Octave Generator. Unlike a few of E-H's crazier offerings from days gone by, though, the POG has proved a major hit with several guitarists of the avant-garde and has been taken up by Jack White and Steve Vai, among others. The POG lets you add one octave up, two octaves up, or one octave down to your original guitar note, or blend any combination of the three as desired to create freakish polyphonic synthy sounds. Unlike many other octave generators, it tracks multiple notes well, so you can also use it for chord work, creating the chime of a faux 12-string or something far wilder. Nifty stuff.

Duesenberg USA Guitars

Duesenberg Starplayer TV

Borrowing the name of a defunct Detroit legend and dipping into a hip retro ethos, Duesenberg hit the scene posing as a forgotten American classic and quickly racked up a string of star endorsements from Bob Dylan, Mike Campbell, Marc Ford, and several others. Whatever its origins, the Starplayer TV—designed and assembled in Germany—has a look, feel, and sound all its own. With a 25.5-inch scale length, a semi-hollowbody with a solid center block and solid arched spruce top, a Duesenberg humbucker in the bridge, a single-coil in the neck, and Duesy's clever reworking of the Bigsby vibrato, the guitar is often described as "Gretsch meets Fender Telecaster." That goes partway toward summing it up, but it will also do plenty of Rickenbacker and Gibson ES-335-style tricks, too. More than anything, though, it is very much its own beast: plugged into either a good vintage combo or a contemporary high-gain stack, it segues seamlessly from grinding roadhouse blues to scorching alt-rock, taking on everything in between with equal composure yet adding its own full, round, and slightly edgy voice to it all. Dare we call it a "modern classic"?

Gretsch 6128TBEE Elliot Easton Model

We could examine many of the contemporary Japanese-made Gretsch guitars for examples of how this great brand has regained its vigor, but the Elliot Easton Model adds several factory modifications to the template that also show us how well the originals can be adapted to current playing needs. The 6128TBEE was made available in the mid-'00s as a signature model for Elliot Easton, who frequently played an original Gretsch Duo Jet with the Cars in the late '70s and early '80s. Rather than being a strict reissue, it was updated with several refinements that Easton wanted to see on the Duo Jet format. To that end, the 6128TBEE has a scale length of 25 inches rather than the original's 24.6 inches, its bridge is pinned down for stability, and it carries locking Sperzel tuners and a self-lubricating graphite nut to keep the Bigsby-loaded guitar better in tune. In addition, many Japanese-built Elliot Easton Models have TV Jones Classics, often considered an improvement on stock Gretsch Filter'Trons. The result is a Gretsch with a little more meat to its chime and jangle and more overall functionality for the hard-gigging guitarist.

Courtesy Fender Musical Instrument Corporation

Ribbecke Halfling

As a quick visual analysis might imply, the Ribbecke Halfling takes its name from its hybrid design ethos, which employs elements of both flat-top and archtop acoustic guitar making in an effort to achieve best-of-both-worlds results. As such, this guitar has a broad, deep, well-balanced tone, with an archtop's enhanced bass response and a flat-top's sweet high end. Tom Ribbecke first began building guitars in northern California in the early 1970s and earned a good reputation for his flat-tops, archtops, and electrics before allergies to finishing products drove him away from the business for nearly a decade in the 1980s. Having been back at it for some twenty years now, Ribbecke developed the Halfling around 2003, and it has been a mainstay of his lineup ever since. Halflings are currently built by the Ribbecke team of luthiers under the master's watchful eye and managed by Ribbecke's daughter, Daniela. Guitars hand-built exclusively by Tom Ribbecke are now available on a custom-order basis only, with prices starting at $25,000.

Grosh Set Neck

Colorado-based builder Don Grosh first established his name while working in California as a maker of quality Fender-inspired S- and T-style bolt-neck guitars. He later created the popular, more original ElectraJet model, another bolt-neck reminiscent of the offset-bodied Jazzmaster shape but with a few new twists. It speaks volumes, then, that one of his most successful designs is named for the fact that it strays from the bolt-neck format that was so long Grosh's stock in trade. The Set Neck is clearly a Les Paul–inspired creation, but it is rendered with several little reconsiderations of the format that add up to a significant improvement in performance. As such, this guitar gives you a feel and tone that is instantly reminiscent of Gibson's seminal solidbody, yet somehow even *more so*: balance and playing position are more ergonomic, tuning more stable, tone more balanced and consistently *there*. In short, it's a phenomenal creation that hits straight at the heart of its intended target in a way few electric guitars, even other great ones, ever quite do—and it doesn't hurt that it looks damn good in the process.

Courtesy Grosh Guitars

Victoria Regal II

The Chicago-based Victoria Amp Company is largely known for its spot-on, hand-wired tweed Fender-style repros, but founder Mark Baier has branched out with some nifty original designs. The Regal II is one of the cleverest among these and hides a tweak-tastic twist beneath its tasty retro packaging. As if its tube reverb and bias-modulating tremolo circuit aren't enticement enough, the Regal II allows the player to swap virtually any compatible eight-pin tube into its two-tube output stage, ushering up a juicy, genuine Class A, dual-single-ended tonefest in the process. Swap in a single 6V6 for 5 watts in the studio, a pair of 6L6s for around 28 watts, or two EL34s for 35 watts max on larger stages, or even mix and match two entirely different tube types to craft your own tonal palette—the Regal II takes it all willingly and breathes out drippingly juicy, overtone-laden Class A tone in the process. The chunky 1x15 combo harks back to Fender's TV-front Pro amp, and you can certainly edge toward those tones, but there's so much else on tap here that you'll have to remind yourself to stop tweaking and just start playing—a rewarding adventure once you undertake it.

Teye La Perla

Raised in the Netherlands on a carefully blended diet of Flamenco and rock 'n' roll, Teye (no last name required) pursued an equal love of authentic Gypsy music and the Rolling Stones through a musical career that virtually merged the two, and, eventually, filtered into his own line of meticulously hand-wrought instruments. The Electric Gypsy line is clearly inspired by Teye's love of Tony Zemaitis' metal- and pearl-fronted guitars (of which he owned several while still a touring musician), but Teye takes the décor a step further while employing several alternative materials in his work. Hand-crafting guitars in Austin, Texas, with names such as La Perla, La India, and La Canastera, Teye uses hand-tooled silver and aluminum plate, abalone, mother-of-pearl, coral, and other materials, alongside his in-house bridge and tailpiece designs, to create some of the most elaborate-looking electric guitars available today. More than just works of art, though—which they undoubtedly are—Teye guitars also play smoothly and sound great, benefiting from several simple, if less obvious, revisions of switching and controls, heel-less neck joint, tuner layout, and so forth. Each is a showpiece and a performance tool—and one-off work of art.

Gibson J-185EC

After a few years in the wilderness, Gibson's acoustic operation regained its former glories in grand style after purchasing the Flatiron Mandolin Company in Bozeman, Montana, in 1987 and moving flat-top guitar production west to that facility soon after. The J-185EC embodies much of what the company's Bozeman works do so well: marrying the tradition of the rare J-185 flat-top, a slightly more compact version of the big SJ-200, to modern playing conveniences such as a rounded cutaway for improved upper-fret access and a built-in Fishman pickup and preamp system for easy stage use. This 16-inch-wide acoustic made from a solid Sitka spruce top and solid Indian rosewood sides has a bold, lively acoustic tone with plenty of depth and sweetness and punches out plenty of volume for rhythm work and flatpick soloing alike. Plugged in, the Fishman system translates it all with a little extra piezo zing so the J-185EC cuts through beautifully on the live stage. All in all, it's an impressive contemporary representative of Gibson's long-standing acoustic prowess and does its lineage proud.

Gustavsson Bluesmaster

Point out the "For Sale" listing of a Gustavsson Bluesmaster to any group of guitarists unfamiliar with the brand, complete with $10K-plus asking price, and you're likely to elicit plenty of "How good can a Les Paul copy *be*?" responses. The answer coming from anyone who has played one, though, will be "Far better than you could ever imagine." The Bluesmaster guitar by Swedish luthier Johan Gustavsson is far more than merely a "Les Paul copy"—it is this gifted maker's interpretation of the set-neck, dual-humbucker, solidbody tone rendered without limit or compromise. The success of Gustavsson's creations lies in his craftsmanship and his knack for selecting the most sonically and visually appealing tonewoods from well-aged stocks. Rather than aping the specs of the classics, he refines whatever might be necessary to make his guitars more resonant, more sweetly musical, and easier to play. As seen, heard, and felt in this rare beauty, the result—as most Gustavsson owners will attest—is a guitar that is more intimately in tune with the player than you ever thought an amplified musical instrument could be.

Courtesy J G Guitars, photos by Craig Snyder

Tone King Metropolitan

Quirky retro styling helps Tone King amps stand out from the crowd even before you jack into one, but power up and you'll find an extremely tonacious American-voiced performance machine lurking beneath the hip exterior. Designer Mark Bartel's efforts extend beyond the amp circuit itself to cover extensive R&D on cabinet performance. Not just any pine or plywood box, the combo is housed in a carefully tuned cabinet made from thinner-than-usual ½-inch stock—crafted using several techniques that shall remain trade secrets—to maximize balance, resonance, and projection. The circuit is still what most players will latch onto first, though, and it offers plenty of temptations itself. Channel one aims to create the "ultimate black-face-style cleans" with added richness and depth, while the lead channel includes a Mid-Bite control to roll it from chewy tweedlike bite to crisper Marshall-like sting. Full output achieves 40 watts via a quartet of 6V6s, although Bartel's proprietary Output Power circuit (with an individual control for each channel) lets you dial it all down to 0.1 watt with minimal tonal coloration. No matter what tone you seek, it's in here and achievable at the stomp of a switch.

Taylor Grand Symphony

Even if the most of Taylor's guitar lines fit into recognizable camps (dreadnaught, grand concert, super jumbo), all have their own twist on tradition. With the Grand Symphony, however, or "GS" for short, Bob Taylor sought an entirely original design, rethought from the ground up for tone and performance, and landed a great new flat-top offering as a result. The guitar rewards the effort with an extremely even, balanced tone, a richer bass than the average flat-top, bold midrange, and a muscular high end that is never shrill. In essence, the Grand Symphony seeks to be an accomplished all-arounder: it puts out impressive volume for the rhythm player, while single-note flatpick runs cut through with ease and gentler fingerpicking retains excellent depth and clarity. At the same time as introducing the new design in 2006, Taylor pioneered a new pickup system that presents the amplified GS extremely well. The Expression System combines multiple magnetic pickups placed at strategic positions around the underside of the guitar's top with a simple high-fidelity preamp to translate the Grand Symphony's acoustic tone to your amplification system of choice in grand style.

Courtesy Taylor Guitars

Swart Atomic Space Tone

With so many retro-leaning boutique amps taking their cues from vintage Fender, Vox, and Marshall models, Swart of Wilmington, North Carolina, gave a visual nod to an even older B-list classic with his Valco-like Atomic Space Tone and created one of the more popular smaller combos of the past decade. This little 17½x15½x9-inch sweetie weighs in at just 35 pounds but packs enough guts to get you through almost any smaller gig in grand style—or any gig at all if you ram it through a suitable PA, as have notable players like Jeff Tweedy of Wilco and Dean Wareham of

Luna. Inside, the circuit is actually perhaps a tad more tweed Deluxe at heart, generating 15 watts from a pair of 6V6s, but it tacks on luscious tube reverb and tremolo for good measure, making it even more of a grab 'n' go solution for stage and studio. The Atomic Space Tone's cleans are deep and plumby, while its old-school lead tones run chocolaty and smooth as you crank it skyward. All in all, an irresistible little package.

PaulC Audio Tim

The Tim overdrive pedal, produced by PaulC Audio ("C" for Cochrane, so no connection to Paul Crowther of Hot Cake fame), has become a favorite breakup-inducer of many boutique pedal fans of late, and another worthy mention in the post–Tube Screamer world of overdrive in general. With a plethora of good to excellent overdrives on the market, the Tim has earned kudos for its versatility, the plethora of good tones found within—all with excellent clarity and transparency—and the fact that for all it has to offer, it doesn't cost an arm and a leg like many of the more esoteric, small-shop pedals out there. Controls for Gain, Bass, Treble, and Volume determine your main overdrive sound, while there's also a second footswitchable boost, with Gain and Tone controls on the pedal's top edge, and a series effects loop for chaining other drive or effects pedals between the Tim's Gain and Output stages. Since Cochrane operates a small shop in Murfreesboro, Tennessee, there is usually a wait of up to a few months to obtain the Tim or its more compact little brother, the Timmy, which lacks the boost channel and effects loop.

Hahn 228

You could fill a book listing the "Fender Telecaster copies" that have been produced through the years, yet just a few seconds with a Hahn 228 in hand tell you this guitar is far from—and far more than—a mere copy. By intensely internalizing his own love of vintage Telecasters and channeling it into a thorough reconception of the form, New York–based maker Chihoe Hahn has produced a guitar that simultaneously pays tribute to the original yet, in the view of many players, surpasses it in several ways. Outwardly, the 228 appears very much just a high-quality Tele clone, but Hahn's attention to wood selection, his ultratight neck pocket (so snug you can carry a 228 around by the neck with the mounting screws removed), and his thin nitrocellulose finish process make the core of the instrument truly a premier piece. Add to this Hahn's in-house bridge tooling, with several subtle alterations to the form to maximize efficiency and resonance, and the use of top-notch pickups from the likes of Lindy Fralin and Jason Lollar, and you're looking at the Platonic form of the Telecaster, if you will, a guitar that maximizes the potential of what *the* Tele set out to be. You want twang, grind, chime, and snarl, all within the same riff? Step this way, sir.

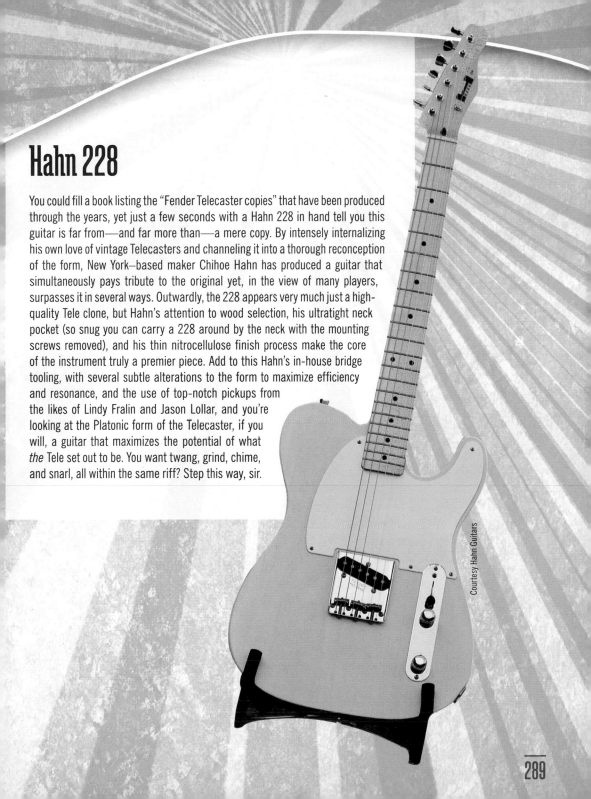

Courtesy Hahn Guitars

Gibson Custom Shop Michael Bloomfield 1959 Les Paul

The Gibson Custom Shop has shown its ability time and again to re-create impressive swathes of Gibson history, but its Limited Edition artist guitars are generally among its finest work. At first glance—and even second and third—it's difficult to tell this one from an original late-'50s Les Paul, and the slight "imperfections" added in the name of re-creating blues great Michael Bloomfield's own legendary guitar make it all even more believable. As rendered by Tom Murphy, one of the world's most renowned ageing and restoration artists, the wear to the faded cherry sunburst finish, the distinctive dings and dents, the patina on the nickel-plated hardware, and even the replaced bridge-pickup Volume knob and truss-rod cover all echo Bloomfield's long-lost Les Paul with an eerie accuracy. What matters most, of course, is that when you plug it in the illusion doesn't fade: it might not quite be a quarter-million-dollar 'burst in the flesh, but the Custom Shop's Bloomfield re-creation has the creamy moan and gutsy roar that are characteristic of a great Les Paul—which make for an exhilarating playing experience.

Dr Z Stang Ray

Not unlike Leo Fender in the 1950s and early '60s, Dr Z founder Michael Zaite is a gifted engineer who, although not a guitar player himself, seeks the input of notable tonehounds and employs his formidable skill and finely honed ear in bringing great players' desires into being. The company was virtually launched on an amp designed for rocker Joe Walsh, a model known as the Maz 38 Sr, but a more recent offering taps country phenomenon Brad Paisley for a very different take on vintage-inspired EL84 tone. The Stang Ray is based on Paisley's beloved 1962 Vox AC30, an early model with an EF86 pentode preamp tube (as more commonly found in vintage AC15s) rather than the later Top Boost circuit and, as such, is a little different than most Vox-inspired boutique combos out there. Much like this Tele-wrangler's signature tone, the Stang Ray excels at beefy cleans early on the dial but segues into a trenchant, overtone-laden, edge-of-breakup tone when you roll the dial toward halfway. Its blooming dynamics and come-hither touch sensitivity make it a real joy and, as might be expected, a stunning partner to a good Tele riff. Paisley guitar finish optional.

Dr. Scientist Tremolessence

Although it's one of the oldest guitar effects ever conceived, tremolo has experienced a surprising renaissance in the early twenty-first century. It might seem, in principle, to be one of the simplest, too—signal goes up, signal goes down—but the myriad flavors available on the market today bring a surprising variety to the table and prove that all tremolo effects truly do not sound the same. The Tremolessence by Dr. Scientist seeks to put many of the best styles of tremolo ever available into one handy box for players who just can't decide whether they want it Fender, or Ampeg, or Valco, or whatever. With knobs for Volume, Treble, Depth, Rate, Shape, and Hold, this stereo circuit lets the player determine just about every governable parameter of his or her tremolo sound. Further, one toggle switch selects between triangular or square waveform, while another offers a hold function that engages the effect when you step on and hold down the On/Off stomp switch, ramping up slowly to full depth using the Hold knob setting. And you thought you just wanted your signal to go up and down.

McInturff
Carolina Custom

Several makers have their take on the ultimate Les Paul–styled guitar, but this North Carolina–based maker's rendition of the classic is considered by many players to be among the best available. Throughout his twenty-five years in the business, Terry McInturff has continued to evolve his designs, grow his skills, and bring several refinements to the table that put him in the upper echelon of the boutique guitar world. McInturff prides himself on carefully selecting his tonewoods, which he tap-tests for resonance in the manner of the best archtop, flat-top, and classical guitar makers. The results, according to most who have experienced a Carolina Custom firsthand, are heard in a depth and clarity of tone that goes beyond the traditional LP-styled electric while capturing the expected meat and muscle of the breed along with an easier playing feel than virtually any prized vintage example is likely to afford. All that, and the traditional set-neck, dual-humbucker, maple-topped-mahogany construction is given a stylistic twist that helps it stand out from the crowd.

Courtesy Gene Baker

Gene Baker b3 Wood

Born just outside Detroit, Michigan, Gene Baker started playing the guitar at the age of eleven, a diehard Kiss fan as so many preteens were in the mid-1970s, and first dabbled in building guitars for himself just two years later. Since then, his sonic explorations have expanded far beyond paint-faced pop-metal to cover virtually the entire palette of electric guitar tone possibilities. The b3 Wood model is named not simply because it is made of the stuff but is one in a series that includes Fire, Earth, Water, and Metal guitars (*all* made primarily from wood, we should point out), each of which embodies a particular tonal ideal. This one shoots for the big, fat, open tone of Gibson's iconic semi-acoustic, the ES-335, while expanding the vocabulary to achieve anything from warmer archtop jazz tones to meaty, biting rock. The formula, in this case, includes extensive body chambering to enhance the sense of "air" in the tone while retaining note clarity within chords and inducing a broad, versatile voice overall. A clever new take on a classic.

65amps London Pro

By tapping into the real needs of gigging guitarists, as well as their own playing experience, 65amps founders Dan Boul and Peter Stroud (the latter a touring and recording guitarist with Sheryl Crow) have honed a line of tube amps intended to capture classic tones while offering improved versatility for contemporary styles, along with rugged roadworthiness. The 18-watt London Pro earned its status as flagship of the line by becoming recognized as a modern classic just a couple years after its introduction in the early 2000s. With distinctly British leanings long familiar to boutique amp fans, the London Pro marries one "Voxy" channel based on an EF86 pentode preamp tube and one "Marshall 18-wattery" channel based on a 12AX7, but it seeks to broaden the vocabulary of both with top-notch modern componentry and a no-expense-spared design ethos. The result is an amp with a breathing, multidimensional sound and an inspiring playing feel; the London Pro will do Vox or Marshall yet also subs easily for many American voices and adds a large dollop of something all its own into the brew. In short, it's one of those amps that becomes an integral and expressive part of your "instrument," and that inspired you to just play and play.

Matchless Independence

Footswitchable, multichannel amps long seemed the territory of printed circuit board–based manufacturing, but noted boutique maker Matchless elevated the format to a whole new plane with its three-channel Independence. One of a newer breed of designs from this reputable maker, the Independence is totally hand-wired in the hallowed point-to-point style, just like the company's flagship DC-30 models and others, yet offers the convenience of three independently selectable channels for clean, crunch, and lead tones. Plug in your favorite guitar and spend some time with this powerful beauty, and you soon realize the real bonus is that Matchless head honcho Phil Jameson hasn't sacrificed any of that lush, swirling, multidimensional Matchless tone in the course of featuring up the platform. With its cathode-biased (a.k.a. "class A") output stage generating 35 surprisingly loud watts from a pair of EL34 tubes, the Independence heaps on the Marshall-esque rumble and wail when desired yet still easily attains more Voxy tones—and all at the stomp of a switch. A channel-switcher for the purist.

TopHat Emplexador MkII

Though not a household name, TopHat's Brian Gerhardt is one of the best-respected designers in boutique amp circles, and rarely fails to hit the mark with an original design. His Emplexador wraps vintage-voiced Marshall plexi and JTM tones and contemporary JCM800-style high-gain overdrive into a single amp head that has proven the last stop in many a Brit-minded tone worshiper's search for the Holy Grail. Partner with a good 2x12 or 4x12 cab, plug in your guitar of choice—a Gibson with humbuckers never fails, but a Stratocaster finds favor for more Hendrix-inspired riffing—and try not to salivate too copiously as the mighty Emplexador gushes the buoyant, bovine crunch and gut-thumping rumble of our Marshall-haunted dreams. Being a purist, Gerhardt pooh-poohs channel switching and gives you just a front-

Courtesy TopHat Amps

panel switch for an either/or vintage/modern selection, with two further mini-switches for voice tweaking. But the tone in here is so workable and touch-sensitive that the road from clean to crunch to wail is an easy ride on the guitar's Volume control. Hats off, Brian, to a job well done.

Carol-Ann OD-2

Guitarists of a certain stripe are fond of playing the "who will be the next Dumble?" game 'round the pub over a few pints of craft ale, but many of those who have already sampled one of Carol-Ann's amps don't even need to ask the question. The company's flagship OD-2 model is by no means a "Dumble copy," but rather very much its own beast. Yet its build quality, tonal depth, and overall class inevitably lead us down that path to unavoidable comparisons. When we say "company," we of course mean Alan Phillips, the man behind the Carol-Ann brand, a former electronics engineer for GlaxoSmithKline who started up amp building full time after emigrating from England to Pelham, New Hampshire. Like all Carol-Ann offerings, the OD-2 is entirely hand-wired by Phillips, using only top-notch components. It offers two relatively straightforward yet tonally superlative channels, footswitchable for clean and lead, with independent three-knob EQ and independent master volumes to generate around 50 watts from a pair of 6L6 output tubes (EL34s optional). Smooth, creamy, dynamic . . . all are fitting descriptors, yet they also seem to pale in the face of the OD-2's gold-throated performance. Simply a cut above, even in the boutique world.

Fano Alt de Facto JM6

Pennsylvania-based maker Dennis Fano cut his teeth building a custom electric for XTC main man Andy Partridge, and since that time he has evolved a line of guitars that represent some of the more fun and funky retro-minded designs going. Fano asks the question, "What if Fender, Gibson, Gretsch, and Rickenbacker merged on a series of guitar designs in the late '50s and early '60s?" and answers it confidently with his Alt de Facto range, a series of high-concept instruments that do exactly that. The JM6 runs from Fender to Gibson, melding the Jazzmaster's offset double-cutaway styling and 25.5-inch scale length with Gibson-esque P-90 pickups and a Bigsby vibrato tailpiece with Tune-o-matic bridge. The resultant whole is much more than the sum of its parts, yielding a lively and rich-voiced guitar that has that hard-to-achieve vintage feel right out of the case, complete with body and hardware relic'ing and a pre-worn neck back. Great for anything from garage rock to grunge to blues, the JM6 has earned itself myriad fans since its introduction and continues to offer an excellent answer to that great "What if?"

MotorAve LeMans

Sick, rad, off the hook . . . whatever your favorite superlative these days, Mark Fuqua's sleek creations will drag it out of you. MotorAve guitars have perhaps inspired more gut-felt exclamations of awe and wonder than have been heard expressed over any new design in quite some time, and this sweet little LeMans, really the baby of the line, has garnered more than its share. Born and raised in Northern California, Fuqua played in bands for several years before moving into luthiery, first working with Chandler Industries in San Francisco in the early '90s, then with James Trussart in Paris and back in the States by the latter part of that decade. The MotorAve brand was born in 2002, named for the famous L.A. cruising strip where his first shop was located (since relocated to Durham, North Carolina), and Fuqua's guitars have had Detroit-inspired themes ever since. While the BelAire is an elegant semi-hollow and the McQueen a scorching single-cutaway solidbody, the LeMans has the vibe of Gibson's seminal devil-horned double cutaway, but one warped by speed, tilting into the G-force as if shot from a cannon—a description that aptly covers the LeMans playing experience, come to think of it.

Courtesy MotorAve Guitars, photo by Kate Fuque

Creston Sarah Ryan Custom T-Style

Based in the snowy northern Vermont town of Burlington, Creston Lea has been building F-style custom guitars for discerning regional and national artists for several years and earning greater and greater acclaim in the process. In addition to the quality craftsmanship and his own tonaliscious touches—witness the dual P-90s, Bigsby tailpiece, and solid one-piece rosewood neck on this Tele-inspired example—many Creston guitars are custom-adorned by local artist Sarah Ryan, who gives each example sent her way a unique, one-off paint job that Lea then shoots with a clear coat to preserve the work for posterity. In this instance, the paint job hides an extremely light one-piece sugar pine body. That, along with the other unusual ingredients, gives the guitar a resonance and zing that make for plenty of clarity amid the muscle of the P-90 growl. The guitars seem to appeal to the alternative-roots and Americana crowds in particular—no surprise there—and David Bryant, Jay Farrar, Ray Lamontagne, Brian Henneman, Tony Gilkyson, and Chuck Prophet have all caught on to Creston's creations.

Courtesy Creston Guitars, photos by Jessica Anderson

Monster Effects Swamp Thang

As the promotional blurb for this small effects manufacturer puts it, Monster Effects are "tested by ears, not machines," and the results show. With a surprisingly large number of guitarists seeming to chase the crème de la crème of tremolo these days, the Swamp Thang, designed by John Spears, aims to nail an early rendition of the effect that sought to be something more: namely, early brownface-Fender vibrato in a box, and as such it is a swampy monster, indeed. As with the original amp-based effect of the early '60s, this Thang is governed by the basic Speed and Depth controls, but as created in prized vintage Fender amps like the Super, Concert, and Pro, it was anything from "simple," requiring two and a half to three full preamp tubes and a host of related circuitry to get the job done. Hence the sigh of joy uttered by countless happy guitarists when Monster Effects boiled all that warbling, bouncing, pitch-wavering goodness down to the size of a standard small effects pedal.

Courtesy Monster Effects

Strymon El Capistan dTape Echo

Manufacturers have long strived to produce the sound of a genuine tape-loop echo unit in a compact pedal effect, and for many, the El Capistan comes the closest. To get there, California-based Strymon put boatloads of R&D into analyzing the sound of several of the best-loved vintage tape echoes, reproducing them with an extremely powerful DSP (digital signal processing) engine. The result is the El Capistan dTape Echo, a veritable smorgasbord of tape-fueled warmth, flutter, and gritty-sweet degradation in one box. The usual knobs for Time (delay), Repeats, and Mix control those standard parameters, but extras "Tape Age" and "Wow & Flutter" help the player attain the desired degree of tape realism (and decay), while there are also three-way switches for "Tape Head" (fixed, multi, single) and Mode, and a Tap tempo footswitch in addition to the Bypass switch. And while "digital" is a dirty word to many fans of vintage analog effects, Strymon's extremely high processing frequency, and the fact that the "dry" portion of the signal, as determined by the Mix control, remains in the analog realm the entire time, ensures a far warmer, more dynamic tone than digital renditions of old. And hey—it's stereo!

Fryette Sig:X

After selling his VHT brand name to a new owner, amplifier designer and builder Steven Fryette pressed on with his own eponymous range of creations aimed largely at the contemporary rocker who demands extreme versatility alongside his stellar tones. The Sig:X is perhaps the best embodiment of this ethos. The words *flexible* and *versatile* almost sell short the Sig:X's capabilities—indeed some entirely new term is required to denote its off-the-charts morphability—and whatever of its myriad shades you conjure, it all roars with girth, depth, and fidelity through the stout 100-watt dual-KT88 output stage. Three footswitchable channels offer clean, crunch, and lead tones with three selectable voices on each channel *plus* independent footswitchable boosts with boost level controls on the front panel. Further, each channel can be individually assigned for full or half power, and the amp remembers your selected parameters for each channel even when you switch to a new voice then back again. From sparkling Fendery cleans, to massive Marshally crunch, to full-throttle modern shred tones, Sig:X puts it all at your fingertips and instantly selectable at the tap of a toe. Even if you don't need this flexibility, it's a nifty toy to fiddle with through an idle evening.

Courtesy Fryette Amplification

Fender Cabronita

Some might puzzle over why Fender decided to give this contemporary variation of the Telecaster a Spanish name that translates roughly to "nasty little goat," but the fact that it's also a colloquialism for "little bastard" does make some sense. Regardless, this fiery, snarly rendition of the Telecaster—with two Gretsch-like humbucking pickups replacing the usual Tele complement—has become extremely popular since its release and makes a great alternative to the traditional slab-bodied bruiser. With the core ingredients of an ash or alder body and bolt-on maple neck with 25.5-inch scale length still firmly in place, la Cabronita retains plenty of characteristic twang, but the pickup change thickens up the voice somewhat, and the bridge modification (still with through-body stringing, but no metal plate to hang the pickup from) removes a little of the vintage Tele's edgy clank. From punk to rockabilly to nastier country and good old rock 'n' roll, the Cab proves pretty versatile, too, and comes off looking like a hip hot rod in the process.

Fender Musical Instruments Corporation

Thorn Junior Ninety

Based in Glendale, California, custom builder Ron Thorn has developed a sterling reputation for his ability to blend classic elements into creative and original new designs, and to consistently tap stellar tones and sublime playability in the process. The Junior Ninety is one of his simpler models, if you will, yet still every ounce a high-performance piece that represents the cornerstone of his work. The guitar's body might be reminiscent of the Fender Telecaster, but the Junior Ninety departs dramatically in just about every direction from that point. A body and neck made from light, highly resonant black limba (a relative of korina) provides a lively, responsive foundation, while the glued-in neck joint and 25-inch scale length round out the snap and pop of the traditional F-style guitar. High-grade hardware, including Thorn's own one-piece vibrato bridge and a Kevlar-reinforced Delrin nut, mirror the care applied to the woodwork itself, and the entire package sings through a pair of Thorn's own staple-top single-coil pickups, a take on Gibson's rare alnico pickup of the 1950s. Simple, down to earth, and toneful.

Huber Krautster II

German luthier supreme Nik Huber made his name crafting highly wrought electrics with breathtakingly figured tops, as so often seen on his Dolphin, Orca, and Redwood models, yet the Krautster II benefits from his shop's same superior wood sources and uncanny knack for details, turning them to a much simpler, pedal-to-the-metal rock machine. In the guise of what outwardly appears to be a single-cutaway inspired by the Les Paul Special and Junior (which, of course, it is), Huber packs a surprisingly versatile solidbody with a tapped hot humbucker in the bridge position and a P-90 in the neck. Alterations to the classic theme include the 25-inch scale length for a hair more shimmer and low-end solidity, an ergonomically carved neck heel for outstanding upper-fret reach in a single-cut, and fret slots that are routed rather than traditionally sawn, allowing an absence in tang ends even on this unbound rosewood fingerboard. The thin, grain-textured satin finish not only looks groovy but feels great to the touch, and the whole shebang roars mightily in the alt-rock groove just as Herr Huber intended.

Courtesy Make'n Music/www.makenmusic.com

Line 6 POD HD

Digital signal processing has been with us, on a practical level at least, since the early 1980s in the form of digital delays and other popular effects, but it took another decade and a half before the technology broke through to tube-amp emulation with any great success. California-based Line 6 was an early leader in the field, and its cute, bean-shaped POD amp modeler, in its various forms, has possibly found its way into more homes and studios than any other amp or processing product out there. The newer HD (high-definition) digital processing brought to the POD around 2011 takes this already impressive tool to new heights and has undoubtedly made believers of many sticklers for genuine tube-amp tone. The improved resolution brings a greater sense of "air" to the POD HD's tone, along with improved dynamics, and it sure is a blast to have everything from a bevy of vintage tweed Fender, Marshall, Vox, Gibson, and Valco-like tones to boutique beauties and hardcore shredmonsters at your fingertips. Even if you still prefer "the real thing" for live or session work, the POD HD is also an invaluable studio tool.

Blackout Effectors Twosome

You want some fuzz? I mean, you *really* want some fuzz? If you're man or woman enough to handle it, the mighty Twosome pedal will hair you up like nobody's business. Feeling that one fuzz is never really enough for true *amant de la fourrure*, Blackout Effectors packed two of its nastiest, most powerful fuzz pedals—the Fix'd Deluxe and Musket—into one box, with stomp switches to select between them and to turn the entire unit on and off. Essentially, though, this is three fuzz circuits in one, since the Fix'd Fuzz on the left lets you bring in two different fuzz circuits, alone or together, or in fact none at all, to give a thick boost with its remaining controls. From spitty and voltage-starved, to smooth and warm, to razory and cutting, it's a survey of great vintage fuzz tones all on its own. Switch to the Musket fuzz on the right side, though, and there's even more, a thicker, somewhat darker, and more muscular fuzz that leans instantly toward early metal and hard rock tones. Wrap it all up, and it's about as much fun as a fuzz freak can have with a single box of tricks.

Voyage-Air VAOM-2C

Most troubadours spend a lifetime on the road trying to *stop* their guitars from folding in two, but the Voyage-Air VAOM-2C is designed to do exactly that. Shunning the typical route to the travel guitar—which typically involves simply building a *tiny* guitar—Voyage-Air instead constructs a real, full-size flat-top that folds over double and stows in an ingenious carry-on case. But it's got to sound like warm donkey dung, right? Well, no, not at all. Once folded into playing position, the patented hinged neck locks down tight and feels as secure as any conventional neck-to-body joint. From this point, the VAOM-2C really behaves just like any conventional flat-top. The solid Sitka spruce top, traditional X-bracing, solid rosewood back and sides, and 25.5-inch scale length combine to give this orchestra-size model (a.k.a. OM) guitar much of the tone you would expect—which is to say, a sound far better than expected from a "folding guitar." In short, it is crisp, even, and harmonically appealing, and really just a darn good guitar by any standards.

Bogner Goldfinger 45

Reinhold Bogner made his name with ultra-high-gain rock machines (as in the Ecstasy created within an old Fender head shell) but has branched out to produce amps that cater to a wide range of musical styles. The Goldfinger 45, a relatively recent model, brings channel switching and mega-featured convenience to classic-rock players and fans of more vintage-voiced tones in general while providing near-high-gain scorch when required. To this end, Bogner bills the Goldfinger as a "vintage valve guitar system" rather than a mere amp and loads it with facilities for adjusting and switching two different effects loops (one in the preamp, one in the output stage), independently footswitchable boost for each channel, reverb, and four output ratings from its four 6V6 output tubes (from 9 to 45 watts), in addition to the footswitchable clean and lead channels with independent EQ (the latter with two mods). For all the bells and whistles, plenty of Goldfinger fans rave about the pure tone of the amp's clean channel and are happy to bypass the tweaking and just *play* the thing, and that's always a good sign in our book.

Divided by 13 RSA 23

The man behind Divided by 13, Fred Taccone, grew up in Fullerton, California, and played in bands on the Orange Country punk circuit—as well as working for Fender and Music Man—before founding his own amp company several years ago. Much like another Fullerton amp maker of several decades before, Taccone has devised several of his models by taking intensive input from professional players, then giving the task an original spin that results in unique and useful products for the modern player. The nifty RSA 23 uses a pair of big KT88 output tubes (which can generate upwards of 80 watts in other designs) biased for a sweet, rich tone and a mere 23 watts of output, which is more than enough for most players today. The front end hits them with your choice of a fat, juicy 5879 pentode preamp tube as used in the old late-'50s Gibson GA-40 Les Paul amp or a more traditional 12AX7, depending which of two channels you plug into. Versatile, characterful, and brimming with tone-enriching harmonics, the RSA 23 is a groovy addition to a brave new world of tube amps.

Gibson Firebird X

Gibson billed the Firebird X of 2010 as "the most revolutionary guitar ever created," and there was plenty of justification to that claim. Since guitarists are surprisingly conservative characters, though, this might not have made quite the splash that it would have in other circles. The Firebird X operates as a fully analog guitar in the traditional sense, though its three new FBX bi-filar-wound pickups are different from anything already out there. The guitar performs its extremely clever party tricks, however, thanks to a digital signal processing engine that provides several onboard effects, plus switching for more than 2,100 different analog pickup combinations. Add to these features the Firebird X's Bluetooth wireless audio connection and MIDI control stream, plus enhanced connectability via the G Node breakout box to your analog amp or digital recording interface of choice, and the possibilities are nearly endless. All this, and it's packaged in a hip, sleek rendition of what was already one of Gibson's most revolutionary guitars back in the early '60s. Who says you can't teach an old dog new tricks?

Gas FX Drive Thru

The Drive Thru is the first pedal released by Gas FX of South Wales, although at the time of this writing, its creator Huw Price, a trained studio engineer, is contemplating further offerings. But what a pedal it is. While Price openly admits that the Drive Thru is very much a descendent of more mass-produced overdrives, the difference seems to be found in the nuances of his circuit, the care of the construction, and the quality of the components used. As such, the Drive Thru is totally hand-wired and features larger signal capacitors and carbon comp resistors of the type you might expect to find in an old tube amp, all hand-loaded and soldered on a thick circuit board. Whatever the magic

Courtesy Gas FX

behind the mojo, the Drive Thru exudes a rich, earthy overdrive that instantly puts you in mind of classic cranked-tube-amp tones, with a juicy playability and easy harmonic feedback. Set its Volume, Tone, and Gain controls for what sounds like unity gain, and position the Germanium/Silicon switch for your favorite flavor of breakup, and the pedal is extremely transparent, too, just adding a delightful sweetening to the tone without changing your guitar's character. Tasty stuff.

Breedlove Voice CM

Oregon-based luthier Kim Breedlove has proven himself one of the most innovative makers in the acoustic world since entering the business more than twenty years ago, and time and again he has attained high standards of performance and lured major artists to the flock by advancing the form rather than tracing tradition for tradition's sake. The Voice CM is a case in point. The guitar combines several trademark Breedlove build techniques—a bridge-truss system to balance string tension across the "floating" top, an asymmetrical pinless bridge, and an entirely unconventional body style—with a newly developed pickup system in an effort to produce an instrument that sounds as much as possible like its unamplified acoustic self when plugged into an amplifier, a PA system, or a recording interface. The result is a rousing success. Unplugged, the Voice CM has an extremely well-balanced and crystal-clear voice yet sounds far more *acoustic* than most electric-acoustics when plugged in. As much as we admire tradition in the guitar world, it's great to see a maker who is bold enough to continually push the envelope—and with such success, too.

D'Pergo S-Style

Mention the guitars of Stefan D'Pergo among players who have at least heard the name, and you're sure to start a flamethrower war about "just how good can a six-thousand-dollar 'Fender copy' *be*?" The thing that's hard for anyone who hasn't held a D'Pergo to comprehend, though, is that while these guitars might pay tribute to the two iconic Fender designs, they are far from copies, and are in fact some of the most artfully wrought custom-made electric guitars in the world. Stefan makes virtually every steel and wood ingredient in his D'Pergo guitars in his shop in rural Windham, New Hampshire—using exclusively certified old-growth tonewood stocks, for example, and precision tooling components from custom alloys—crafting them into instruments that have a playing feel, tone, and finish that, as virtually all who have played them would agree, really can't be bettered. You might prefer a *different* style of guitar, but if you're looking for the epitome of the craft in S- and T-style electrics, this is it. The cost might be more than many players can afford, certainly, but if you've got it, what price sublime tone and heavenly feel?

Paul Reed Smith DGT

Designed as the signature model for Austin-based guitarist David Grissom, the DGT model (for David Grissom Tremolo) isn't as fancy as PRS Artist or Custom models, or as exclusive as its Private Reserve guitars, but has nevertheless become one of the most highly acclaimed efforts from this Maryland maker since its introduction in 2007. Grissom, who has played with Joe Ely, John Mellencamp, the Dixie Chicks, and his own band Storyville, among others, was himself a longtime PRS endorsee and brought several updates to the table. Among these were a new humbucking pickup design that leaned more toward the vintage side of things than many PRS efforts of the past, highlighting depth and clarity but still with plenty of bite; a new über-comfortable neck profile; versatile new switching; and a thin nitrocellulose finish. On paper, these read as subtle variations on the foundation of PRS's long-standing McCarty Trem model, yet all added up, resulting in a guitar with very much its own feel and tone—and one that has proven extremely popular, too.

Knaggs Chena

Joe Knaggs served as a master builder at Paul Reed Smith for many years before breaking away in 2009 to form Knaggs Guitars alongside former PRS marketing man Peter Wolf. It's no surprise, then, that many Knaggs-branded instruments display a kinship with PRS guitars, but they are very much their own beasts, too. A member of Knaggs' set-neck Influence series, the Chena—named, like all Knaggs guitars for the Native American name of a river on the eastern seaboard—is an exceedingly beautiful creation and an impressively versatile instrument. Its mahogany body is carved out internally to be entirely hollow, except for a sound post that rises to meet the clever Knaggs bridge and tailpiece. It's capped with a carved and figured maple top finished in what Knaggs calls Winter Solstice. An even deeper elegance shines through when you plug her in and the Chena rewards with everything from creamy, lush jazz tones to grinding rock 'n' roll to breezier styles. From every angle, both visual and aural, it's an impressive piece of work.

Courtesy Knaggs Guitars

John Page P-1SV

After spending more than 20 years at Fender as a guitar designer, master builder, and co-founder of the Custom Shop, John Page set up shop for himself in Sunny Valley, Oregon, to turn out handmade electric guitars that artfully blend vision and tradition. The P-1SV is one of Page's core models and a prime example of his work. Less fancy than some of his guitars, it nevertheless reveals unabashed elegance at every turn, and shows just how much guitar can be had from a simple design done right. While clearly influenced by the Fender Telecaster—a guitar for which Page professes a long-standing love affair—the P-1SV broadens the vocabulary of the single-cutaway slab-bodied original with a humbucking pickup in the neck position and the added depth, richness, and woody resonance that skilled craftsmanship brings to the table. Dig in through a Deluxe Reverb or Vox AC30 set just shy of breakup, and the P-1SV twangs with the best of them, but also turns easily to jazz, fusion, or good old rock 'n' roll without batting an eye.

Courtesy John Page

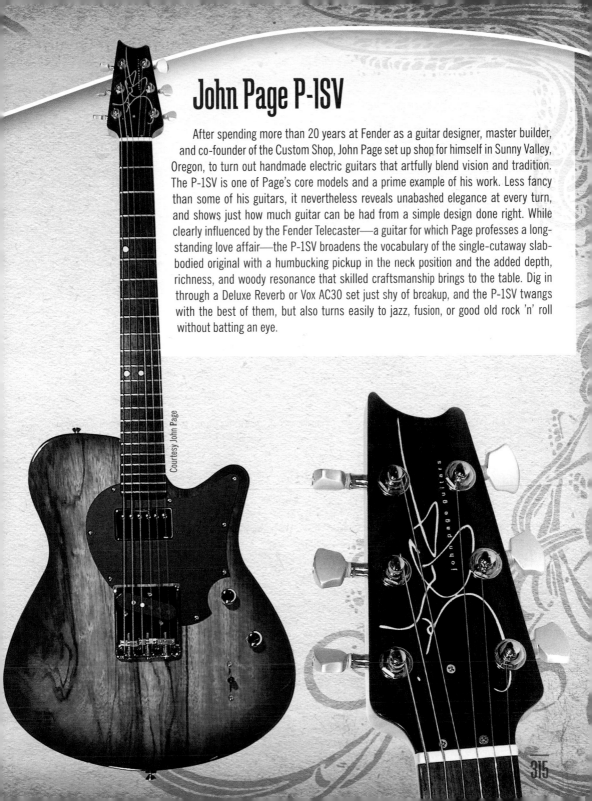

Photos by Ron Ballin, courtesy Rick Kelly/
www.kellyguitars.com

Rick Kelly Bowery Pine Custom

Play a lot of truly great guitars, and you realize that an enormous part of the magic of any outstanding instrument comes from the wood—and that very often means well-aged wood. For several years New York City–based luthier Rick Kelly has specialized in T-style electrics made from what he calls "the bones of Old New York," wood salvaged from old buildings that have either been torn down or refurbished, and have disgorged their 150- to 200-year-old Adirondack white pine timbers for Kelly to recycle into superbly resonant guitars. Pine might seem an unlikely wood for the body of a first-class guitar, and yet there is some precedent in its use: Fender's first few Telecaster prototypes were made from pine, and Kelly's "new" guitars have an uncanny knack at capturing what many players would hope to hear in a great six-decade-old Tele. The success of the venture has led high-caliber players like G. E. Smith and Bill Frisell to his shop in the Bowery, as well as twangmeister Bill Kirchen, who tells us he likes to imagine that "Bob Dylan once slid down the maple bannister in the Chelsea Hotel" that was salvaged for the neck of his own pine-bodied tone monster.

Fender Musical Instruments Corporation

Fender Custom Shop LTD '50s Esquire

The Esquire, ostensibly Fender's first solidbody creation, has retained a major following throughout its 62-plus-year existence, and its deceptive blend of power and simplicity is beautifully represented in the Fender Custom Shop's reissue-style '50s Esquire. While it might have seemed pointless for a buyer to dispense with the option of a neck pickup for a mere $30 savings (although $30 meant more in 1950, when a Broadcaster was $169, versus the Esquire's $139 price tag), the lack of a neck pickup counts as a veritable *positive* for many players, especially those not seeking such a tone in the first place. The absence of a neck pickup lets the strings ring and sustain with minimal impedance because there are no magnets at that point in the structure to drag them into submission, and many players will tell you their Esquires are punchier and sustain longer as a result. In addition, one switch position bypasses the tone potentiometer for maximum zing from that lone pickup . . . although the forward position, a preset "bassy" sound, is usually considered useless. With its hand-aging, this recent Custom Shop creation both looks and feels the part.

Index

Acknowledgments

Acoustic Vibe Music (Tempe, Arizona), Amwatts Amps, Tom Anderson Guitar Works, Gene Baker, Rick Batey, Bourgeois Guitars, Breedlove Guitar Company, Brook Guitars, Carmine Street Guitars (New York), Chicago Music Exchange, Collings Guitars, Cowtown Guitars (Las Vegas), CR Guitars, Creston Guitars, Dayton Vintage Guitars & Amps (Franklin, Ohio), Deke Dickerson, Duesenberg USA Guitars, Elderly Instruments (Lansing, Michigan), John Elshaw, Jim Elyea, Fender Musical Instrument Company, Brian Fischer, Fretted Americana (Calabasas, California), Froggy Bottom Guitars, Steven Fryette, Gary's Guitars (Portsmouth, New Hampshire), Gas FX, Roger Giffin, Golden Age Fretted Instruments (Westfield, New Jersey), The Gretsch Company, Grosh Guitars, Ross Gruet, Guitar Exchange (Baltimore), Gruhn Guitars (Nashville), Guitar Gallery (Nashville), Hahn Guitars, Hugh Hardy, Matte Henderson, Nik Huber Guitars, Travis Indgjer/GearHead Music, Charles Johnson, Rick Kelly, Brad Klukow, Knaggs Guitars, Dean Ellis Kohler, Jason Lollar, Los Angeles Guitar Shop, Andy Manson, Manzer Guitars, Mojave Ampworks, Monster Effects, Tim Moore, Paul Moskwa, MotorAve Guitars, Musée de la Musique (Paris), Olivia's Vintage (Carbondale, Illinois), Steve Olson, Nigel Osborne, John Page, Prescription Electronics, Retrofret Vintage Guitars/New York String Service (Brooklyn), Rumbleseat Music (Albuquerque, New Mexico/Ithaca, New York), Bruce Sandler, Terry Scarberry, Vaughn Skow, Southside Guitars (Brooklyn), John Spears, Michael Tamposi, Teuffel Guitars, Teye Guitars, Tommy's Guitar Shop (Everett, Washington), James Trussart Custom Guitars, Victoria Amp Company, *Vintage Guitar* magazine, Vintage Tone Music (Painesville, Ohio), Voyage-Air Guitar, Robin Weber, Keith Welchel, and Z. Vex Effects.